# SATHYA SAI SPEAKS

## VOLUME IV
### (Revised and Enlarged Edition)

OVER
1,00,000
COPIES
SOLD

Discourses of
**BHAGAVAN SRI SATHYA SAI BABA**
(Delivered during 1964)

**SRI SATHYA SAI BOOKS & PUBLICATIONS TRUST**
Prashaanthi Nilayam - 515134.
Ananthapur District, Andhra Pradesh, INDIA
Phone:87375 / 87236, Fax: 91-8555-87236 & 87390

©Sri Sathya Sai Books & Publications Trust
Prashaanthi Nilayam (India)

All Rights Reserved

The copyright and the rights of translation in any language are reserved by the Publishers. No part, para, passage, text or photograph or art work of this book should be reproduced, transmitted or utilised, in original language or by translation, in any form, or by any means, electronic, mechanical, photo copying, recording or by any information, storage or retrieval system, except with and prior permission, in writing from Sri Sathya Sai Books & Publications Trust, Prashaanthi Nilayam (Andhra Pradesh) India, except for brief passages quoted in book review. This book can be exported from India only by the Publishers Sri Sathya Sai Books and Publications Trust, Prashaanthi Nilayam (India).

International Standard Book No. 81-7208-152-9
81-7208-118-9 (SET)

**Published in India by**
The Convenor, Sri Sathya Sai Books & Publications Trust
Prashaanthi Nilayam, India, Pin Code 515134
Phone: 87375/ 87236, FAX : 91-8555-87236 and 87390.

Price: Rs. 34.50

*Printed by*
SAI SHRIRAM PRINTERS,
Madras-26 Phone: 4839871

# Contents

|    |                          | Page |
|----|--------------------------|------|
| 1. | Heroes, not Zeros        | 1    |
| 2. | Names do not matter      | 8    |
| 3. | The house of the Lord    | 16   |
| 4. | Brahmaanda Linga         | 21   |
| 5. | The Mani Mantapa         | 27   |
| 6. | Kaashi and Badhri        | 30   |
| 7. | Beacons of light         | 34   |
| 8. | Dharmakshethra           | 39   |
| 9. | Yanthram and Manthram    | 43   |
| 10.| A Rupee or hundred paise | 51   |
| 11.| Role of the Pandith      | 59   |
| 12.| Amrithasya Puthraah      | 66   |
| 13.| Fragrance with Grace     | 73   |
| 14.| Be like lamps            | 77   |
| 15.| Sai Sankalpam            | 83   |
| 16.| Take wings and fly       | 87   |
| 17.| His Residential Address  | 92   |
| 18.| Upanayanam               | 97   |
| 19.| Jeeva and Dheva          | 103  |
| 20.| The Guru is the guide    | 108  |
| 21.| Sravana and Smarana      | 115  |

| 22. | Eliminate the Ego | -- | -- | 121 |
| 23. | The Rain Cloud | -- | -- | 126 |
| 24. | The sandalwood tree | -- | -- | 131 |
| 25. | The bubble of pride | -- | -- | 139 |
| 26. | True remorse and false | -- | -- | 146 |
| 27. | The I behind the Eye | -- | -- | 150 |
| 28. | Be a caretaker | -- | -- | 156 |
| 29. | Japa and bhaja | -- | -- | 163 |
| 30. | Genuine kinsmen | -- | -- | 168 |
| 31. | How old are you really? | -- | -- | 177 |
| 32. | The path to the presence | -- | -- | 186 |
| 33. | Faith is the foundation | -- | -- | 193 |
| 34. | Neither different nor diminished | -- | -- | 201 |
| 35. | The bond that unbinds | -- | -- | 206 |
| 36. | Prick the bubble of pride | -- | -- | 213 |
| 37. | Keep the flag flying | -- | -- | 220 |
| 38. | Karma and karuna | -- | -- | 223 |
| 39. | Through mirth and moan | -- | -- | 228 |
| 40. | Naama and naami | -- | -- | 233 |
| 41. | Swinging from yes to no | -- | -- | 241 |
| 42. | Life's balance sheet | -- | -- | 246 |
| 43. | Actors and action | -- | -- | 250 |
| 44. | Are Words Mere Sound? | -- | -- | 254 |
| 45. | Ishwara grants aishwaryam | -- | -- | 259 |
| 46. | The human raft | -- | -- | 269 |
| 47. | You are born for your own sake | -- | -- | 273 |
| 48. | Diagnose your own disease | -- | -- | 276 |
| 49. | No srama in aashrama | -- | -- | 281 |
| 50. | Beacon in the dark | -- | -- | 289 |
| 51. | Travel Light | -- | -- | 294 |
| 52. | Anna and amritha | -- | -- | 298 |
|  | Glossary |  |  | 302 |

# Publisher's Note

"SATHYA SAI SPEAKS" Series is, according to late Prof. N. Kasturi, the original translator and compiler, "a fragrant bouquet of flowers that never fade or falter". These discourses were delivered by Swaami out of profound compassion towards seekers of Truth during the last few decades.

The need for revised and enlarged editions of the Series was strongly felt and expressed by devotees, especially by foreigners. An attempt has therefore been made in these volumes to meet their needs. The discourses have been presented year-wise so that there is no overlapping of the discourses delivered in a year, in more than one volume pertaining to the same calendar year. This rearrangement has resulted in an increase in the number of volumes, from the previous twelve to the present fifteen volumes, covering the years 1953 to 1982. Further new volumes will also be added in due course, to cover the discourses delivered after 1982.

The retention of Sanskrit words on page after page, in the previous volumes, without their English equivalents in most cases, was causing great confusion to readers, especially foreigners, who were not familiar with Sanskrit. In the present revised volumes, an attempt has been made to aid easy reading by replacing Sanskrit words with English equivalents wherever they do not affect Baaba's original expression. Sanskrit words have been retained wherever it was felt necessary to preserve the essence of the original expression of Baaba and where the English equivalents may not do full justice to the text in the particular context. However, in all such places the English equivalents have been given along with the Sanskrit words. Some very commonly understood Sanskrit words or Sanskrit words which are repeated too often are retained without English equivalents to retain the original flavour of Baaba's discourses. Further, in this revised volume, phonetic spellings have been adopted for all Sanskrit words uniformly to enable readers who are new to these words to pronounce them correctly and to remove any vagueness in the pronunciation of these words.

A Glossary has been added in these revised editions to provide comprehensive and detailed explanation of the more important Sanskrit words for the benefit of lay readers who may be interested in *Vedhic* religion and philosophy. It is hoped that this will be of great help to devotees to understand more clearly the topics of Baaba's discourses covering a wide spectrum of *Vedhic* philosophy.

The revised series of volumes are being brought out in a larger format, Demy Octavo size, so that they can be companion books with other publications in private libraries. Computerised typesetting using a larger size of type, a more readable type face and better line spacing have been adopted for more comfortable reading of the books, especially by elderly readers. Very long paragraphs have been split into shorter paragraphs and suitable sub-headings have been added in every page, to relieve the monotony on the eye and make reading a pleasure.

Better quality paper, improved binding, dust cover with new design and foil printing and plastic cover have been adopted for the revised volumes for better preservation and durable shelf-life of the volumes.

With these changes, it is hoped that the revised and enlarged volumes of **"Sathya Sai Speaks"** Series, will be of great benefit to earnest seekers in spiritual realm.

# Does Sai Speak ?

**Sathya Sai Speaks**

Does Sai speak these words into avid ears and arid hearts? No!... **It is our Mother that speaks,** caressing, cajoling, crooning lullabies to relieve the pain, bless with bliss, *Mokshayishyaami, maa suchah!* (I will see that you are liberated, don't worry). Don't weep, she cradles us ! She leads us softly along the road, over pebbles, thorns. When the path is bitter, uphill, hard, she sings us through *Yogakshemam vahaamyaham* (I bear the responsiblity of your welfare))--- our Mother speaks.

**Sathya Sai Speaks**

Does Sai speak these words into tingling ears and twinkling hearts? No!... **It is our Father that speaks,** refining, revealing, reminding our name to us, long forgotten, long begotten! *Abhayam Sarva bhoothebhyo!* (I protect all the creation). Don't fear, He armours us. Upward, onward, goodward, Godward---guides us, guards us. When the path is tortuous, twisted, He pulls us through. *Na Sukhaal - labhyathe sukham* (without good times happiness is not possible) --- **our Father speaks.**

## Sathya Sai Speaks

Does Sai speak these words into mazy ears and crazy hearts? No!... **It is our Master that speaks,** advising, admonishing, heating us crucibly, treating us crucially, leading to God within. *Eesaavaasyam idam sarvam!* (Lord is in everything...the whole world is His). There's no two; He opens the lid of Divine Box, with treasures encased in *kosas* (sheaths) five, *Sathyam* (Truth), *Jnaanam* (knowledge), *Aanandam* (Bliss), *Brahman* (God)---**the Master speaks.**

## Sathya Sai Speaks

Does Sai speak these words into searching ears and seeking hearts? No!... **It is God that speaks,** stilling the mind of waywardness, *Brahmavid brahmaiva bhavathi!* (Knowledge of Brahman or God makes one merge with Him). Become and be, He wakens. "Dear wave! emerging; merge; dear ray! run back". He calls. "Dear spark! re-enter fire; You are I, I am you". *Soham* loses '*sa*' and '*ham*'; Om alone is He and We, *Ekam-eva-aksharam Brahman* (*Brahmam* is symbolised by ONE syllable *Om*).

**This is how Sai speaks.**

# 1. Heroes, not Zeros

PANDITH Sathyanaaraayana Avadhaanulu could have spoken for some more time, but he stopped rather suddenly perhaps to give Me more time. You must not grow listless when others speak; for, whoever speaks here, he is giving you the nectar of the *Vedhas* or *Shaasthras* (scriptures) and that is sweet and liberating ever. Moreover, he said that this evening, we have met here since it is New Year Day, the first of January, 1964! Well. This is a delusion within the larger Delusion! This Day is welcomed as marking some big change, as if yesterday was something quite different for it belonged to 1963 and today is something quite distinct, for it is 1964! This day is celebrated by people, in picnics, in gambling, in drinking and feasting; they attend cinema shows, wear new clothes, give presents to each other and greet all with joy and hilarity. They exhaust their money and their energy in the pursuit of frivolity, thrill and excitement.

All this is due to the custom that views this day as something unique. In fact, the 'year' is just a convention. There are as many New Year Days as there are days in the year; many communities and countries have their own distinct calendars. It is not the first of January or the first of *Chaithra* (first month of Thelugu New Year) that is unique. The year is just a name to indicate a number of months, the month a number of days, a day to indicate a number of hours, the hour is a period of time counted in minutes, and the minute is a name for sixty seconds. Each second is new. It is a gift, a chance, an opportunity, a thing to be celebrated, to be used for your uplift. That is to say, each second is a fresh chance given to you for training the mind, refining the intellect, purifying the emotions, strengthening the will, for getting confirmed in the conviction that you are the deathless *Aathma* (Self, the Infinite Consciousness).

## Be like the lotus with head high above waters

Be thankful to the Lord that He gave you Time, as well as action to fill it with. He gave you food, as well as hunger to relish it. But, that does not entitle you to engage yourself in action indiscriminately. When you build a house, you install a door in front. What is the purpose of the door? To admit all whom you welcome and to keep out all whom you do not want. It has a double purpose; you do not keep the doors wide open, for all and sundry to come in as and when they like. So too, select the impulses, the motives, the incentives that enter your mind; keep out the demeaning, the debasing, the deleterious. Admit the highest wisdom of the scriptures, the wisdom culled out of the crucible of experience, called *anubhavajnaanam*.

All water is not potable; the stagnant pool is to be avoided, the flowing river is better. Select and drink. Use the mosquito curtain, but, see that the mosquitoes do not get in when you go to bed. Keep them out; do not imprison them inside the net. Sail in the boat that floats on water; but, do not allow the water to enter the boat. Be in worldly life, but, do not allow it to get into you. Use the doors intelligently, to let in those whom you want, and keep out those whom you do not need. The lotus, born in slime and mud, rises up through the water and lifts its head high above the waters; it refuses to get wet though water is the element which gives it life! Be like the lotus.

By action, done with all this care, the Vision gets clarified. Man is blinded by the objective world and he believes that world to be real, meaningful and worthy of pursuit. The cataract grows in the eye and robs it of its efficiency. The cataract is the enemy of the eye. Ignorance, the cataract of the inner eye, blinds the intellect and robs it of its efficiency. So, it cannot see the Divinity that is your real nature. It misleads you into the impression that you are a man (*Maanava*), whereas you are really God (*Maadhava*).

## Tread the path of Liberation

The rope is mistaken to be a snake and the perceiver flees in fear. The truth is, it is not the organ-eye that sees; there are many whose eyes are good, so far as doctors can discover, but they cannot see! The eye sees because it is illumined by a microscopic spark of the rays of the Sun. The scripture says: "*Chakshos Suryo ajayatha*": From the eye, Surya was born. The soul is the motive force of all the senses; the eye is but a window through which the soul peeps out at the external world. Of what use is the eye, when the vision is not correct? That is to say, when you have no *Samadhrishti*. *Samam* means *Brahman*, the Absolute Reality; *Samadhrishti* means, seeing only *Brahman*, the One, in all things at all times. This *Ekathwam* (Oneness) is the baisc truth. All other experiences are partial, distorted, false. Dwell on that, in your meditation. Fix it in your inner consciousness. That is the path of Liberation, which you must start treading and, today is as good a day as any, for deciding to do so. You have meditated too long on riches, status, salary, children, relatives, fame and the standard of living. They are all of minor interest, momentary value, dubious profit. Meditate, fix your urge on the *Nithya*, the *Sathya*, the *Nirmala*, the *Nischala*---the Eternal, the Real, the Pure and the Immovable.

## The Eternal Charioteer

Pandith Avadhaanulu referred to some incidents mentioned in the Mahaabhaaratha and so, I too shall mention just one point which will make you appreciate the Mahaabhaaratha more. The Lord had *Maayaa* (Illusion) as His Consort, so to say, and He had a son, called *Manas* (Mind). This *Manas*, to continue the parable, had two wives: *Pravritthi* and *Nivritthi*---Attachment and Detachment. Of course, Attachment was his favourite wife, and she had a hundred children. Detachment was ill-treated and neglected and she had five children. That is the symbolism of the Kauravas (hundred sons) and the Paandavas (five sons) of Mahaabhaaratha. Though the children all lived in the same kingdom, ate the same food and learnt from the same teacher, their natures differed widely from one another; the Kauravas, children of Attachment were greedy, cruel, self-centred and vain; the Paandavas, the five of them, each one represented a supreme virtue, so that they could be said to symbolise *sathya*, *dharma*, *shaanthi*, *prema* and *ahimsa* (truth, righteousness, peace, love and non-injury). Since they were so pure and born of Detachment, the Lord became their guide. In fact the Lord will be the Guide of whoever installs Him as his *Saarathi* (Charioteer). He will not consider that position inferior. He is the *Sanaathana Saarathi* (Eternal Charioteer) come to be the Charioteer of all. He is the Lord, for all who seek a Master, a support. The soul is the Master in every one and Krishna is the Universal soul, personified.

## Let the Lord shape your mind

There are two birds sitting on one tree, the *Upanishadh* says: the *jeevaathma* and the *Paramaathma*---the individual soul and the Supreme Soul---on the tree of this body, this World. One bird eats the fruits of that tree, while the other simply looks on, as a witness. But, the wonder is, the two birds are really one, though they appear as two; they cannot be separated, since they are two aspects of the same entity. Steam in the air cannot be seen; it has no shape or form; but it is the same as ice, which is hard, heavy and cold. *Niraakaara* and *Saakaara* (without Form and with Form), are just two ways in which the One manifests Itself.

The minute hand of the clock is the individual soul, the bird that eats the fruits. It goes round and round but, the hour hand moves silently and slowly, with a certain dignity. The hour hand can be said to be the Supreme Soul. Once an hour the two meet, but, the individual soul does not get that consummation fixed for ever. It loses the precious chance and so has to go round and round again and again. Liberation is when the two merge, and only one remains.

When the obstacles in the path of truth are laid low, deliverance is achieved. That is why *moksha* (liberation) is something that can be won, here and now; one need not wait for the dissolution of the physical body for that. Action must not be felt as a burden, for that feeling is a sure sign, indicating that it is against the grain. No action which helps your progress will weigh heavily on you. It is only when you go counter to your innermost nature that you feel it a burden. A time comes when you look back on your achievement and sigh at the futility of it all. Entrust to the Lord, before it is too late, your mind and let Him shape it as He likes.

Assign to your mind the task of serving the Lord and it will grow tame. You do not hand over the goldsmith an ornament that is quite nice; you give him for repairs or reshaping, the ornaments you feel have been broken or dented or gone out of fashion. So too, give the Lord your mind that certainly needs repair, if not complete reconstruction.

## Man should have no fear

The blemish that affects the mind is illusion. It is like a fierce dog that will not allow any one to approach the Master. You can manage to by-pass it, only by assuming the *ruupam* or Form of the Master, which is called *Saaruupyam,* or by calling out for the Master so loudly that He comes down and accompanies you into the house, that is to say, by winning His Grace, *Saameepyam* (proximity). Illusion is His pet and so, it will not harm you if He orders it to desist from harming you.

The Master comes to save not one good man from Illusion, but the whole of mankind. Of course, He has to come assuming a Form that man can love, revere, and appreciate. He can give joy and courage, only if He speaks the language of human intercourse. Even as it is, many are afraid to approach Me, for they know I am aware of their innermost thoughts and deepest desires. But, let Me tell you, only helpless animals have fear. Man, who is child of Immortality, should have no fear. People pray before stone images of the snake god, but when the actual snake appears in answer to their prayers, they run away terror-stricken from the shrine! The Lord manifests Himself only to shower Grace, never to strike terror.

On the banks of the river near Lucknow, there was a sage who addressed dogs, crows and men equally as God; he had realised the unity of all in the Divine Essence. That is the result of Divine knowledge, or intense *Bhakthi*, where you do not see anything other than your *Ishtadevatha* (Chosen Deity), wherever you turn. Be ever in that Divine Bliss, the bliss that comes from God-consciousness, always and everywhere. That is the Eternal Bliss (*Nithyaanandha*) which the wise enjoy.

Like the silk-worm that spins from out of itself the cocoon that proves to be its tomb, man spins from out of his own mind the cage in which he gets trapped. But, there is a way of escape, which the spiritual teacher (*Guru*) can teach you or which the God in you will reveal to you. Take to the spiritual practice which will bring relief. Away with the roles of clown and clout, which you have acted all the ages. Take on the role of the Hero, not the Zero! Forget the past, do not worry about possible errors or disappointments. Decide and do.

There are some spiritual teachers who advise you to keep a daily diary, where you note down every item of evil that you did; they ask you to read it as a spiritual exercise and resolve to correct yourself. Well, reading it, and writing it will only tend to impress it more effectively on the mind. It is better to substitute good thoughts for the bad and cleanse the mind of all evil by dwelling on righteous deeds and holy thoughts. Forget the things that you do not want to remember. Bring to memory only those things that are worth remembering. That is the sane way to achieve spiritual progress.

*Prashaanthi Nilayam, 1-1-1964*

## 2. Names do not matter

TODAY is a holy day because people honour it as such. Every day is holy for those who utilise it for holy purposes; but there are some days set apart as specially significant and *Makara Sankraanthi* is one such. Sankraanthi is so called because the day takes you from darkness to increasing light; the path of light is open from today. The Sun enters upon the *Uttharaayanam* (journey towards North) this day; he moves from the *Makararekha* in the *Madhyarekha*. Bheeshma waited for this day, spending 56 days on the bed of arrows in pain, because he felt that death, when the Sun starts the journey towards north, is auspicious. He wanted to offer his life at the Feet of the Lord at an auspicious moment.

Man must proceed ever towards *bhalam* (strength); he should not take to untruth, wickedness, crookedness---all of which denote a fundamental fatal trait of cowardice, weakness (*balaheenam*). Weakness is born of accepting as true a lower image of yourself than what the facts warrant. You believe you are the husk, but, really you are the kernel. That is the main mistake. All spiritual practice must be directed to the removal of the husk and the revelation of the kernel. So long as you say, 'I am,' there is bound to be fear, but, once you say and feel, *'Aham Brahmaasmi'* (I am *Brahman*), you get unconquerable strength.

The body is the field (*kshethra*) of the Master who knows all *kshethras*. One day, when Vivekaanandha was in his room, at night, sleepless because he was tossed about by conflicting thoughts, Raamakrishna who was 'asleep,' was talking as if in a dream but his talk was clearly heard by Vivekaanandha. He said, "*O Manas!* (O Mind)! *O Maanasa raajahamsa* (Royal swan of the mind)! *O Nithya-aanandha rasaika nilaya* (Repository of Etenal Bliss only)! You are Divine in nature---*Daivaswaruupa*. Sport in the pure lake of meditation of the Divine; instead, why do you crave for the dirty pond of sensual pleasure!" That was the advice of the *Guru* to Naren. Naren immediately resolved to take that advice to heart.

## Characteristic of Incarnations

The influence of the Divine is such that while you are contemplating it, all traces of envy and greed will disappear from the mind. The boy Krishna had entered a *Gopee's* house and was just standing beneath the pot of curds when she discovered Him. Krishna ran out into the street and the *Gopee* pursued Him, and wanted to catch Him soon, for she was so pained that the boy was running in the hot Sun. She never worried about the loss of curds or milk or butter, but the very thought of Krishna's tender feet walking over the hard stones in the Sun was something she could not bear. The divine love that Krishna showered, made every one forget everything else. He too gave such disarming replies to the queries of the mother and the *Gopees* (cow-herd girls) that no one could have anything but divine love towards Him. That is the characteristic of Divine Incarnations, at all times.

"She was carrying the milk to the temple to be offered to God; perhaps God Himself took the vessel away from her," He would say, announcing indirectly His own Reality. "I was sleeping by your side, Mother. How then could I have gone away to their houses, to steal their butter?" He would plead---suggesting that He could be in more than one place at a point of time. When caught in the act of searching for butter, He would say that He had put His hand in the pot, just to find out if a calf that had run away was inside it! With such lovely retorts, He won a place in every heart and the *Gopees* vied with each other in fondling Him and serving Him.

## Tread the path of Gods

Krishna was the same *Premaswaruupa* (Divine love personified) even for the Grandfather Bheeshma. The illiterate simple *Gopees* and the old revered warrior Bheeshma, persons of all types, grades and professions found in Him their chief source of Wisdom, Grace and Inspiration. That is the sign of the Incarnation. When he waited for the northward movement of the Sun to come, Bheeshma was giving man a valuable message: the Sun is the presiding deity of intellect (*buddhi*) and when in the *hridhayaakaasha* (space in the heart) the Sun takes a northward turn, that is, the *Utthara-ayanu* or the *Utthama-ayana* (the Superior Path), the path which leads to God instead of the downward path to the objective world, that period is best for the journey of the soul too. So, what you should also do today is to resolve to tread the path of Gods (*Deva-ayana*). Have the resolve to begin remembrance of the Supreme Lord's Name, Ritual

Worship, and Divine Service (*Naamasmarana* of *Paramaathma, archana* and *aaraadhana*). The day on which you begin these, and thus inaugurate the Superior Path for your intellect, that day is *Uttharaayana* for you. Do not wait for the almanac to tell you the date.

## The most dangerous illusion

The very first lesson I gave when I declared My Identity at Uravakonda was: "*Maanasa bhajare Gurucharanam, Dusthara bhava saagara tharanam.*" That is to say: First know that you are in this cycle of birth and death, the ocean of worldly life (*bhavasaagaram*); then, resolve on crossing it (*tharanam*); then fix on a *Guru* or the Name and Form of God which appeals to you; lastly, dwell on His Glory, do *bhajan*, but do it with all your mind. He, who is deluded by this relative reality is the worldly person (*samsaari*); he who is aware that it is only relatively real is the spiritual practitioner (*saadhaka*).

Egoism is the most dangerous illusion that has to be exploded and destroyed. Bheema had it, but when he could not lift and lay aside the tail of an old decrepit monkey, who was really Anjaneya Himself, that bubble was exploded. Arjuna had it; one day, after the battle, when Krishna brought the chariot back to camp, he wanted that like all charioteers, Krishna should get down first; the master must get down later, after the charioteer opens the door for him, is it not? Krishna refused, and insisted that Arjuna should alight, before He Himself should. At last Krishna won. Arjuna got down and then, as soon as Krishna left His seat and touched the ground, the chariot went up in flames! If only Krishna had got down first! The fact was that the various fiery arrows that had the power of burning the chariot had hit the target, but due to the Presence of Krishna, their igniferous powers could not manifest themselves. Knowing this Arjuna was humiliated; his egoism had a rude shock. He knew that every action of Kirshna was full of significance.

Krishna was the *Avathaara* (Incarnation of Vishnu) come to destroy evil; but now, the evil is not identifiable in certain persons alone; it is widespread. The scorpion has poison only in its tail; the cobra only in its fangs; but, man has poison all over! He has in his eye, his tongue, his mind, his intelligence, his gait, his brain---everywhere. You may ask, O when will this poison be counteracted and destroyed? It will disappear, do not doubt it. That is the very purpose for which I have come. Bring your 'flower of the heart' (*hridhayapushpam*) to Me, rid of all the pests that infest it, the Six Enemies of Man---desire, anger, etc.

## There is a Destiny that shapes events

No one is prepared to make the effort for spiritual victory. If you demand the job of a Collectorr to be given to you straightaway, how can it be done? There are certain qualifications---age, scholarship, efficiency, talent, experience. The flower must become the fruit, the fruit must ripen, the ripeness must be expressed in sweetness. It all takes time. Even an atheist must accept a superior or mysterious power which guides things and events. The argument that you have not seen it and therefore you will not accept it as true is not quite inelligent. The eye is at best a poor instrument. Again, you need not yourself see a thing; others who have seen it, if they are unprejudiced and wise, can be believed.

An old man was warned when he proposed to go through a narrow road that there was a cobra on the road side; but, he said that he had not seen it and so, he was not prepared to believe it. He had to believe it when it bit him, but then it was too late to benefit by that knowledge! Nagayya said just now that recently in one of his speeches Nehru had to acknowledge that there is a Destiny that shapes events, irrespective of individual efforts. Well, everyone has to come to that conclusion, sooner or later; for, there is a limit to the capacity of man to control events. Beyond that, an unseen hand takes over the wheel of events. You may call it Destiny, another may call it Providence and a third, God. Names do not matter. It is the humility that matters, the wonder, the sense of awe that matters.

## Result of extreme miserliness

Then there are some who say that having a trait in the mind, revering it as valuable, is enough; practising it is not so necessary. It is like saying, it is enough that food is in the dish, it need not be eaten and assimilated! Two brothers were famous for their miserliness; the elder was the worse culprit. One day, he had to go some distance to another village. So, he rose early and moved out of the house. Half way along the road, about five miles off, a doubt arose in his mind whether his younger brother had put out the oil lamp at home as soon as he left. So, he returned fast and asked the brother inside. He said, "Do you doubt my intelligence? I put it out as soon as your back was turned; but, pray, why did you walk back? Consider how much your chappals have worn out by these extra five miles!" The elder brother replied, "What? Do you doubt my intelligence? I have tucked the chappals under my arm; I walked back barefooted." But, do you know the result of their miserliness! The younger brother was stung by a scropion in the dark; the elder was bitten on the bare foot by a cobra on the road!

This Nagayya when he acted the part of Thyaagayya in the film, never forgot that he was Nagayya. If he forgets that, the film will fail. So too, never forget that you are the Infinite Consciousness (*Aathman*); with that consciousness, you can play any role on the world stage. This fact will get stablised in you, if you read the Geetha in the light of Krishna's actions in the Bhaagavatha and the Mahaabhaaratha. Fill your mind with Divine plays of the Lord and His glory. Once, He and His comrades stole into a house and brought down the vessel of curds. When the mistress of the house came in, "Why did you come in?" she asked. "My mother had a stick in her hand; so, I ran in here out of fear," Krishna replied. "Who are these boys?" she asked. "I brought them to bear witness to what I say," replied Krishna. "Why have you placed that vessel between your legs?" she asked in feigned anger. "So that these fellows may not get hold of the butter," was the answer! "Why do you go from house to house and eat the butter from their stores?" asked Yasodha. "I like only things I select and choose; I do not like to be fed," replied the Boy Krishna. Krishna could not be confined to one house or to one routine. He is All-pervading (*Sarvavyaapi*); He loves the devotees (*Bhaktha Vathsala*). Make your heart the Seat of the Lord; then it will have value. Soil which has veins of mica is valuable; but, that which has veins of gold is even more precious. The soil is valued according to the preciousness of the metal which it has in its fold. So too, hearts are evaluated by the contents. Keep God in your hearts; they will then be most precious possessions.

## Youth must realise the depths of their personality

If God is implanted in the heart, you will see only God everywhere, even in the objective world. For, *Sarvam Brahmamayam* (all is *Brahman*), is a fact. Resolve this day to engage only in virtuous deeds, good thoughts, good company. Let your mind dwell on elevating thoughts. Do not waste a single moment of your waking time in idle gossip or vain boasting or demeaning recreations. Death stalks behind you to fell you and carry you off. Consider Kennedy, how death was lurking around, waiting for the chance! Did he not have men to guard him, soldiers, security men, bodyguards? But, it was all in vain. So while life persists, do good things, speak soft and sweet, never injure or insult another, serve those in need and keep the image of God ever before the mind's eye.

The secular state is hesitating to teach the principles of Eternal Religion (*Sanaathana Dharma*) to young children and students in schools, though those principles are of universal application and do not go against any particular religion. The Shri Prakaasha Committee may, it is said, recommend a course of moral instruction! But if it is not emphasising the superconscious basis of the individual, much of the invigorating strength of *Sanaathana Dharma* would have been lost. A regular course in the discipline of meditation must also be given to youth, so that they may realise the depths of their own personality and its infinite possibilities for ensuring peace and happiness (*shaanthi* and *soukhyam*).

*Prashaanthi Nilayam, 14-1-1964*

---

*Freedom is independence from externals. Perfect freedom is not given to any man on earth. Lesser the number of wants, the greater is the freedom. Hence perfect freedom is absolute desirelessness.*

**Shri Sathya Sai**

## 3. The house of the Lord

I HAVE been coming off and on to Trichinopoly since fifteen years but this is the first time I am imparting *Aanandha* to such a large number of the citizens. The *Grihapravesham* (entering the new house ceremonially), for which A.K.C. Nataraajan is glad I have come, is just an excuse; giving you all this happiness was the primary purpose of My coming over. Your joy is My joy. Today A.K.C. entered the new house that he built for himself; I want that you should all build new houses for happy living, and install the Lord therein. I do not mean houses of brick and mortar, but houses of good thoughts, good words, good deeds and good company, where you could live calm and collected. Invite Me for the *Grihapravesham* of such houses and I shall most readily agree. In fact, then, the house is Mine already and I do not need even an invitation to come and enter it. These houses are for worldly comfort; that house is for spiritual joy. And My Place of Residence is the pure, aspiring heart.

'*Deho devaalaya*': the body is the temple, it is said. That is the real house of A.K.C. and of each one of you. You are going about with a temple, where God is in the innermost shrine. The body is not a mass of flesh and bone; it is a medium for *manthras* (sacred words or formulae) which save when they are meditated upon. It is a sacred instrument earned after long ages of struggle, equipped with reason and emotion, capable of being used for deliverance from grief and evil. Honour it as such; keep it in good condition, so that it might serve that high purpose; maintain it even more carefully than these brick houses; and, always preserve the conviction that it is an instrument and nothing more. Use it for just the purpose for which it has been designed and given.

## Feel strong with faith and devotion

Above all, at this moment, it is urgent that every one should inquire into the true, the pure and the permanent. For, there is at present a delusion about values. Even the leaders of people are hugging the false hypothesis that happiness can be got by means of wealth or health, or housing, or clothing, or the cultivation of skills in handicraft and manufacture! The bird sits upon the bough that sways in the storm, confident of its wings, not confident of the bough whereon it sits! So, you too should feel strong because of the bough of the objective world, whereon you have perched.

You know from the experience of the Cauvery river floods that nothing can save a man from drowning in the floods, neither status, nor caste, nor wealth nor even health, unless he knows the simple art of swimming. Need I say that crossing the ocean of worldly life, reaching the other shore of the sea of Birth-Death, is similarly possible only for those who know the art of spiritual discipline? Those, who are trying to build the human community on a foundation of wealth (*dhana*), are building on sand; those are who seek to build it on the rock of righteousness (*dharma*) are the wise.

## Practise a fraction of what you preach

*Dharma moolam idham jagath*: Righteousness is the root of this world. Obey it and you are happy. The evil man is a coward, haunted by fear. He has no peace within him. Respect for the parents who started you in life and brought you into this world, to gather the vast and varied treasure of experience, is the first lesson that *Dharma* teaches. Gratitude is the spring which feeds that respect. It is a quality that is fast disappearing in the world today. Respect for the teacher, for the elders, for the wise---all these are on the decline. That is why righteousness is fast disappearing and losing its hold.

People talk loud and long from all kinds of platforms about right conduct, divine love, peace, compassion, truth (*dharma, prema, shaanthi, dhaya, sathya*), etc.; this gets published in the newspaper next day and there their purpose ends. The paper of today is waste paper tomorrow! It is used for packing, thrown into the dust-heap, and burnt as refuse. That is the story of all platform professions. Put into practice a fraction of what you preach.

Just as the body is the house you live in, the world is the body of God. An ant biting the little finger of your foot is able to draw your attention to the spot, and you react to the pain, making an effort to remove the tiny enemy. You must similarly feel the pain, misery, or joy or elation, wherever it is evinced in the entire land; you must make an effort to protect the land from the enemy, however remote may be the place where the enemy has presented himself. Be kind with all your kin. Expand your sympathies, serve others who stand in need to the extent of your skill and resources. Do not fritter away your talents in profitless channels.

Every person consumes quantities of food, but does not stop to calculate what he does in return to the society that helped him to live; the food must be transformed into service, either of one's best interest, or of the interests of others. You should not be a burden on others or an enemy of yourself. Mere care of the body is profitless, for the body is only a container, a despised container, when the spark of Divinity which it contains goes out. No one will take in a corpse, if rain interrupts the funeral; a wayside shop may permit you to keep your shoes for a while, while you go into the nearby temple; but the corpse never! That is something disgusting, whose sight has to be avoided.

## Start the first step with *Naamasmarana*

Turn the key in the lock to the right, it opens; turn the same key to the left, it is locked. So too, turn your mind towards the objective world, it is locked, caught, entangled. Turn it to the right, away from the objects of the senses, the lock is loosened, you are free, deliverance is at hand. How to turn it right? Well, begin with remembering the Lord's holy name (*Naamasmarana*), as the first step. All journeys start with the first step. That will itself take you through the second and the third, to the very goal.

I have to tell you one other point. I find that certain devotees have announced that I will be going from here to their places and even arranged processions and public meetings, without My permission. You have seen here itself how the Municipality had to present their Welcome Address to Me, at the Pandal here; I was not consulted about this programme before, nor had I agreed to it. Tens of thousands had gathered at the Municipal Hall. At Salem and a number of places between this town and

Bangalore, people have organised such functions. When I have given My word, I keep up to it. That is why I came all the way from Thirupathi, starting at 11 a.m. and motoring till 10 in the night. I knew that A.K.C. had announced here that I would reach by 10.30 p.m. and so I stopped for about an hour some miles away on the road, so that his guess might prove true. A.K.C. was wondering when I came, how I came exactly at 10.30 as per his announcement over the mike a few hours previously. Perhaps he forgot that I could hear his announcement miles and miles away. And who prompted him to make it, may I ask? When I say that I am coming, I do come; but, these over-enthusiastic devotees at Salem and elsewhere are causing great hardship to the thousands whom they mislead. Please hereafter do not be led away by all kinds of rumours that I am visiting this place or that, on My way to this place or that. Test the authenticity of each such piece of news before you believe.

*Trichinopoly, 3-2-1964*

---

What are problems?
Whatever they are, they are all transient
in relation to eternity and of no lasting consequence.

What are thoughts?
They are creative force within man, and represent the
free will given to man by God.

Life should be full of joy and it will be,
if you live your life in complete harmony with God.

**SHRI SATHYA SAI**

# 4. Brahmaanda Linga

PANDITH Umaamaheshwara Shaasthry and Veerabhadhra Shaasthry both spoke on the Principle of Godhead, (*Bhaagavath-thathwam*), as far as they had grasped it, and as far as language can express it; for, it is something beyond expression and explanation. It has to be exprienced and once experienced, the richness, the fullness, the extent, the depth of that experience can never be communicated to another. Man must feel that his highest destiny is to have that experience. He is not a despicable creature, born in slime or sin, to eke out a drab existence and be extinguished for ever. He is immortal; he is eternal. So, when the call comes from the region of immortality, he responds with his whole heart. He refuses to believe that he will die. He laughs at Death and treats him as a harmless casual visitor. For, there is something in him that whispers a challenge to death. He is a mixture of *deha* and *deva*---of the mortal and the immortal. If liberation means the stoppage of grief and the acquisition of joy, then, it is easy. What you have to do is to place all your burdens on God; that makes you care-free, grief-free. Then, when you take everything as the *Leela* (Divine play) of the Lord you love, you clap your hands in bliss whatever may happen, for it is all His Divine Play and you are as happy as He is, when His Plans are going through!

## The genuine status of Man

"*Eashwara sarvabhoothaanaam hriddese Arjuna thishtathi.*" "O Arjuna, the God resides in the heart of all beings," says Lord Krishna in Bhagavadh Geetha. He is not to be found specially in cities like Amarnaath, Kaashi, Thirupathi, Kedharaam or Gokarnam. Just as every drop of the ocean has the salty taste, the composition and the name of the ocean, so too every single being has the Divine taste and composition, and the name of the Lord. Only you do not realise it so clearly. The river Godaavari realises itself by reaching the Sea; man realises himself by merging in the Absolute. That which merges with the goal is *Lingam*: *Leeyathe gamyam ithi lingam.*

The space encased in the pot must become one with the Space that traverses the entire Universe, by the negation of the attachment, which is just an artificial creation of the deluded mind. That attachment must disappear; that inferior status of manhood that now satisfies him must give place to the status of Reality of God (*Muadhavathwam*) which is the genuine status. That is the task for which Sai is calling you; that is the work for which I have come. A Judge of the Supreme Court may, while at home, play with his grandchild and bend on all fours for the little fellow to mount his back and then He may crawl on the floor when the child cries "Holla"; but, all the while his status as a Judge does not suffer diminution, nor does he forget it. So, you too must always be conscious of the high calling on which you have come; you should not disgrace it by any mean or meaningless act or word or thought. I have come to give you the courage to conceive yourself as the Supreme Truth *(Paramaathma)* you really are; to give you the intellectual power *(dheeshakthi)* to grasp the reality. That alone can destroy the delusion born of ignorance.

## Have the deliberation first

Step by step, you reach the end of the road. One act followed by another leads to a good habit. Listening, listening, you get prodded into action. Resolve to act, to mix only in good company, to read only elevating books, to form the habit of remembering the Lord's name *(Naamasmarana)* and, then ignorance will vanish automatically. The Divine Bliss that will well up within you by the contemplation of *Aanandhaswaruupa* (Bliss Personified) will drive out all grief, all worry. Shiva, it seems, laughed when He took a good look at the Chariot that was provided for Him when He started out to slay the *Thripura-asuras,* the demons of the three bodies, *Sthuula, Suukshma* and *Kaarana*---the Gross, the Subtle and the Causal. Vishnu, the Charioteer, was mostly in *Yogic* Sleep *(Yoganidhra),* the stable Earth was the Chariot, and the two wheels were the Sun and the Moon, two spheres which never revolved in unison! That laughter laid the demons low; there was no more need to proceed against the demons. How did the evil forces that dwelt in the three bodies die? They could not exist where there was Divine Bliss; for, they are products of grief. Develop *Aanandha;* then evil impulses and tendencies will vanish, for they will not get any foothold in the heart.

Move forward towards the Light and the shadow falls behind; you move away from it and you have to follow your own shadow. Go every moment one step nearer to the Lord and then, *Maayaa,* the shadow (illusion) will fall back and will not delude you at all. Be steady; be resolved. Do not commit a fault or take a false step and then repent! Have the *thaapam* (the deliberation, the decision, the discipline) first, that is better than *paschaath-thaapam*, (regret for the mistake made). Arjuna had *thaapam*, he saw the consequences even before the battle began and wanted Krishna to advise him what to do. But, Dharmaraaja, the eldest brother, had *paschaath-thaapam*, sorrow after the war was over, repentence after the loss incurred.

## Reason out and discriminate

Above all, you must take every step in spiritual practice or in the worldly life, only after deep deliberation and satisfying yourself that it will be for your good. Otherwise, it will be like the story of the weeping city. One day, a close female attendant of the queen came to the palace weeping in great sorrow, and so, the queen began to shed tears. Seeing the queen in tears, the entire female attendants wept and the weeping spread to the male attendants also. The king, finding the queen inconsolably sad, also wept profusely in sympathy, and the sight made the entire city weep loud and non-stop. At last, one sensible fellow set in motion an inquiry, which passed through person after person until the queen herself was accosted. She said that her attendant was in sore grief, and when she, a washerwoman by caste, was interrogated, she confessed that it was all due to the sudden demise of her favourite ass! When this news spread, the weeping ceased and there was wide-spread laughter and shame. Reason out, discriminate; do not rush to conclusions or be led away by mere hearsay.

I have come to re-form you: I won't leave you until I do that. Even if you get away before I do that, do not think you can escape Me; I will hold on to you. I am not worried if you leave Me, for I am not anxious that there should be a huge gathering here, around Me. Who invited you all here? There was not even a little notice in print, but yet you have come here in thousands. You attach yourselves to Me. I am unattached. I am attached only to the Task for which I have come.

But, of one thing, be assured. Whether you come to Me or not, you are all in Mine. This *Shivamaatha*, this *Sai Maatha* (Mother of all) has the love of a thousand mothers towards Her children; that is why I do so much *laalana* (fondling) and so much *paalana* (protecting). Whenever I appear to be angry, remember, it is only love in another form. For, I have not even an atom of anger in me; I just evince My disappointment that you do not shape as I direct. When I direct you along a line of action, reflect on My advice; you have full liberty to do so; in fact, I shall be happy if you do so; I do not like slavish obedience. If you feel that it will help you to reach the goal, follow it; if not, go to some other place; but, let Me tell you one thing: Wherever you go, you meet only Me. I am everywhere.

Have you heard the story of the rabbit that had borrowed from Mother Earth four naye paise? She thought that if she moved into a new region she would be free from the obligation. So, one day she ran as fast as her legs could carry her and went far far away from the place where the amount was originally received. At last, she sat down in great relief and said to herself, "Now no one will ask me to repay." What was her surprise when from the ground underneath she heard a voice, "Mother Earth is right under your feet, here. You cannot escape from me, however far you run!"

So too, you cannot run away from Me. I will demand good conduct, good habits, good thoughts, good company, wherever you go seeking for refuge! And what reason have you to leave? Only those who ignore the joy, the consolation, the courage, the love and the blessing they have received here, will do so. Only those who believe the ear and not the eye, will do so. In a short time, you will be witnessing the emergence of the *Linga* that is formed within; the auspicious time for the emergence for the *Linga* is approaching; you see it and you receive the blessings; but, yet, there will be some among you who will doubt it and deny it. That is the *karma* of such; what else can they do? (Here, Baaba stopped the discourse; the movements started, first in the region of the abdomen, then the chest and the throat; Baaba swayed from the side; leaned on the table; drank water; and finally, after about twenty minutes, an eggshaped pink *Linga* emerged from His mouth. Holding it between the thumb and forefinger of His right hand, Baaba discoursed further about it).

Ah! This is the *Brahmaanda Linga*! Symbol of the Universe. Inside it, the nine planets (*Navagrahas*) revolve; the entire Universe is represented herein, all the planets and their satellites, the primal fire, the clouds of primal dust, and over the *anda*, there is an eye imprinted, the *Jagadekachakshu* (the Eye of the One Eternal Witness). You are indeed blessed, the merit of many births has brought you here to see the Great Phenomenon, this rare Creation. Years of worship, or ritualistic vows and fasts, may not give this unique chance which you now have had, remember. Use this good luck to hear good Godly advice, to select good company and to strive more earnestly to reach the Goal.

*Prashaanthi Nilayam, Shivaraathri, 11-2-1964*

## 5. The Mani Mantapa

KUPPU Bairaagi Shaasthry and the Srouthi from Mysore gave you the pleasure of hearing both *Vedhaantha* (system of Hindu philosophy based on *Vedhas*) and *Vedha*, while Veerabhadhra Shaasthry selected as his subject the *Dolothsavam* (swing festival) of Krishna, evidently because today, these devotees from Bangalore, mostly florists and decorators who have been attached to Me for more than twenty-two years, insisted on My sitting for some time in this *jhoola* (swing) they have constructed with such care and devotion. I shall speak only for some little time, for, there is a *Harikatha* (musical discourse) later and as I have often told you, you must learn to respectfully listen to whosoever addresses you here, for they speak only of things that elevate you and strengthen your spiritual discipline.

What exactly is the aim and purpose of all the *Shaasthras* (scriptures), the *Bhaagavatham* (containing tales about *Avathaaras* of Vishnu), the *Puraanas* (mythological tales), these discourses and the *Harikatha*? Just try to answer that query. It is to tell man the truth about himself. There is no plot to mislead you. That is not the desire of the sages who wrote down these annals and their own experiences. You know only the present, what is happening before your eyes; you do not know that the Present is related to the Past and is preparing the course of the Future. It is like the headline and titles of a film on the screen; as the letters gleam one after the other, you read them and pass on to the next that comes to view. Each new letter or word wipes out the one already before your eye, just as each birth wipes out the memory of the one already experienced.

## All have to merge finally

Man does not realise that the end of this cycle of birth and death is in his own hands. The tree came from the seed and the seed from the tree and so on, from the beginning of time. Yes; you may not know which came first, tree or seed; but, you can easily put an end to the cycle, by frying the seed. It won't sprout again. Being extraordinary, man is now descending to levels which are below ordinary. The marshy lake. Like the animals of the desert, he is running towards the mirage to slake his thirst. He claims to have mastered the senses and all low desires but they sprout at the first chance, like grass after the first shower after summer.

Just as you seek the udder of the cow for the milk it gives, seek the Lord and His Glory only in nature. As a matter of fact, Nature is useful only when it adds to the wonder and awe that it is able to provoke and sustain. Everything is an image of the Lord. Krishna revelled in seeing His own images in the *Mani Mantapa* (pavilion set with precious stones) of His house, when He was a child. Just as the Lord is pleased when He sees Himself in His manifestation called Nature, there is such joy welling up in all when they hear the story of the Lord and how He calls all to Himself. It is the call of the *bimba* (object) for the *prathibimba* (image); to merge in it. So, all are entitled for merging; all finally have to attain it. Otherwise, there is no meaning for the yearning to become greater and greater.

You might ask Me to speak about My own mystery. It is not easy to understand it. When you have the chance, gather all the joy you can. There is no use of bolting the door after the thieves have robbed and fled. Seize the chance and do not repent later that you missed the opportunity. Remember, you have to come to Me, if not in this birth, atleast within ten more births! Strive to acquire Grace; Grace is the reward for spiritual practice; the highest spiritual discipline is to follow the instructions of the Master.

Years of rigorous training make the soldier, who can then stand all the rigours of warfare. The heroic fighter is not made in a day. So too, the practising spiritual aspirant (*saadhaka*) who can win victories, is not made in a day. Restrictions and regulations, drill and techniques have been laid down for him also. Follow them sincerely and steadily and victory is yours.

*Prashaanthi Nilayam, 12-2-1964*

---

*Pain is a gap between two moments of happiness.*

*Happiness is an interval between two moments of pain.*

SHRI SATHYA SAI

## 6. Kaashi and Badhri

LIFE is only relatively real; until death, it appears to be real, that is all. For the procession of the bride and groom, the father of the bride had brought an elephant or rather the model of an elephant, correct to the minutest detail; the model was taken by all who saw it to be alive. Then, while all were admiring the wonderful work of art and arguing that it was alive, it exploded, shooting forth lovely little stars and snakes of light that gleamed through the sky. It was filled with fireworks and when it was lit, the entire stock filling the inside emerged, with a burst of noise and a brilliant riot of light and colour. Man is like that elephant, true, until the explosion!

Before that explosion happens, man must realise himself. The fireworks are desire, anger, delusion, pride and jealousy etc., and they now fill this artificial animal, useful only for the show. Man is saved from such calamity by *Vedhaantha*, which is like the roar of the lion; it gives Courage and Enterprise; it makes man a hero. It does not whine or howl or cry. It drives cowardice away; instils the highest types of self-confidence. It is the strongest armour against the arrows of fate. It acts like a waterproof against the hailstorms of sensual pleasure. It is a curtain keeping out the mosquitoes of worry, which would otherwise rob you of sleep. With *Vedhaantha*-saturated heart, you are a rock on the shore, unaffected by the waves of temptation. *Vedhaantha* challenges your spirit of adventure, your own reality. Get into the train of spiritual discipline now; station by station, you will reach the terminus, which is *jnaana* (realisation) of you and of all this. Go to Penukonda, purchase a ticket for Bangalore and sit in the train. Do not get down in the middle when some station attracts you. The stations are *karma, upaasana* (action, contemplation), etc. You have to pass through them, but remember they are not the termini. The terminus is Realisation.

## Harmonious outlook essential

Man is now possessed by the ghost of Delusion; he is prating a language which is unbecoming, behaving like an animal moving in a zigzag manner, climbing and sliding. I have come to exorcise the ghost; that is part of My work. This delusion, that the man who is possessed is really intelligent, has caused great harm. For example, Pandiths spend a good deal of time to argue that Raama is superior to Krishna or that Krishna is superior, whereas the truth is that each of them reveals a certain phase of Divinity. The comparison itself diminishes the integrity of the inquirer. If he has any reverence, he would not attempt an intellectual estimate; he would try to get an intuitive experience, as Raamakrishna Paramahamsa did; and, then he would realise that one is as sweet as the other. Saint Thyaagaraaja discovered this because he was a mystic, one who experienced, instead of arguing over it. He sang that Raama is composed of two sounds, '*Raa*' taken from Naa-*raa*-ya-na and '*Ma*' taken from Na-*ma*-sshi-va-ya; that Raama is the harmonisation of *Vaishnavism* and *Shaivism* (worship of God as Vishnu and worship of God as Shiva). Harmony is the test of any religious outlook; if it breeds hate or faction or pride, the outlook is definitely evil. Keep away from such, if you are interested in your spiritual practice.

## Regulate love with virtue and service

I am not attracted by learning or scholarship, which does not lead anywhere except towards egoism and pride. I am drawn only by devotion. Bring to Me whatever troubles you have; I shall take them on and give you *Aanandha*. When I like My devotees, I like their faults too, though some here turn up their noses and laugh at the peculiar follies and foibles of people who come from all the various States. I am drawn by the Love which brings you here from long distances through great difficulties, which makes you happy in spite of the want of the comforts to which you are accustomed, which makes you put up with the life under the trees or in the open sheds.

I know that you do not go to the old *mandhir* (temple) in the village, for as you say, from there you cannot see Me whenever I happen to pass from this side of the building to the other! I am here since three hours and you are having sight of Me (*darshan*) so long; but, yet, as soon as I go up into My room, you rush to the Nilayam to get another *darshan*, as I come out into the verandah! What greater sign of devotion is needed than this yearning for *darshan*?

But, this love alone is not enough. In fact, it does not mean much at all. What is wanted is the regulation of that Love, in the form of virtue and service. If you achieve that, then there is none to equal you, in this age. As the seed, so the sapling; as the status, so the behaviour; as the teacher, so the students; as the food, so the belch. Here, renunciation and divine love from the atmosphere, and silence is the discipline. Do not criticise others; criticise yourselves rather. Have the name of the Lord on your tongue; the form of the Lord before your eye. If you shape yourself this way, the place where you stand will become Kaashi, the house which you inhabit will become Badhri. Let all your activities be directed towards the purification of your hearts. You have My Blessings in this endeavour.

*Prashaanthi Nilayam, 3-2-1964*

*The play is His,*
*The role is His,*
*The lines are written by Him.*
*He directs,*
*He designs the dress*
*and decoration,*
*the gesture and the tone,*
*the entrance and exit.*
*You have to act well the part*
*and receive His approbation*
*when the curtain falls.*

**Shri Sathya Sai**

## 7. Beacons of light

I AM glad I am speaking to a gathering of artists, poets and literary men, as well as those who are interested in promoting the fine arts. You have met here to commemorate the Coronation of Krishna Devaraaya, the Vijayanagara Emperor who patronised poetry, drama, sculpture, painting, music, dance, and literature and revived Hindu *Dharma* through all these media. The culture of Bhaarath (India) that has grown from the ageless *Vedhas* (the four ancient books of Hinduism) was for some time overwhelmed by the influence of Western standards of life and thought, on account of the artificial support they got when Westerners ruled over this land. Now, it has to be re-discovered and re-established, mainly through the removal of the weaknesses among the people of Bhaarath. People have become too weak to be the recipients of the tremendously powerful Message of the Eternal Religion, *Sanaathana Dharma*! The individual is called by us, *vyakthi*, do you know why? Because we expect him to make *vyaktha*, that is to say, to manifest his Divinity! *Ishwarassarvabhuuthaanaam hrddese, Arjuna, thishtathi* : "The Lord is residing in the heart of all beings, O Arjuna!" thus said Lord Krishna to Arjuna in the Bhagavadh Geetha. Demonstrate that it is true, realise Him within your heart, let Him become manifest, that is the obligation of the individual.

The Kings of Vijayanagara had virtue, courage, patriotism, love of *Dharma*, generosity, vision, statesmanship. They built many temples; they restorted dilapidated ones; they constructed many tanks and towns. It is good to remember them and be grateful for what they did. But, there is one mistake which you should not commit: do not be contented merely with the contemplation of the past. Why survey the road which you have traversed already? Why allow the achievements of the past to curb enthusiasm in the present? You ask, can we today carve or build or paint or sing as well as they in the Vijayanagara Empire did? That is a sign of weakness, being benumbed by fear.

## Give no room for cowardice

A hermit once met the Cholera Goddess on the road, returning from a village where she had thinned the population. He asked her how many she had taken into her lap. She replied, "Only ten." But, really speaking, the casualties were a hundred. She explained, "I killed only ten; the rest died out of fear!" Man is *Aathmaswaruupa* (Self-embodied), that is, *Abhayaswaruupa* (Fearlessness-embodied). If he knows his real nature, he will give no room for weakness or cowardice.

That is the main aim of culture, to cultivate mental calm, mental courage, to make every one feel kinship with every one else. You are born with the cry, '*koham*' (who am I?), on your lips; when you depart, you must have the declaration, '*Soham*' (I am He), on your smiling face. This is the message of the *Dharma* which

Krishnadevaraya fostered. Take that lesson home from this meeting. You are now seeing with the EYE---a three-lettered physical apparatus, the three letters representing the three qualities: *Sathwa, Rajas* and *Thamas* (purity and poise, restless activity, ignorance and inertia). See with the clarified, unprejudiced, unattached 'I'; then, you see only One; though you see yourself, you are indeed everything that refers itself as 'I'.

## Win the title the *Upanishadhs* proclaim

It is because this single aim (*lakshya*) has been given up, that all this confusion (*avalakshana*), has come about! Bezwada Gopala Reddy said just now that the Pandiths who have specialised in the ancient scriptures and sacred texts are the *Maanasa-sarovara* (the holy lake where the holy river Brahmaputhra arises) of our culture; but, very few honour such men today. There is a general neglect of the higher aspects of culture. People know more about the details of the personal lives of film stars; more and more of them are getting interested in such trash. They do not care for the Pandith toiling in the same street; they do not know the names of the poets and the painters of their own town. That is the tragedy of the educated classes; they have no sense of values.

This day, when you have called here literary men like Puttaparthi Naaraayanaachar, I feel it is a day of *Aanandhodhayam* (dawn of Bliss) for every one; for, leterature gives, or ought to give, bliss and peace. You honour a ruler for promoting culture and literature; well, you must recognise, therefore, that the rulers have a responsibility even today to continue the tradition. They must canalise the energy of the people and their intelligence into moral activities and socially harmonising programmes. I always encourage religious, social and cultural activities (*Sanaathanam, Saanghikam* and

*Saamskrithikam*) the three S's; if it is reviving the values recognised as great by time or recreating the damaged structure of the good society, or restoring vigour to some fine art that is declining, you can count on My Blessings. I always exhort people to win, not the titles that come to those who canvass support, but the title that the *Upanishadhs* proclaim as the highest decoration for spiritual aspirants: *Amrithasya Puthraah*, Children of Immortality.

Of what use is it if a man boasts that his grandfather was a great scholar? *Manuja*, the Sanskrit word of Man, implies a noble ancestry, from Manu Himself. Boast of your inner Divinity which is your greatest treasure. I must say this to the poets and writers who are here: Saraswathi is a Goddess, the Consort of *Brahma*, the creator; you are the votaries of a Goddess, whom every one worships; She confers wisdom and liberation. Be true to the highest boons She confers. Do not be contented if you give some food for the worldly hunger of the senses. Do not lower your ideals for the sake of cheap fame or vulgarise public taste. Instead of *loukika sringaram* (worldly enjoyment of sex), give *aloukika Aathmaanandham* (Bliss of the Self). Contribute to the expansion of love, the purification of motives, the enlargement of sympathy, the tolerance of difference, the respect for individual striving.

By all means, pay gratitude to the heroes of the past and the benefactors of the present. But fill yourself with enthusiasm to reach the Goal, by means of good thoughts and good deeds and good words. Kalluru Subba Rao spoke of the 25 years of struggle he has had, to celebrate this Festival in various parts of Rayalaseema, the struggle he had to change the name of these districts into Rayalaseema, instead of the old name, Ceded Districts or Dattamandala. He must be helped much more, not by means of *maatalu* (words) but by *mootalu* (bags of money). Festivals like this have to be celebrated more frequently, and I too shall join you more frequently.

In fact, Puttaparthi is just 16 miles off; still, I have come like this to Penukonda only twice—once when Krishnarao brought Me to preside over the District Athletic Competitions and now, when Krishnadevaraya brought Me! I am looking forward to share My joy with all and so, I feel that you have but to invite Me and I shall be with you. I know that you have not understood Me yet; you only see Me from a distance, see Me through the thousands who pass through your town to come to Me. If only you catch a little of their faith and joy, you will be amply rewarded. I have been worried—if worry is the name for that feeling—that while people from the farthest corners of this country and even from foreign countries are benefiting, the people of Penukonda are denying themselves the chance of sharing My *Aanandham*.

Penukonda, the town that derives its name from the mountain, has been too long a heap of stones, albeit a huge heap. Your hearts must become *kondas*, that is, huge mountain peaks, and on the top, as in Arunagiri, the *Jyothi* (light) of knowledge must shine like a beacon. Learn, experience, and be happy. Control, canalise and secure. It does not matter a bit if you have no faith in Me or in God. Have faith in yourselves, that is enough. For, who are you, really? Each of you is Divinity, whether you know it or not.

*Penukonda: Jubilee Celebrations of the Coronation of Krishnadevaraya of the Vijayanagara Empire, 17-2-1964.*

## 8. Dharmakshethra

THIS is the Inaugural Meeting of the Prashaanthi Vidwanmahaasabha established to promote the knowledge and practice among all mankind of the fundamental truths, beliefs and disciplines of *Sanaathana Dharma* (Eternal Religion). The Raaja Saheb just now gave expression to his great joy and satisfaction that the Wheel of Revival is being set in motion by Me at this place, from the Palace, in spite of the claims of many other places for that honour. It was at Rajahmundry last year, on Shri Raama Navami Day, that I announced to the Pandiths gathered around Me on the sands of an island in the river Godaavari, the aims and objects of this Sabha. Naturally, devotees resident there were hoping and preparing themselves in that hope, that the Inaugural Meeting could be arranged in their town. Without doubt, Rajahmundry is a place competent to bear that honour. With its historic past and large number of *Aasthika Sanghas* (Associations of believers) and institutions that it is fostering, it ranks high among the upholders of tradition. But, like all good things and all lucky chances, this too is won, not so much by effort, as by merit---merit accumulated through years, and even through centuries and ages!

## The Godward path is *Karma* based on *Dharma*

This is an epoch-making event. For, it is no less than the Dawn of the Golden Era of the Liberation of Humanity. Venkatagiri has been for centuries the seat of a Royal Family dedicated to the support, protection and promotion of *Dharma* and so, it has earned this honour. Consider how many temples were built or renovated or maintained by the Raajas of Venkatagiri! Take count of the number of Pandiths they have patronised and encouraged, the number of religious books their donations have helped to see light! Consider the atmosphere of *Dharma* which they established in this State for centuries. See the interest the family is taking even now, when their State and status have been swept away by the storms of political change.

*Bhaarathavarsha* (Mother India) has kept before her this ideal of *Dharma*. That is the taproot of her culture, the source of her vigour and vitality. The Godward path is action based on righteousness (*Karma* based on *Dharma*). That is the path, also towards joy, contentment and therefore of strength. Now, the path has become hidden by an overgrowth of briar and bush; the bridges and culverts are in disrepair. People have forgotten the goal, the path, and the habit of walking on it. That road is the only refuge; it must be trodden tomorrow, if not, today, for the goal lies at the end of that road. It was laid down centuries ago, beyond the memory of history, in the *Vedhas. Sathyam vadha, Dharmam chara*---"Speak the truth, practise righteousness," the *Vedhas* call on you. These Pandiths well versed in *Vedhas* and *Shaasthras* know what *Dharma* is and they can explain it to you without distortion. That is why you have to go to them reverentially and seat them amidst you and get enlightened by them. Knowing is not being. You must try to translate into daily life what you learn from them. The moral life is the best prescription for joyful life.

## Learn to live in His Glory

Every one's heart is a *Dharmakshethra* (the scene of Mahaabhaaratha war) where the battle between the forces of Good and Evil is fought. Why, the whole country is *Dharmakshethra*. So, the mothers and children of this land must be devoted to *Dharma*, above all. The Geetha begins with word, *Dharmakshethrae*, and ends with the words, *Sarva Dharmaan parityajya*: through *Dharma*, you have to transcend *Dharma*. That is why Kaushalya exhorted Raama when he went into the forest, "May the *Dharma* which you are upholding by this act, be your guardian when you are in the forest, as an exile." And, Raama too upheld *Dharma* even under the most trying circumstances. When, after the death of Raavana, Vibheeshana's Coronation was arranged, he prayed that Raama himself should crown him in the city of Lanka. But, Raama declared that His vow and His father's orders did not allow Him to set foot in a city during the years of exile. That period was not yet over, He said. So, the function was attended only by Sugreeva and others. Raama thus demonstrated by His actions how scrupulously *Dharma* had to be observed. We want mothers who are so wise, and children who are so steadfast in the practice of *Dharma*.

Practice---that is the real thing in spiritual matters. Scholarship is a burden, it is very often a handicap. So long as God is believed to be far away, in temples and holy places, man will feel religion a burden and a hurdle.

But, plant Him in your heart and you feel light, burdenless, and even strong. It is like the food basket; when carried on the shoulder, it feels heavy; you are too weak even to carry it. But, sit near a stream and eat it. Though the total weight has not decreased, you feel lighter and stronger. That is the consequence of taking the food in: do likewise, with the idea of God. Do not carry it on the shoulder, have it 'in.'

Keep the memory of the Lord and His Glory always with you; that will quicken your steps and you will arrive soon at the Goal. The mother, coming from the well, with a pot of water on her head, another on the hip and a third in her hand, hurries home, since she is always conscious of the infant in the cradle. If she forgets the infant, her gait slows down and she wanders around, chatting with all her friends. Similarly, if God, the Goal, is not cherished in the memory, one has to wander through many births and arrive home late.

God is the life-breath of every soul. So, learn to live in His Glory, in His Memory, in His Contemplation, every moment. That is what the *Vedhas* and *Shaasthras* teach.

*Venkatagiri, 18-2-1964*

---

*If there is righteousness in the heart there is beauty in character.*

*If there is beauty in character there is harmony in the home.*

*If there is harmony in the home there is order in the nation.*

*If there is order in the nation there is peace in the world.*

**Shri Sathya Sai**

## 9. Yanthram & Manthram

MAN has immense capacities latent in him, waiting to be tapped and used. He has many talents which he has to bring to light. He feels the urge to love all beings, to share his joys and griefs with his kind, to know more and satisfy the curiosity of his intellect, to peep behind the awe and wonder that Nature arouses in him. He is able to gather information about all kinds of things from all corners of the world, but, he is unaware of what happens in the corners of his own mind. He knows who is who among all the rest, but, he does not know the answer to the simple question, "Who am I?"

The fact is, he has to ask it himself and seek out the clue to the enigma himself. He has not felt that it is essential to know the answer; he is content to move about blindly in the world, groping his way in the dark. Without knowing who he himself is, he is rashly judging, labelling and even libelling other men! This is the fundamental reason for the hollowness of human life today, for the hate and fear that stalk the world.

The *Vedhas* and *Shaasthras* of India have the key to that answer; they can teach you the process by which you can discover it for yourself if you are so inclined. There are only twenty-six letters in the English alphabet; yet by combining them in various ways, thousands of books are written. So too, the ideas and hints given in the *Vedhas* may be a few; their application explains the entire literature of *Akshara*, which means both 'letter' and 'indestructible.' Every person born in Bhaarath must be an exemplar of these disciplines; for, '*Bhaa*' implies 'splendour,' *prakaasham*, the splendour that is encased in man, and '*Rathi*' implies 'the desire to manifest it, to taste it.' Live up to that glory and you will all be transformed into fullness.

## The Divine Principle

You are the Formless (*Niraakaaram*) come in the form of Man (*Naraakaaram*), the Infinite, come in the role of the finite, the Formless Infinite appearing as the formful infinitesimal, the Absolute pretending to be the Relative, the *Aathma* behaving as the body, the Metaphysical masquerading as the merely physical. The Universal *Aathma* (Self) is the basis of all being. The sky was there before houses were built under it; it penetrated and pervaded them for some time; then, the houses crumbled and became heaps and mounds; but, the sky was not affected at all. So too, the *Aathma* pervades the body and subsists even when the body is reduced to dust.

The same inexplicable, invisible, electric current, when it enters a bulb, a fan, a stove, a cooler, or a sprayer, activates each one of them or all of them together. Similarly, *Ishwara sarva bhoothaanaam* : the Divine Principle activates all beings. That is the inner core, the Divine Spark, more minute than the minutest, more magnificent than the most magnificent. To observe the minute you must use a microscope; to bring the remote nearer your eye, you seek the help of a telescope; these are *Yanthras* (material instruments). The instruments that help you to visualise the Core that has such strange contradictory attributes are called *Manthras*---formulae that save you when you meditate on them. They are also called *Thanthras* (Ceremonies and rites) when their practical application has to be emphasised. Faith in the efficacy of these *Manthras* and in the utility of the procedure prescribed, as well as in the existence of the Core are all essential for success in the great adventure, just as faith in the efficacy of the *Yanthra*, in the correctness of the procedure, and in the existence of the material he is seeking to know more about are essential for the scientist.

## "The liberation from night"

You must tackle this problem, straight from where it starts. Ignorance can be cured only by knowledge; darkness can be destroyed only by light. No amount of argument or threat or persuasion can compel darkness to move away. A flash, that is enough; it is gone. Prepare for that flash of illumination; **the light is** there already, in you. But, since it is heavily **overladen by** repressing factors, it cannot reveal itself. "The liberation from night" which happens when the light is revealed, is called *Moksha*. Every one has to achieve it, whether he is striving for it now or not. It is the inevitable end to the struggle, the goal to which all are proceeding.

But, please do not be afraid of reaching the goal of liberation (*Moksha*)! Do not conceive that stage as a calamity. It is the end of calamity. It is death to all grief; the birth of joy---a joy that knows no decline, the death of grief, grief that will never more be born.

Well, how do you prepare yourself for the stage? I must tell you that the answer is in that very word

*Moksha*, itself. It is self-explanatory. '*Mo*' indicates *Moha* (delusion; being deluded by the scintillating, the gaudy, the transitory, the temporary trash); and, '*ksha*' means *kshaya* (decline; disappearance, destruction). It requires you to keep the flights of your mind away from these deluding attractions, and on the straight path towards liberation.

## Avoid illusion by denying it

See how the insufferable heat of the Sun is controlled and modulated and reduced by your bodily mechanism to the congenial temperature of 98.4 degree; so, you too should keep the destructive force of your elemental passions born out of the clamour of *sabdha, sparsha, ruupa, rasa, gandha* (sound, touch, form, taste, smell) rigorously in check and bring it down to tolerable levels, yielding comfort and congenial living. You yourselves create the illusion of which you are the slave; deny it, don't give it a chance to Lord over you, then it will not harm you. Someone was told, "There, inside that well, lies your shadow." He said, "No; it cannot be." But, he decided, nevertheless, to go and verify the fact. He walked up to the well and peeped in. And, lo, he found it was true. The well had his shadow inside! Poor fellow, he did not know that the shadow would be there only when he looked in! Do not test *Maayaa*. Try to locate it, it will present itself. You can avoid it only by denying it; you can escape only by concentrating on the substance; do not attach any value to the shadow, whether inside the well or outside it. For, after all, it is just a shadow!

Illusion haunts man as *kaama* or *thrishna* (desire). Desire calls for *sabdha, sparsha, ruupa, rasa, gandha*---the qualities of the Five Elements of which man is the complex; *sabdha* of *Aakaasha* (space), *sparsha* of *Vayu* (air), *ruupa* of *Agni* (fire), *rasa* of *Jala* (water), and *gandha* of the Earth. Man is prompted by the element of Space in him to seek sweet sounds that satisfy the ear, by the element of Air in him to run after smooth and soft things that yield pleasure to the skin, by the element of Fire in him to pursue things that by beauty of form appeal to the eye, the Water element in him to crave for food and drink that are tasty to the tongue, and by the inner urge of the element of Earth in him to cater to the nose, by trying to enjoy perfume and fragrance and pleasant smells. *Kaama* (desire) has a two-headed son, *krodha-lobha* by name, the twin-headed monster anger-greed. Through the malignant designs of these three, you are robbed of lasting happiness.

## Be the Prince you really are

Unaware of your Divine Status, you revel in low company; you toil and sweat as the slave of mean passions which drag you into disgrace. Be the Prince you really are. Be like the lotus, which though born in the slush at the bottom of the lake, by sheer will-power rises above the waters to see the Sun and be inspired by its rays. The lotus discards contact with water, though it is born and bred in that element; so, you too should avoid being attached to the elemental passions, that the elements constituting you urge you into. How long are you to sit content with the minor role of a clown or a clout? Are you not ashamed? Have you no ambition? Why smother your genuine talents under a self-imposed mask? All these are zero roles; take on the role of the hero which is your right, and shine!

I shall tell you how to deserve that role, how to earn it from the *Suuthradhara*, the Director of this play. Enter on a course of spiritual discipline; your experience itself will tell you the validity and the value of that course. Instal a radio receiver, select the wavelength of the station you propose to listen to, switch on correctly to that wavelength, and you hear the programme clear and distinct. Your ear will tell you the accuracy with which you have tuned. Similarly, take on a form of *manthra* (*manthraswaruupam*); pronounce it and meditate on it with accurate care and steady attention; tune in to the Voice of God within you. One of the obstacles in the way of the spiritual aspirant is the satire and criticism poured on him by quacks that crowd round him. Do not pay heed to their advice or their barbs. They are experts only in the silly short-lived trivialities of social life or sensual pleasure. Most people nowadays are more interested in the history of film stars than in the history of *Yogis* and *Paramahamsas* (ascetics of the highest order) who can save you from the disaster of deep-seated ignorance.

### Three-stranded rope of Yama

Yama or the God of Death is described as dragging his victims to his abode by means of the rope of *paasa* (snare). Well. He has no rope factory there, for supplying him with the rope he needs. You manufacture the rope yourself and have it ready round your neck; he has only to take hold of the rope and pull you along! It is a three-stranded rope, the strands being *Ahamkaara*, *Vishayavaasana* and *Kaama* (Egoism, Sense-attachment and Desire).

Do not respect men who are caught up in the tangle of the senses. Give respect according to the knowledge each possesses of himself, i.e., of the Immanent and the Transcendent. How do you fix the price of cane? According to the sugar content, is it not? You evaluate oranges in proportion to the juice they contain, is it not? So too, a man is worthy of honour in proportion to the knowledge of the Self he has acquired. This knowledge alone can confer steadiness and strength. Without it, all profession of renunciation, all pretence of devotion, all performance of charity are but tongue-deep or skin-deep!

It is not the resolution that matters; it is resoluteness. Resolution is just a string of words. You may know the 700 *slokas* of the Bhagavadh Geetha by heart; but, believe Me, the time you spent in learning it by rote, and in reciting it, is all a waste, if you do not resolutely act upon even a single *shloka*. Why? That learning might even be handicap; for the skill has affected your head, and made it swell with pride.

## Dharma will never play false

Bhagavadh Geetha is a means by which you can get immersed in your own *Bhagavadh-bhaava* (relationship with God). If you are so immeresed, you will have undiminished, undiminishable *Aanandham, Nithyaanandham* (Eternal Bliss). Now, in your ignorance, you feel small, you feel miserable, you feel that the wicked, the greedy, the cruel, are all happier than you and unjustifiably so. You feel it is unjust that you who are so truthful, so loving, so good, should suffer. Just ponder over this. Are they as happy as you imagine, and is your condition so bad as you picture? Just investigate and you will find out for yourself. They are only painted pots of poison; the paint of honey is just a thin coating, a mere show. Their hearts know no peace; they are as miserable as you, if not more.

Believe that *Dharma* or Moral Rectitude will never play false; it will ensure greater joy than can be gained through all other means. Raama destroyed Raavana; it was a victory of one head over ten; concentration over distraction. Raavana craved for *Prakrithi* (Seetha) discarding the *Purusha* (Spirit) which gave it values and meaning, viz., Raama. If you crave for *Prakrithi*, the objective world, you degrade yourself, you deny your reality, and you join Raavana's brood. Do not also imagine that the Lord is outside *Prakrithi*, or even of you, who are really a part of the objective world. He is in you, behind you, beside you, before you. He is the eye of your eye; the I of your I. Yearn for the *yoga* or union with Him, through the unwavering awareness of His being the real You. Yearn for *yoga*; and whatever *bhoga* (pleasure) you really need will be offered to you in due course. If on the other hand, you yearn for *bhoga* itself, you are gone! You are blessed only with *roga* (disease), remember!

Live in the consuming conviction that you are the *Aathman*. That is the hard core of the Eternal Teaching. The *Aathma* it is that sees through the eyes, hears through the ears, handles through the fingers, moves through the feet. That is the basic 'you.' That 'you' is not elated by praise or deflated by blame. When some one carps at you, reason out thus within yourself: 'Is he casting aspersions on my body? Well. Why should I be worried? He is doing just what I should myself do, casting out the attachment to the flesh, to this paltry prison. Or, is he throwing them at the *Aathma*? Nothing can affect its purity; or tarnish its glory. So remain calm and unperturbed.' You may ask, what happens then to the strings of abuse? Like the letter sent by post and refused by the addressee, it returns to the sender!

I enjoin you to go home and ruminate over these suggestions and ideas. Reflect upon what you have heard, especially from these who convey to you the gems contained in the ancient scriptures, tested on the touch-stone of experience all along the centuries. *Sanaathana Dharma* recommends the three-fold course of listening, recapitulating, concentrating. Listening makes you learned only. Concentrated meditation on the meaning of the thing heard gives you the fruit of the teaching as intended by the Teacher.

*Venkatagiri, 19-2-1964*

## 10. A rupee or hundred paise?

PICHAYYA Shaasthry of Nellore spoke so feelingly of his ardour and anxiety to meet Me, an ardour he has had had for many years, he also spoke of the joy he now has at the realisation of his desire. Of course, for every desire to come true, the time, the cause and the circumstances have to coincide. It is just today that, in his case, these three combined to give him this satisfaction. I have known him all these years and I was aware of his yearning to come to Me, especially during the last four years, and I called him today to have his wish fulfilled.

Remilla Suuryaprkasha Shaasthry spoke on the *Apaurusheyathwa* (not having a person as their author) of the *Vedhas* and Vaaranaasi Subrahmanya Shaasthry on *Dharma* as reflected in the actions of Raama as depicted in the Vaalmeeki Raamaayana. These are subjects of great interest to all of you. But, I must chide you for not paying them the attention they and the subjects deserved; you were restless and worried and not concentrating on the teaching. This is a part of the atmosphere that you carry about with you, wherever you go, nowadays. There is lack of earnestness, of single-pointed attention.

The trouble is, you are moving in the wrong direction, away from the desirable destination. You have come into the world to realise yourselves, fully equipped with all the instruments needed for that endeavour—*viveka, vairaagya* and *vichakshana*—(discrimination, non-attachment and ability), the urge to enlarge your love, to enrich your emotions, to ennoble your actions.

But, you have lost your way; you are caught in a morass; you are confused by mirages and dreams which you take as real; you run after false colours and cheap substitutes.

## *Vedha* is the source of *Dharma*

Subrahmanya Shaasthry, using his erudite scholarship, selected from the Raamaayana fine incidents to show that Raama is the perfect embodiment of *Dharma* and proclaiming *Dharma* to the world. In his arguments with the dying Vali, he declared that all beings, endowed with discrimination, are bound by righteousness and shall meet punishment if they should ignore it. He was aware of all the various applications of *Dharma* in the various fields of human activity.

Now, the *Vedha* is the source of *Dharma, Vedha* which Suuryaprakasha Shaasthry declared was revealed to the *Yogic* Consciousness of sages. And Raama is the Personification of that *Dharma*. So Raamaayana partakes of the excellence of the *Vedhas*. The Mahaabhaaratha is generally known as the *Fifth Vedha*. And the Bhaagavatha describes the Glory and the Grace of the Lord and His splendour as the Indweller in All. So, that too is as efficacious as the *Vedhas* to elevate man and to release him from the bondage to the mean and the sordid.

It is the *Vedhaswaruupam* (essence of the *Vedhas*) that is enshrined in these three works, thus making them equally effective as drugs to cure you of ignorance. But, why do you promote clamour and discord by accusing these Brahmins of exclusiveness and monopolistic greed? Even they, in spite of all their faith and sacrifice, are finding it difficult to follow the regimen recommended by the *Vedhas*. They have generations of practice and encouragement behind them.

## Develop the Divinity in you

The study of the *Vedhic* lore has been with them and their families for centuries; but, yet, they are finding it hard to live up to *Vedhic* standards of Brahminhood. How then can you take it? Four persons have a rupee coin each; if each changes the coin into naya paise and keeping 25 for himself, gives 25 each to the other three, no one loses. Each of them has a hundred paise, instead of a single coin, but, there has been no diminution of the purchasing power each had at the beginning. The Raamaayana, the Mahaabhaaratha and the Bhaagavatha are 100 paise; the *Vedha* is the rupee. That is all the difference. Why then lose yourself in this campaign of hatred? Why try to carry a burden which is beyond the capacity of your shoulders? Look at all the time-tables, the restrictions and regulations, the ceremonies and rites that the Brahmins have burdened themselves with. Their purpose is not merely to ensure security and solace to themselves but, even more, to ensure the orderly working of the forces of nature for the benefit of all mankind, of all beings in all the worlds. That is the high ideal for which they have imposed on themselves all the toil and tribulation.

Your duty is to concentrate on the development of the Divinity latent in you; once you do that, all hate and all pride will disappear; you will become humble fellow-pilgrims with the Brahmins, to the same goal, though along parallel paths. Remember these things cannot be decided by the counting of votes or measuring popular support. You cannot judge fish as more precious than diamonds, merely because there are more crowds in the fish-market, and only a handful of customers in the shops selling diamonds.

## Aanandha has to be earned the hard way

The cottage and the castle are both built on the earth: so too, all faiths and religions, all disciplines have the *Vedha* as the basis. The special feature of Indian culture is that here the dress and demeanour, the language and literature, the manner and mode of living, the ideals and institutions are all attuned to the spiritual progress of man, emphasising as they do the superiority of the spirit over the body, the subtle over the gross. Everything is subordinated to that supreme task. The body should be fed and kept free from disease. Why? So that it may be fit for spiritual discipline. Spiritual discipline for what? For the realisation of the truth about oneself. The subtle is the basis for the gross; the Divine is the basis for the Human. Indian Culture turns your eye to the basis, not to what is built upon it.

This outlook was, for long, the natural outlook for every Indian; it was automatic, even. It was imbibed at the mother's lap, from the father in the field, the teacher at school, from neighbour and freinds and relatives, from the old and the young, from whatever was done or written or spoken by those around. It is because that attitude is fast disappearing and is in danger of being completely thrown overboard that this Prashaanthi Vidwanmahaasabha has been started by Me to remind you once again of the duty of cultivating it.

You will all doubtless agree when I say the Divine Bliss is your greatest need. But, you cannot order it from any shop. It has to be earned the hard way: doing good deeds, moving in good company, desisting from evil, keeping the mind attached to the Glory of God. Good and bad cannot be kept together in the same vessel; then, the good also will turn bad. Night and light cannot coexist. The Sun was proud that he had no enemies left. But, some one told him that he had one enemy left, viz., Darkness. Then, he sent his rays, the emissaries, to seek out the foe, but, wherever they went, they saw only light, the darkness was nowhere to be found. They returned and reported : "There was no such thing as Darkness upon the earth; we made the most rigorous search!"

## Make intellect Master of your mind

Suuryaprakaasha Shaasthry said that the worlds this side of *Suuryaloka* are all inhabited by beings that are subject to life and death, to the processes of involution and evolution and that the world on the other side are inhabited by beings that are free from these aspects of change. He also asked, who can give us the secret of transcending the barrier that divides the region of death from the region of immortality? Of course, the Lord has often sent Messengers to tell humanity about it and He has Himself come down in human form to communicate it and save mankind from perdition. It is because the task of guiding man has gone on so consistently that today in India there is at least this quantum of earnestness to achieve it and to escape from the cycle of birth and death.

You can gain that victory only by rigorous *Saadhana*. Spiritual discipline is more arduous than physical discipline; imagine the tremendous amount of effort undergone by the lady who runs along a wire stretched across the ring, underneath the circus tent. After all, the gain is just a few rupees. The same steadfastness and systematic effort aimed at a higher reward can endow you with mental balance and you can maintain your equilibrium under the most adverse or the most intoxicating circumstances. The *Jnaanendhriyas* (organs of perception) are more important for this type of *saadhana* than the *Karmendhriyas* (sense organs), the intellect more important than all the rest of the inner instruments given to man. Make the intellect the Master of your mind and you will not fail; you will fail only when the senses establish mastery over the mind.

## Clarify intellect by spiritual discipline

A lame man and a blind man became friends and they moved from place to place, the lame man riding on the shoulders of the blind. One day, while passing through some fields, the lame man saw hundreds of what are called *Dosakaayis* (an edible variety of gourd) in a field and he suggested to the blind man that they pluck a few and eat their full. The blind man had greater sense and so he did not welcome the idea immediately he heard about it. He asked, "Brother! Have they fenced the crop?" The lame man said, "No." Then, the blind man said, "Let us go our way. The *Dosakaayis* must be bitter; that is why they are left unguarded." You know there are sweet as well as bitter *Dosakaayis* and the blind man, by his intellect, was able to discover that they were bitter, even without tasting them. His intelligence perceived the truth faster and clearer.

Clarify the intellect by spiritual discipline so that you get a vision of the Lord who dwells within; that is the *Suudarshana* (Discus, a weapon of Vishnu) which saved Gajendra, the wild elephant (man) that was caught by the alligator (egoism) while rollicking in the lake of

*Samsaara* (the objective world). Look upon joy and grief as teachers of hardihood and balance. Grief is a friendly reminder, a good taskmaster, even a better teacher than joy. The Lord grants both protection and punishment; for, how can He be the Lord, if He does not insist on strict accounting and strict obedience?

You are as distant from the Lord as you think you are, as near Him as you feel you are. Well, let Me tell you this. The distance from Me to you is the same as the distance from you to Me, is it not? But, you complain that I am far far from you, though you are approaching nearer and nearer. How can that be? I am as near you as you are near Me.

## You are a prisoner under sentence

That nearness is won by Devotion, which cannot be steady except after getting rid of "I" and "Mine". When a prisoner is taken from place to place, he is accompained by two constables, is it not? When man who is a prisoner in this jail moves from one place to another, he too is accompained by *Ahamkaaram* and *Mamaakaaram*: Egoism and Attachment. When he moves about without these two, you can be sure he is a free man, liberated from prison.

Now that I have referred to jail and jail life, let Me tell you something more. You are all under sentence of imprisonment and are in this jail. There is no use hoping for reward when you work in jail; you have to work because you are ordered to; and you must work well too. You cannot argue that rewards are not distributed justly and you are not entitled to desist from your allotted task. If you do so, your sentence will be extended or you will be transferred to another jail. On the other hand, if you quietly accept the sentence and go about your work without clamouring or murmuring, your term is reduced, and you are sent out with a certificate that ensures a happy life, unpestered by constables. This is the attitude that the *jeevi* (individual) must adopt, if he is aware of his sentence and if he is earnest about freeing himself.

Remember, Freedom is your birthright. Concentrate on that and practise the means of attaining it.

*Venkatagiri, 20-02-1964*

---

*Remember that with every step,
you are nearing God.
And when you take one step towards Him
God takes ten steps towards you.
There is no halting place in the pilgrimage!
It is one continuous journey,
through day and night,
through tears and smiles,
through death and birth,
through tomb and womb.
When the road ends and goal is gained,
the pilgrim finds
that he has travelled
from himself to himself,
that was long and lonesome;
but God that lead him unto,
was all the while in him,
around him, with him and besides him.
He himself was always Divine.*

**Shri Sathya Sai**

## 11. Role of the Pandith

THE springs of Indian culture have very nearly gone dry, under the scorching influence of foreign cultures to which Indians are fast selling themselves. The agencies which are keeping the tree green, have become weak; institutions and customery rites and rituals which kept the facets of that culture alive in the eyes of the people, have faded into feebleness. People, who were charged with the social duty of reminding the masses of their heritage, have been rendered dispirited and mendicant. The *Dharma* laid down in the *Vedhas* has to be experienced, in order to be appreciated; it cannot be merely talked about, in tall language. The use of the *Vedhas* does not consist in mere recitation, though the reciters are doing a valuable service, preserving them in correct form and style of pronunciation. *Vedhas* yield *Aanandha*; *Vedha maathaa* (Mother of *Vedhas*) is the *Aanandha maathaa* (Mother of Divine Bliss).

They provide the answer to the Question of questions: "Who am I?" Every one of you has to know that this question has to worry you sooner or later. And, every one has to discover the answer. The senses, each specialising in one small field of cognition, are powerless to give the answer; they at best very inadequate even in their own specialised provinces; there are sounds the ear cannot hear; there are colours the eye cannot take in and interpret to us and tastes beyond the ken of the buds of the tongue. They are imperfect instruments for the study of the external world. How can they serve to teach us about the intangible, invisible, inner world of the Self? The *Vedhaanthic* vision alone can reveal to you "the smaller than the smallest, the bigger than the biggest" (*Anoraneeyaan mahatho maheeyaan*).

When you have vision, you do not realise its value; you take it as just natural. It is only when you lose it or when it gets dim, that you run to the ophthalmic hospital. When the *Vedhaanthic* vision of India had become dim, Shankaraachaarya restored it and so saved the country. If he had not done so, believe Me India would have become another China.

## *Dharma* is eternal, basic, fundamental

When you are boring and fixing a pipe to draw the water up, you have to take good care, lest water or air gets into the pipe and spoils the creation of the vaccum that is needed. So too, if you desire success in your effort to unravel the truth of your inner Self, you have to take good care that the outer self, does not enter and spoil the concentration. You have to prevent thoughts of the outer world from entering the mind. The senses are positive handicaps in that field of research.

One of the dangerous tricks of the modern times, which is misleading a number of people, is the claim made by many, that they have been sent to re-establish *Dharma*. Each one is doing it in his own fashion, and as it suits his skill and idiosyncrasy. When a bridge on the highway gets damaged, no single pedestrian, however eminent, can start repairing or re-building it; nor can the villagers living in proximity to it, start the operations, according to their own ideas of bridge-building. The very authority which laid down the road, and planned the bridge has to come down and draw up the plan. *Dharma* is the road for individual and social progress, in this world and through the world, to the next. It is eternal, basic, fundamental. The principles may not be altered or adjusted to suit personal whims, or pressing problems, that appear formidable to the eyes of some individuals, or group of persons. It is like the mother who has to be accepted, not like the wife whom you can choose or discard.

## Man is basically Immortal

Vaaranaasi Subrahmanya Shaasthry spoke of *Dharma* as expounded in and through the Mahaabhaaratha. That is a prop which can sustain any drooping heart. If you can inquire deeply and reason fearlessly, you can appreciate the Indian point of view that, instead of seeking a lower standard of *aanandha* (happiness) by feeding the senses, one can get lasting *Aanandha* (Divine Bliss), by training the mind to be ever in the eyes of the Cosmic, the Universal, the Lord, as It is called, when you impose a Name and a Form upon it, to enclose it in you Consciousness. Why does man get *Aanandha* when he contemplates the Cosmic and the Universal? Because he himself is the Cosmic, the Universal! It is the *thwam* (thou) called to the *Thath* (That); the *Thath* responding to the kindred voice of the *thwam*.

Man is basically, essentially, fully, Immortal; he is *Amruthaswaruupam* (of the nature of Nectar of Immortality). But, yet he is afraid he would die! He is *Aanandhaswaruupam* (of the nature of Bliss); but, yet he is it that weeps that he is miserable. He is *Shaanthiswaruupam* (of the nature of peace); yet, everywhere he is overlaid with anxiety. This absurd self-deception is the root of the tragedy from which the world suffers today. The truth has to be driven into the consciousness of both the spiritual teachers and disciples, wherever they may be, in this country or elsewhere.

## Accept what scriptures declare

Many *Gurus* do not instruct people in this doctrine of courage, they do not bring up those who go to them in the discipline of the knowledge of Self (*Aathma-jnaana*), for, they themselves are not established in the Reality of Self (*Aathma-thathwa*). They intensify the egoism of their disciples and devotees and hasten their doom, rather than avoid it. The disciples too asked for quick results and shortened courses and less and less austerity. The *Gurus* have therefore to water down the rigour of spiritual discipline, and behave as minions of the disciples themselves! They wink at many a moral transgression, and very often share in the plots and intrigues which are the daily routine of the devotees! It is a sad state of affairs, indeed! A people destined for glory, for the role of guides of humanity but, grovelling in the dark, seeking to sqeeze lasting joy from food, clothing, shelter and hours of trivial entertainment.

A business magnate from the West, Mr. Kilman, came to Puttaparthi and, during the discussion on various spiritual problems, he asked Me, "Why build temples, when what we want are wells, dams, hospital and factories?" I told him to find out from the well-fed, and well-employed whether they are happy, whether they have inner calm! The *Aathma* alone is the source of inner strength, it is the fountain-spring of Joy---joy unaffected by reverses or victories.

You may ask, "How do you know, or rather, how are we to know that there is an entity called the *Aathma*?" Well, how do you know that today is the 24th day of February? The Sun did not rise today, after an announcement from the skies that is the twenty-fourth day of the month called February. Some person whom you respect, said that today is the 24th February, that is all. You accepted their word and you were glad that your acceptance made things smoother for you. Similarly, when the *Vedhas* and the Scriptures declare that you are *Aathman*, instead of mistaking yourself to be the gross body, accept it and find in it a great source of peace and step by step, the truth will be revealed to you in your own unmistakable experience.

## The world is a training ground

The Lord has declared in the Geetha, '*Mama Maayaa*': My Illusion; that is to say, this relative world is His Handiwork, His *Leela* and His *Mahima* (Divine Play and Greatness), devised as a training ground, an inspiration, for those who desire to see Him, the Source and Substance of all this. "This objective world is My Play," He says. From illusion, you must get interested in the Author, the Master, the Lord. Once you see the world as the arena of His activity, the stage for His play, then, you will never more be misled; you will not be deceived by any tricks of the play or of the stage-effect; you will not be distracted; you will not be led to believe it as genuinely real. It is valid so long as it lasts, and you are in the theatre.

Take the base (*Aadhaara*) as more real than the structure (*Aadheya*); the Lord as more real than the world. This is the basic lesson of Indian thought. Among all the principles of *Vedhantha*, this is a pearl. The world is like a mirage; the mirage does not originate from any rain;

nor does it reach any lake or sea. It was not there before the Sun shone, nor will it be there when evening falls. It is just an intervening phenomenon; it is best left alone.

This Prashaanthi Vidwanmahaasabha has been established in order to give each thirsty soul a cup of solace and strength, from the well of the *Vedhas* and *Shaasthras*, to lead the waters of fertility to every parched area. Ghandhikota Subrahmanya Shaasthry read out some verses he wrote about Me. These Pandiths are not with Me to extol Me; nor is there any need to extol Me or them. I have no other purpose than this: to lead you to the path of *Aanandha*. I have no special attachment to the Vidwanmahaasabha because I have established it. All *Sabhas* and *Sanghas* (Associations) and individuals that do this same task, according to their capacity and means, are dear to Me. I do not call upon you to cultivate faith in Me or to worship Me. I want only that you should cultivate faith in yourselves, and worship the Lord who is utilising you as His instrument.

## Practise the teachings you heard

Realise that your essential core is the *Aathma*. I have no need to seek fame through these meetings or associations. Not that the statements made by Ghandikota Subrahmanya Shaasthry are wrong. But, I know that some of you sitting here suspected, when he was reading his poem, that he and others have collected here, just to eulogise Me! Let Me tell you, I do not like such demonstrativeness and show; they are against My very Nature and Purpose.

After hearing these Pandiths for three days, morning and evening, do not go home without becoming richer; let it not be the story of, "I went; I sat; I saw; I heard; I came." That is what the dull-witted do. Make the teaching your own by practising it. Let the meaning circulate in your veins and enliven your earnestness. There are some weakwilled persons, who are dragged hither and thither by others. They see some one going and they too go to Puttaparthi. They see some one staying away and they too stay away. Why be moved by the vagaries of others and why lose the lucky chance that may not recur at all?

Of course, I love all; those who come to Me, as well as those who stop coming; those who stay at the Nilayam, as well as those who stay away; those who praise, as well as those who blame. For no one is beyond the boundary of My love.

Hold your right palm, spread it vertically before you! You find that the thumb points towards you and is keeping apart from the other fingers. That represenets the *Paramaathma* which is aloof and unaffected. The forefinger is the *jeevi*, the self, attached to the three *gunas*, the three-stranded complex of the objective world. It seeks to mix with this, that and the other, to show this and mark out that; it is ever busy identifying objects and so it gets the company of only the three qualities (*gunas*). But, once let it turn towards the *Paramaathma* (Supreme Self), let it achieve *Saameepya* (proximity) with it! Then it will lose the contact with the *gunas*; it and the thumb will form the *Chin-mudra*---the sign of the *Puurna* (Full), the completed Consciousness.

I bless you that your attention and activity be always focussed on the Self within you; that is the purpose for which the Prashaanthi Vidwanmahaasabha has been established.

*Rajahmundry, 24-2-1964*

## 12. Amrithasya Puthraah

THE Hindu Samaaj, Rajahmundry, was established, as its President told us now, in 1903. So this can be considered the *Shashtiabda Puurthi Celebration* of this institution, which means the celebration of its attaining the sixtieth year of its life. It is the custom to have such celebrations a little time after the completion of the period, not on the exact date on which the period is completed. Therefore, this conforms to that custom also.

This rite is named a *Shaanthi* (Pacification), the attainment of an equipoise, of calm. At sixty the senses have lost thier wildness and waywardness, they have become powerless to drag the individual into ruin. That is believed to be just the time to fix one's mind on God and start on the course one has missed in the confusion of material pursuits.

The Samaaj too has wandered far from the path it was set on; it was a premier institution in this town of many institutions for the encouragement and promotion of *Sanaathana Dharma*, the Eternal Religion. It held competitions in the recitation and interpretations of the Bhagavadh Geetha, the authoritative book on that *Dharma*, and it distributed copies of the Geetha itself to hundreds of high school students, just when they were stepping out of their schools into the larger world. I know that it took a leading role in the task of spreading the doctrines of *Sanaathana Dharma*.

## Real form of Devotion is Divine Love

Now, owing to causes like the apathy of the people, the attractions of more showy forms of activity, and the drying up of funds for rewarding students, scholars and Pandiths, this Samaaj has been reduced to a recreation centre for office-goers and others: re-creation, not of the ideals for which India stood in the past and stands at present, but of the activity and liveliness of the body and the nerves and the mind. This Samaaj has now to take up the responsibility again, for it is as important now, as it was sixty years ago. For such service the demand is continuous; it can never become out-of-date, or superfluous. If one looks around and observes the fall in standards, the need is even greater today. This is the reason, perhaps, why the President came to Me with a prayer to bless the Samaaj and to speak to you on the work you have to do.

Devotion to God is not to be calculated on the basis of the institutions one has started or helped, the temples one has built or renovated, the donations one has given away, nor does it depend on the number of times one has written the Name of the Lord or on the time and energy one has spent in the worship of the Lord. These are not vital at all, no, not even secondary. Devotion is Divine Love, unsullied by any tinge of desire for the benefit that flows from it or the fruit or consequence of that love. It is love that knows no particular reason for its manifestation. It is of the nature of the love of the soul for the Oversoul; the river for the sea; the creeper for the tree, the star for the sky, the spring for the cliff down which it flows. It is sweet, in bad times as well as good. It is not like pepper or salt with which you savour your dishes; it is the very bread and butter, the essential substance itself. It is not the pickle, which only lends a twang to the tongue and helps you to consume a little more of the food. It is an unchanging attitude, a desirable bent of the mind, standing steady through joy and grief. For the Divine Bliss comes through knowledge of the Self; the Devotee is the true witness.

## *Dharma* is a means of living

Vaaranaasi Subrahmanya Shaasthry said now that Yudhishtira, the eldest of the Paandava Brothers, had that devotion and so, he did not falter even an inch from his faith when in exile; nor did he lose his head, when he won back his throne. Others like Dhuryodhana used *Dharma* as a handy excuse to escape the evil consequences of their acts. Righteousness is not to be treated as a means of escape; it is a means of living. Never once did Dhuryodhana observe the principles of righteousness towards the Paandava Brothers; at last, he had to face the inevitable doom, when Bheema challenged him for the duel which was to lay him low. At that moment, the author of the deceitful gambling game, the house of lac which was set on fire, the insult heaped on the honoured Queen, the slaughterer of Abhimanyu by a pack of ferocious foes who fell upon him, the dark designer of all these iniquities, took refuge in *Dharma* and started quoting texts.

Wavering and indecision affect you in the realm of *Dharma* when you are not stabilised in the knowledge of the Self, which gives you a correct sense of proportion and also a sense of direction and achievement. That is why the Geetha lays so much emphasis on the necessity to know both the *kshethra* and the *kshethrajna* (the field of knowledge and the Knower of that Field). Know both, and then, you are entitled to the title, *Amrithasya Puthraah*: "Children of Immortality." Other titles are burdens on the head that wears them. Of what benefit are they, those that vanish in a whiff, and do not deceive any one, for more than a few years?

## The grandest things in Creation

Through devotion to God alone can that knowledge be attained. *Bhakthi* purifies the heart, elevates the feelings and universalises the vision. It also brings down the Grace of God; for, the clouds have to come over the fields and pour rain; the plants cannot rise up to drink the life-giving fluid. The mother has to bend to the cradle to fondle the child. *Bhakthi* has that power, to bring the Lord down. Once Naaradha was asked to name the most noteworthy among the things of the world. He answered that the earth was the biggest. But, he was told water has occupied three-fourths of the earth; it threatens to swallow up the balance too, bit by bit. So, water, he had to agree, was more powerful. However, water too was drunk up by the sage Agasthya and the oceans were rendered dry by him, and he, in turn is now just a star in the sky! Is the sky the biggest, then? No. For, it was covered by one single foot of the *Vaamana-avathaara* of the Lord (Vishnu's Incarnation as *Vaamana*, the Dwarf). And, the Lord? O, He enters the hearts of the devotees and resides there. So, Naaradha had to conclude that the hearts of devotees are the grandest things in Creation!

That is why I condemn all signs of weakness and call the sense of weakness itself a sin, an unpardonable sin. It is an insult to the heritage of Immortality, the title

*Amrithasya Puthraah*, which mankind deserves and must earn. Weakness, vacillation, despair, all these bring dishonour on Him who conferred on you the honour of child of Immortality; you are *Bhala-swaruupa* (of the Nature of Strength). Whenever accosted, you must declare yourself so, and not otherwise. Do not bend and cringe and barter your self-respect. Do not believe that you are this little lump of body. You are the indestructible, immortal *Aathma*, of the same nature as the Absolute Reality, *Brahman* itself.

## The four resolutions to be made by everyone

Have gratitude to the Creator who poured into you the nectar that ensures immortality; He requires you to stand firm in the face of joy and grief. Even animals exhibit gratitude; not only the pet animals, but wild ones, like the lion. Have you not heard the story of the lion suffering from a wound in the foot? A slave who was fleeing through the forest saw it and when he approached it with sympathy, the lion put out its foot. He then slowly pulled out the thorn that had caused all that pain and left the place, only to be arrested later and taken to Rome. There, they decided to throw him into the amphitheatre and let lose upon him a lion that had been recently captured. It was, however, the same lion which the slave had saved and so, its gratitude did not allow it to harm its saviour. Be grateful to the Lord for endowing you with powers of discrimination, of detachment, of evaluation.

Make four resolutions about your life hereafter :

(1) **Purity**: Desist from wicked thoughts, bad habits, low activities that weaken your self-respect

(2) **Service**: Serve others for they are the reflections of the same entity of which you are yourself another

reflection. No one of you has any authenticity, except with reference to the One Original.

(3) **Mutuality** : Feel always kinship with all creation. See the same current flowing through all the objects in the Universe.

(4) **Truth** : Do not deceive yourself or others, by distorting your experience.

## Respect our ancient culture

The Hindu Samaaj must set about doing the duty for which it was started, the revival in the minds of the educated classes and the students, of respect and attachment for our ancient culture. Do not be led away by the cynicism of critics; that should serve only to encourage you. There was once an incident in train that was going over the Godaavari bridge. A poor ryot searched for a naya paisa coin and he threw it into the river for he felt it as a sacred duty to honour the holy river. Immediately a fellow-traveller sitting comfortably in the corner got wild. He condemned the act as silly superstition and economic waste. "This is why this country is poor and powerless," he said, puffing his cigarette, as he poured out his wrath against the custom of throwing coins into the rivers. The ryot did not keep quiet. He said, "Look here, my man! I pass over this bridge perhaps once a year or so; I lose only one naya paisa at a time; I derive so much joy and satisfaction by that little sacrifice; but, pray, tell me, what benefit and economic gain you derive from this constant smoking which you are indulging in. The smoke you puff into the air poisons the atmosphere for all of us; it harms your health, it spoils the health of others; it wastes your money; it is a *Raajasik* habit (of passion and restless activity), which increases your pride and makes you nervous and unstable."

Examine the faults that may lie dormant in you and try to get rid of them. Do not merely declaim from platforms the excellence of such qualities as charity, service, sympathy, equality, secularism, etc. Descend and practise a few sincerely. When your neighbour is in the throes of a serious illness, do not rest content with the idea that you are happily free. No one is free if even one is bound. Remember that the food you give to each living being reaches God Himself, the service you do to any one being fills God with joy.

## Do not vulgarise devotion

Now, all worship and rituals are for *bhakthi* only, for the better comfort and more luxurious consumption of the worshipper himself. Devotion has been vulgarised into a business deal. I shall give you so much, provided you give me so much in return. If that shrine promises more, this shrine is given up; if even there, you do not get quick returns, somewhere else, some other God might be more profitable. That is the way in which worldly men wander about in their panicky rounds. "If I stand in the midst of others, God will not notice me; so, I must stand alone and shout, to attract His attention. Otherwise, He might ignore me," they argue and behave foolishly. Hold fast to the Ideal; do not try to degrade the Almighty to suit your limited vision. Rise up, strengthen your detachment, establish yourselves in discrimination. Then, your goal is brought near.

*Rajahmundry, Hindu Samaaj, 25-2-1964*

## 13. Fragrant with Grace

NOT all places where images are installed are sacred; or, if they are sacred, not all of them are equally potent. Raama incarnated as Man for the re-establishment of *Dharma*; centuries later, Gopana had the chance to worship Him on this hill and to talk and move with Him, as his Master and Lord. Badhragiri, by his *thapas*, forced Raama to install Himself on his head. Truly, this place is a monument for the uniqueness of *Bhakthi* as a means of realising the Lord. All stones are not Ahalyas; nor are all feet those of Raama. It is only when the stone that is Ahalya is trodden by the feet of Him who is Raama that the resurrection takes place. What is the resurrection, really? It is the revelation of the divinity inherent in man. That is the result of contact with God-head; that can come only after years of contrition, which serves to remove the evil from the heart of man.

Raavana had vast knowledge of spiritual texts. His ten heads represent the learning he had earned from the six *Shaasthras* and the four *Vedhas*. But, he never put that knowledge to any use. He craved for the possession of *Prakrithi* (material objects), only; he wanted to master the world of matter, the objective world. He was a master of the material sciences. But, he was not tamed by the spirit. He discarded the Spirit, *Purusha*-Raama; he was content with the possession at Lanka, of *Prakrithi* (Matter), represented by Seetha. That was why he fell.

## *Prema* alone will remove hatred

When people do not place faith in the Self but pursue the senses only, the danger signal is up and the Lord sends a Messenger or comes Himself, if a great big step in reconstruction has to be taken. Arjuna forgot the basis of Self. Raavana went counter to it. The world is building itself up on the sandy foundation of the sensory world. So, *Avathaars* have to come. Like the monkey which could not pull its hand from out of the narrow-necked pot, because it first held in its grasp a handful of doughnuts which the pot contained, man too is suffering today, since he is unwilling to release his hold on the handful of pleasurable things he has grasped from the world. Man is led into the wrong belief that the accumulation of material possessions will endow him with joy and calm. But Divine Love (*Prema*) alone can give that everlasting joy. *Prema* alone will remove anger and envy and hatred.

This is a sacred occasion on a sacred hill. You have been privileged to be born in this holy place; why the very sight of the pilgrims who come here daily full of yearning and God-hunger, that itself is a fortunate chance. They bring so much of Love of Raama (*Raamaprema*) with them; they sing *Raamanaama* (holy name of Raama) and they recite the Lord's name. They never allow you to forget that this is a place fragrant with the Grace of God. Do you realise what a great service this is for your advance? When I was in Ayodhya some years back, I could hear the continuous chanting of the holy name of Raama, that the air there was wafting in all directions. But, let Me ask you how you behave towards these pilgrims who come here, after years of sincere preparation, with hearts laden with faith! Many of you crowd round them and seek chances to exploit their devotion and their ignorance of this place. You squeeze out of them all the reverence they bring towards you and the place. They respect you, they envy you, since you breathe this holy air and drink this holy water and witness this holy worship. But, you laugh at their foolishness, while trading on their devotion. This is very unjust. You are like men who have plenty of delicious dishes before them, but have no hunger for the delicacy.

## Realise the Omnipresence of God

I must speak also to the pilgrims, for, I see them also here in large numbers. If you come as on a picnic, without the mental preparation necessary to receive the Grace of God, you are a nuisance here. You spoil the atmosphere of the place. You have come to see sights, not to strengthen your spiritual inclinations. You go from place to place, like postal parcels, collecting impressions on the outer wrapper, not on the core of your being. A blind man going places is not worried whether it is night or day. So too, you do not differentiate between one place and another. You behave equally unconcerned, equally senses-centred, in all types of places. You do not allow the holiness of the place to act on your mind.

As a result of the pilgrimage, your habits must change for the better; your outlook must widen; your inward look must become deeper and become more steady. You must realise the Omnipresence of God, and the Oneness of Humanity. You must learn tolerance and patience, charity and service. You must determine to seek, after the pilgrimage is over, sitting in your own home, ruminating over your experiences, the higher, the richer and the more real experience of God-realisation. I bless you that you may form that determination and, striving step by step, achieve that Goal.

*Bhadhraachalam, 28-2-1964*

> Reawakening of man is at hand.
> Reawakening to the knowledge
> that man himself is God.
> The human body is not you,
> it simply houses the soul or
> the spark of Divinity within,
> for God dwells in the heart of every man
> and that dwelling spark of the divine
> is you - yourself.
> All else is illusion.
>
> SHRI SATHYA SAI

## 14. Be like lamps

YOU are all pilgrims, moving along this land of action (*Karmakshethra*) to the goal of land of righteousness (*Dharmakshethra*). The literary men, the poets, the teachers and administrators who addressed you so far are all guides who help you along; but, the road has to be trodden by you, every inch of it. "*Kavim puraanam anusaasithaaram*": the Poet is the person who commands, who lays down the law, the ancient, the timeless---that is what the *Vedhas* declare. So these Poets too have to place the rules of right conduct before people and warn them in time when they go astray. They should not themselves stray, while professing to show others the path. Kavi, the Poet, is called the all-seeing (*Kraantha Darshi*); he is the seer of *Manthra* (*Manthra Drashta*); his role is to interpret God to man. He should not indulge in meaningless talk, significanceless writing. That will be degrading his role. He should not be asking questions without end, for, he should seek in silence to get the answers, without infecting others with his doubts and his posers.

Life is a mirage; it comes from no visible rain; it falls into no recognisable sea. There was a man once who was pestered by a host of relatives when he was dying. Parents, wife, children, brothers, sisters---all surrounded his bed during his last moments and wailed. They asked him "What is to happen to us?" The dying man lifted his head a little from the pillow and asked in return, "What is to happen to me? I am now more interested in that problem, than being worried about what is to happen to you." Well, it is better every one asks that questions even now and equips himself with the answer rather than wait until it is too late. "What am I for?" "What ought I to do?" These questions you must pursue, and arrive at the answers.

## You are happiness in essence

Your nature is *Sath, Chith* and *Aanandha* (Existence, Consciousness, Bliss Absolute), believe Me. That is why you behave in the way you do. You desire to exist for ever; you enjoy continuing to live; you avoid all talk of your own death. That is enough evidence to conclude that you are Reality in essence (*Sath-swaruupa*). Then, again, you are filled with wonder and curiosity and a desire to know the world around you. You ask continuously what, why, how and when, about all and sundry. This is the prompting that is given by the Consciousness (*Chith*), that is in your make-up. Lastly, you are always seeking joy, through some means or other. You try to avoid grief, you try to taste joy instead. It is the nature of man to do so. For, he is essentially of the nature of Bliss (*Aanandhaswaruupa*). When he seeks *Aanandha*, it is like the call of the deep for the deep. When some one asks you, "How do you do," and you answer, "Quite well, thank you," he does not stop to enquire why you are well. It is only when you answer that you are ill, he stops and expresses concern and probes into the causes, symptoms and cure of the illness. "Well-ness" is natural; "illness" unnatural. Anxiety is caused by the unnatural only. So, you are happiness in essence (*sukhaswaruupa*) also.

## Be strong to resist temptations

*Sath, Chith, Aanandha* are the attributes of the *Aathma* (Self) and you are the Self, not the body. There was a king who had an abiding faith in astrology. So, when his son was born on a day when the *Moola Nakshathra* (Star) was in the ascendant, he feared that the child would bring calamity to the line; he therefore asked his soldiers to slay it and throw the carcass in the jungle. The servants were so overcome by pity that, instead of killing the child, they just cast it away in the jungle and came away. The child was discovered and fostered by a washerman for many years. The boy was engaged in watching the clothes spread out to dry, when one day, the king lost his way and strayed into the village where the washerman lived with the Prince. While resting in the washerman's house, the king discovered that the boy who watched the clothes was his own son. He took him back and crowned him Yuvaraaja. Now, even when the boy was with the washerman, he did not lose his status as a Prince. Only he did not know his reality. You are all in the same plight: Princes, misled into believing that you are washermen, souls ignorant of the magnificence of the status, but declaring that you are only the shortlived, easily-destroyed bodies.

The gods once were so elated at some victory they won, so proud and so forgetful of the Divine Grace that helped them to foil their enemies, that they held a great banquet to celebrate it. When they were engaged in the revelry, the Lord decided to prick the bubble of their conceit. So, He created a strange phenonmenon which presented itself before them and arrested their attention. They went near it out of fear and wonder. It accosted them and when it was told that they were a company of gods celebrating a victory, it challenged them to prove their mettle by using their powers on a blade of grass that it placed on the ground. *Agni,* the god of Fire, tried to burn it but was foiled; *Vaayu,* the god of Wind, tried his best to sweep it off but could not. Thus, each god tried to prove his worth by using all his skill on that tiny blade and it was demonstrated that without the overall Grace of God, each of them and all of them would have failed in the battle, instead of winning it. Humility was thus taught to the exultant gods by the all-merciful Lord.

## Read elevating literature

You must be humble, but yet strong to resist temptation. Do not yield like cowards to the sly insinuations of the senses. Your time in school has to be used not only in the task of collecting information and earning certain skills that will give you an income on which you can live; it must also be used to acquire the art of being content and calm, collected and courageous. You must also cultivate at school an ardent thirst for knowing the truth of the world and of your own self. Your words must be like honey; your hearts must be as soft as butter; your outlook must be like the lamp, illumining, not confusing. Be like the umpire on the football field, watching the game, judging the play according to the rules laid down, unaffected by success or reverse of this team or that.

I want you also to read such books as will prompt you to ask and answer questions about your Self. Read good stuff, elevating literature, like the "Educator," which I am inaugurating today. I shall also write some articles for it, off and on, for it will be read by teachers who will pass on the inspiration to the pupils. I am glad the Teachers Guild of Anantapur District have taken up this task of publishing a magazine for their mutual benefit. They are the people who brought Me here today, to this School, which bears My Name. I am glad that the School is celebrating its Annual School Day. The Headmaster has a special responsibility to cultivate the enthusiasm of the local people and canalise it for the benefit of the school. And, when the plan is for the benefit of the school, all should join hands to help him.

## Grace is proportionate to exertion

I have heard discordant voices emanating from this town, and whispers that if Sathya Sai Baaba is really Divine, why is the Bukkapatnam Tank dry during the greater part of the year? Some of you here might have heard such statements, made by irresponsible persons who have no knowledge of the working of Cosmic Laws. What is the relationship between My Truth and the freshes that fill the tank of your village? It is really an absurd idea: that since Sai Baaba is within four miles of this place, the Bukkapatnam Tank must be full all the year round and the lands below it must yield good profit for the owners! Why should I expend My Grace especially on this tank, as proximity gives greater attachment? All places are equally near for Me and, if they turn away from good ways, all are equally far! For Me, distance is not to be measured by miles. A tank in another continent might be as near to Me as a tank across the Chithravathi.

Again, unless the people of this village have deposited amounts in the bank, how can the bank honour the cheques they draw? Have you deposited devotion to the Lord, service to your kind, faith in your spiritual practice? Then alone can you draw upon the Grace that is won by such exertion: Grace is proportionate to exertion.

And, I may also ask, in what way have you suffered? Whereas other villages hereabouts are declining and people are migrating from them to the bigger towns, Bukkapatnam is thriving continuously. This is due to the stream of pious pilgrims who are flowing into Puttaparthi, through this village. The atmosphere is rendered cool by the company of the holy that gathers there. The Supreme Divine Power (*Mahaashakthi*) that manifested in your neighbourhood and the Supreme Devotion to God (*Mahaabhakthi*) radiating from that place have yielded benefits which you cannot deny. This school is but one of the many evidences of that Grace. I bless you that you may grow more and more in devotion to the Lord, under whatever Name and Form, and earn His Grace to a larger extent.

*Bukkapatnam, 13-3-1964*

---

When the Name is pronounced by the tongue,

and the image is adored by the mind,

these should not degenerate

into mechanical routine;

the Meaning of the Name and

the Content of the Form,

must, at the same time, inspire and illumine

the Consciousness.

SHRI SATHYA SAI

## 15. Sai Sankalpam

TODAY is thrice blessed, because first, it is the New Year Day for those who follow the Solar Calendar; second, it marks the beginning of the *Vasantha Navaraathri*; and third, because of the entry into Brindaavan, which you all witnessed this morning. For the Kannada country, there is an additional reason for rejoicing, for, just now we are inaugurating in their State the activities of our Prashaanthi Vidwanmahaasabha. On such an auspicious day, it is the duty of every one of you to gather and cherish in your hearts the wise words, the drops of *Amritha* (Nectar), which these Pandiths offer you from their knowledge and experience. Not merely hear, but, endeavour to act accordingly, for, the rain has to fall on prepared soil in order to promote the growth of the crop. You have to collect the rain, store it in tanks, direct it along well laid out canals to the fields which thirst for it; you should not allow it all to flow into waste or into a sea of salt. These Pandiths are repositories of ancient learning and I can assure you, whatever subject they speak upon, they will not stray a hair's breadth from the path of India's genuine culture.

We have here today Jatti, the Finance Minister of Mysore, Sawant, the Agriculture Minister for Mahaaraashtra, and Members of Parliament like Dr. Raamakrishna Rao, legislators chosen by the will of the people. Dasaratha, when he desired to crown Raamachandra, consulted the representatives of his people, as well as the Pandiths of the court. He placed before the people, not merely his personal wish, but also the reactions of sages like Vasishta to his proposal. But, at present, the link between the Pandiths and the politicians, the religious heads and the rulers has snapped and each goes his own way, irrespective of what the other thinks or feels. Long years of foreign rule during which the Pandiths were considered to be symbols of an out-dated civilization contributed to this, no doubt. But, even after that rule has ended, nothing has been done to re-establish the link.

## Scriptures are like traffic signs

The system of education which promotes an attitude of contempt towards the learning which does not yield immediate pecuniary benefits is very largely responsible for the neglect of these great men. I must also mention as another cause the fall in the general level of morals. When all are sliding down the easy path of flippancy, those who advise against it and warn the victims about the inevitable disaster are ignored and laughed at. Sunk in the search of pleasures and cheap recreation, people become deaf to the counsels of the past and calls of the sublime.

Another factor which I must condemn is the hatred between castes and religions. The Pandiths are mostly of one caste and the politicians treat them from the angle of communal hatred. This hatred is not based on reason; it is rooted in fear and ignorance, and so, is undesirable. The *Vedhas, Upanishadhs* and *Shaasthras* are like traffic signs on the road; if they are removed, the journey is rendered slow and difficult, replete with accidents. We cannot afford to destroy them. We have to restore them in the interests of humanity itself. Caste (*jaathi*) has to be determined on the basis of *Gunas* (qualities) though a man belonging to a caste can be judged fit or unfit, on the basis of his *Karma*. If *jaathi* has to be decided on the twin bases of *Guna* and *Karma* (qualities and actions), as evidenced by the character and activities of the individual, a person will have to be labelled differently every hour or every minute of his life! It is only in pitch darkness that the ground appears level; day reveals the heights and hollows. So too, it is only ignorance that makes people talk of equality; knowledge reveals basic differences in health, equipment, attitude and tastes!

## *Bhakthi*-directed education is today's need

*Sai Sankalpam* is to bring together once again the *Paalakas* (Rulers) and the Pandiths, the guardians of the welfare of the people in the secular and the spiritual fields. That is why the ministers and the legislators are here on this platform, along with Pandiths and Shaasthris. Without the cooperative functioning of these two, there can be no progress, no success in the attempt to build up a new world. The Kauravas had all the instruments for victory; wealth, might of arms, allies, fanatic hatred of the enemy, Karna! But, they all became dust, for they never paid heed to the higher values of *Dharma*; they did not equip themselves with the Grace of God, which is reserved for those who walk the path of humility and peace. Krishna was not their charioteer: they put their faith in lesser things.

When plans are laid by the rulers for the uplift of the people and for training the children of the land, I want that the ancient wisdom of this land, still preserved and practised by these Pandiths, must be consulted. That will keep the keel of the ship straight. I want that the knowledge embodied in the *Upanishadhs* should be handed down to every one. *Bhakthi*-directed education must take precedence over the *Bhukthi*-directed (enjoyment-directed) schooling that prevails today in most countries of the world. *Bhakthi* is the *Aashakthi* or yearning which goads you on to the spiritual discipline which will endow you with that *Jnaana*. Have both faith and steadiness---and you will win.

## Calamities must heighten your faith

You have been putting up since morning with the Sun and the lack of accommodation in this crowded *pandal;* your faith and steadiness have not been shaken by these. Keep them unaffected by the still greater difficulties and disasters that might blow over you. The gale helps to toughen the trunk of the tree. Calamities must deepen your courage, enlarge your faith; your spiritual practise must be intensified just when the weather is inclement. In fair weather, a care-free attitude is pardonable, but, in foul weather, every precaution is of value.

These Pandiths know the precautions and they will tell you about them. Treasure them well and act accordingly. That is My message to you today. The Prashaanthi Vidwanmahaasabha is bound to extend its activities in Karnataka and enter, as Sawant said, not only Mahaaraashtra State, but all States of India and all countries of the world. For the Wisdom of the Sages is the Heritage of Humanity.

*Brindaavan, Whitefield, 13-4-1964*

## 16. Take wings and fly

KAANTHI, the Minister who spoke just now, is in charge of education in this State of Karnaataka and he knows well that the education he is arranging for the children of his people is not adequate to meet all the challenges of life in this fast-changing, quickly tiring world. These Pandiths who have dedicated their scholarship and their talents for the spread of the means and methods of attaining peace are therefore valuable collaborators with Kaanthi in the field of education. I am glad he recognises that truth.

*Dharma* is a word related to *dhaarana* and derived from the same root. *Dhaarana* means 'wearing,' as a cloth; *Dharma* is the very habiliment of India, the dress that *Bhaarathmaatha* (Mother India) wears to protect her honour, to proclaim her status, to shelter herself against heat and cold, to set a standard to her sisters. When the wicked Kaurava princes seized hold of the sari that Dhroupadhi wore and tried to inflict insult on her honour, Krishna rescued her and foiled the foul design. Dharmaraaja sat as if he was unaware of his rights and duties; Bheema was involved in doubt concerning his obligations to his elder brother and his consort; Arjuna cared more for his own interests; Nakula and Sahadeva waited and weighed the pros and cons. But, the Lord did not wait! His Grace knew no delay or doubt.

Now, *Bhaarathamaatha* is in a similar plight. *Dharma*, the very clothes that she has worn since centuries, which is the expression of her natural style, is now seized on by wicked irreverent hands. They wish to dress her in unbecoming styles, as their own imitative or frenzy dictates. So, Krishna has to come again for rescuing the victim of the wicked.

## Everything has its *Dharma*

Krishna revealed the hollowness of the people who were confident of their capacity to dishonour Dhroupadhi and the weakness of those entrusted with the task of protecting her. Now too, I have to foil the attempts to undermine *Dharma* and to stand in support of those who are the traditional protectors and protagonists of *Dharma*.

Every single thing has its *Dharma*; water has its *Dharma*, the nature and obligation to move; fire, the *Dharma* to burn and consume; the magnet, to attract and draw unto itself. And, every one of these is keeping up its *Dharma* unchanged, including the Solar system and the stars of the firmament. Among the things endowed with Consciousness or *Chaithanya*, the plants and trees, the insects and the birds, born out of eggs or the mammals---all have managed to treasure their specific *Dharmas* unaffected by the passage of time. But man, whose intelligence sweeps from the inert and the infinitesimal to the Super-conscious and the Universal, is the only living thing that has slipped, and is sliding down. The experience of many generations of seekers, who sought the means of contentment and joy, embodied in the precepts of practical living, collectively called *Shaasthra* is neglected, and new-fangled nostrums are recommended and tried on vast scale. No wonder, contentment and joy are far, far away from human grasp.

*Dharma*, for example, says '*Sathyam vadha*' and '*Dharmam chara*': Speak the truth and practise righteousness. *Sathyaannaasthi paro dharmah*: there is no more stabilising factor in society, no more support for individual progress than *Sathya*, Truth. Hiding the truth or perverting it or denying it or defacing it are all signs of cowardice; no bold person will stoop to cover the face of Truth. Besides, you must know the *Vedhic* injunction is: '*Dharmam chara*', "Practise *Dharma*." It is not enough if you learn about it; you must act it, fill every moment with word and deed and thought that reflect your awareness of *Dhrama*. That type of living is the hallmark of what is called *seelam* (character), in such statements as *Seelam param bhuushanam* : "Character is the most precious jewel."

## Resist temptation to ignore *Dharma*

You must examine every moment of your waking time whether you are observing the precepts of *Dharma* or straying away : *Dharma* is now just a convenient excuse to derive benefits from others, not an opportunity to fulfil your duties to others! You remind others of it, when you desire to squeeze some advantage from them. You must remember not only the rights that *Dharma* confers but also the duties it imposes.

The temptation to ignore *Dharma* grows from egoism and the acceptance of false values. The wish to satisfy the lower desire is the root of *Adharma* (unrighteousness). This wish takes hold of you slyly, silently, like a thief in the night; or like a comrade come to save you; or like a servant come to attend on you; or, like a counsellor come to warn you. Oh, wickedness has a thousand tricks to capture your heart. You must be ever alert against the temptation. The wish makes a chink in your consciousness, enters and establish itself and then multiplies its brood and eats into the personality you have built up with laborious care. The fort is no longer under your control. You have been reduced into a puppet manipulated by these inner enemies. Whenever you try to rebuild yourselves, they undermine the structure and you have to do it all over again. That is the extent of the harm they do.

### *Gopikas'* state of God-consciousness

To conquer this egoism, no rigorous system of exercise or breath control is necessary. No, not even complicated scholarship. The *Gopikas* (cow-herds) confirm this truth. They were simple rural folk, untouched by the conclusions of deep study. Naaradha was once so shocked at their ignorance of the science of spiritual progress that he volunteered to go among them and put them through some lessons in *Jnaana*.

He found on entry into Brindaavan that the *gopees* (cowherd girls) selling milk or curds in the streets forgot to shout the names of their ware but said, "Govindha, Naaraayana," instead; so immersed were they in God-consciousness. They did not know that they had sold off all the milk; they still wandered on, calling out the names of the Lord, for the dust of Brindaavan was so sacred for them. They had no *vishayavaasana*, that is, no wish for sensual pleasure; and so, they had no *Ajnaana* (ignorance). Hence, Naaradha concluded that they had no need for the lessons he had planned to give. He prayed to them to teach him the means of getting that yearning and that vision of the all-pervading Krishna.

## Achieve identification with the Lord

There was a *gopee*, for example, called Suguna, who had no other thought than those related to Krishna. Now every evening, it was the usual routine in Brindaavan for every housewife to light the lamp from the flame of the lamp at the house of Nandha; they believed that getting light from the flame of the lamp of the eldest and highest is auspicious. Suguna went with the lamp of Nandha's house and when she reached the house, her mind was lost in the thrill and joy of seeing the very house where Krishna spent his childhood days, to which his pranks and prattle drew all the cowherd boys and girls. She stood there with her unlighted lamp for a long while, near the big oil lamp, illumining the central hall. She was holding the lamp near the flame, but not near enough. She had her finger right over the flame. She was not aware that her finger was being scorched by the flame; she was too full of Krishna-consciousness to be aware of the pain. It was Yasodha who saw her plight and woke her from the reverie, or shall we say, vision? For, to her, the house was alive with Krishna wherever her eyes turned. That is the *thanmayathwam* (identification) one must achieve. There is no use if the fledgeling stays in the nest; it should develop wings and fly into the sky. There is no use if man grovels in the dust; he should take to his wings and fly.

India is the teacher of all humanity in this field. That is her special role. If the body is the temple of God, the world is the body of God. So, He seeks to establish *Aanandha* in all countries and all people. That is why I have been giving these discourses and getting the Pandiths from all parts of the country to give discourses to you.

*Brindaavan, 15-4-1964*

## 17. His residential address

THE Thelugu Vijnaana Samithi, Bangalore, has done well in recognising the greatness and spirit of service of these Pandiths who are propagating, under the auspices of the Prashaanthi Vidwanmahaasabha, the practical disciplines laid down in the *Vedhas* and *Shaasthras*. They are invaluable spiritual text-books for all mankind. *Shaasthra* means that which 'ordains,' or 'commands' or 'instructs with authority.' They do not force you to do as they ordain, but, they "remind you of your worth and work"---"*jnaapakam, na thu kaarakam*," as the saying goes. For, there is great need of that reminder; the Divine that the Human really is, has been forgotten. It was once glowing and shining in the experience, but, it no longer inspires the individual with sublime confidence. The *Vedhamaatha* has been deserted; spurious guardians and sham caretakers have won the hearts of the people

Remilla Suuryaprakaasha Shaasthry just now in his speech on the role of *Suurya* (Sun) according to the *Vedhic Riks* (hymns) mentioned that the Sun is the source, sustenance, and silent slaughterer of life. But, he did not mention about the much greater role played by the inner

Sun, *buddhi* (intellect), in individual and social life. *Chakshos suuryo ajaayatha*---"the Sun was born out of the Eye of the *Purusha*," says the *Purusha Sooktha*. Intellect illumines the Vision (*Dhrishti*). What is the *Nethra* (Eye) that is talked about? It is the *Jnaana nethra* or the *Shaasthra nethra* (Eye of knowledge or Eye of Scriptures), which is endowed with correct Vision.

The *Shaasthras* direct you to the Reality easily and without hesitation. You have heard people pointing to the faint crescent moon in the sky and saying, "There! Right on top of that mango tree, a yard from the lightning-conductor on that spire, to the left of it." That is just the kind of help that the *Shaasthras* give about the Universal and the Absolute. You have to run your eye along the tree, the spire and the lightning conductor, and see the moon yourself. *Shaasthras* guide you to the truth and lead you to it, in easy stages.

## Mere scholarship will not help

It is a hard job to know about your own Self. Take the case of the food that you eat with your own mouth. You feel it in your stomach and after that, you do not experience what happens to it at each stage. How then can you know, without acquiring the special means for it, the Truth that lies behind the sheaths that encase and enclose you---the *Annamaya, Praanamaya, Manomaya, Vijnaanamaya* and *Aanandhamaya*---(sheaths of material, vital energy, mind, intelligence and bliss)? Clear your intellect or intellectual power (*dheeshakthi*) of the cobwebs of the ego, the dust of desire, the soot of greed and envy, and it becomes a fit instrument for revealing the *Swaruupa*---the Inner Truth. "Know yourself, know the Inner Motivator, the *Antharyaamin*"---that is the exhortation of the scriptures of all faiths. For, unless you are armed with that knowledge, you are like a ship without a compass, sailing on a stormy sea.

I must tell you that scholarship in the *Shaasthras* will not help you; scholarship is a very dangerous thing for it makes you aware of your ego all the time, instead of helping you to overcome it. If you notice serried ranks of bottles on the shelves of a man, you can conclude that he is a chronic invalid, addicted to drugs. So too, if you see on a man's shelves serried ranks of books, you can conclude that he is a chronic invalid, suffering from doubt and despair and confusion, and addicted to the drugs that he believes will cure them. Like all long-standing invalids, both these will start giving, at the slightest provocation, tedious accounts of their illnesses and the methods by which they tried to cure themselves.

### Royal road to achieve the Truth

Want of steady faith is what drives people to drugs and books. There is a story about Raadha and her faith in Krishna. The elders in Brindaavan who revelled in scandalising Krishna—successors have been born for them even now—set an ordeal for Raadha to test her virtue. She was given a mud pot with a hundred holes and asked to bring water in that pot, from the Yamuna to her house! She was so full of the Krishna-consciousness that she never knew the condition of the pot. She immersed it in the river, repeating the name of Krishna as usual with every intake of the breath and every exhalation. Every time the name Krishna was uttered, a hole was covered, so that by the time the pot was full, it was whole! That was the measure of her faith. Faith can affect even inanimate objects.

The ancients have laid a royal road for cultivating the spirit and achieving the Truth with that as the instrument. Why wander about in the thorny wastes, or slushy bylanes? Practise the *Saadhana* of *Japam* and *Dhyaanam* as prescribed; know all about it, from these Pandiths and others who have the experience. Do *Puuja* (ritual worship), with flowers, *Japam* with rosaries, etc., but, only until you get set for higher endeavours. You must offer the Lord, not the flowers that plants grow; that will reward the plant, not you! The Lord wants you to offer the lotus that blooms in the Lake of your Heart, the fruit that ripens on the tree of your earthly career, not the lotus and the fruit available in the market place! You may ask : "Where can we find the Lord?" Well, He has given His address, in *Chapter 18, Slokha 61* of the Bhagavadh Geetha. Turn to it and note it down. *'Ishwarassarvabhoothaanaam hriddese, Arjuna, thisthathi'*---"O Arjuna, the Lord resides in the heart of all beings." Now, after knowing that, how can you look down on any living being in contempt or how can you revel in hating him or indulge in the pastime of ridiculing? Every individual is charged with the Divine Presence, moved by Divine attributes. Love, honour, friendliness—that is what each one deserves from you. Give these in full measure.

### The hard path to win Lord's Grace

The Grace of the Lord cannot be won by a little pretence of *vairaagyam* (non-attachment) or just a grain of *vivekam* (discrimination). Know and act; realise and experience; that is the hard path. Surrender yourself to His Will.

Life is a great *Yajna* (*Vedhic* ritual of sacrifice). Allow the Lord to preside over it. Do not ignore Him. This is not a *Bhoga-bhuumi* (land of enjoyment), it is *Thyaagabhuumi, Yogabhuumi, Karmabhuumi* (land of sacrifice, union with God, and of devoted action). See how even the rain which threatened to pour on you and disturb the gathering stood away. When I started from Whitefield some people said: "There cannot be any meeting this evening; there will be heavy rain at Bangalore also." I told them, "Never has rain interfered with the meetings where I spoke." The clouds melted away in a refreshing gale, which scattered on your sweet-smelling flowers from that row of trees, that is all.

Have that love, that spirit of united work and prayer---and I assure you, *Raamaraajya* (kingdom of Lord Raama) will establish itself again in this land.

*Malleswaram, 16-4-1964*

*Listen to the primeval Pranava AUM resounding in your heart as well as in the heart of the Universe*

**SHRI SATHYA SAI**

## 18. Upanayanam

TODAY is Shankara Jayanthi---the day commemorating the advent of Shankaraacharya who came to restore *Dharma*; it is also the day on which *Brahmopadesam* (instruction about *Brahman*) was given here for the boys sitting on this dais, who have come from Bengal, Bombay, Hyderabad and Bangalore. The Shankara Jayanthi Day was chosen by Me for their initiation into the higher *Aadhyaathmic* (Spiritual) Life, for Shankara is an inspiration even today for millions of spiritual aspirants all over the world, who seek to know the Reality of the Universe and its fundamental Unity. They had this lucky chance of getting initiated here in My Presence by Me, as a result of their own good fortune.

The ceremony of *Brahmopadesam* is *Upanayanam*, which means, "taking near," taking the young aspirant near *Brahman*, that is to say, introducing him to *Brahmajijnaasa* (desire to know *Brahman*), the path of *Brahman*. It is one of the *Samskaaras* (purificatory acts), rites which reconstruct the personality, reform the mind, purify it and re-build it. It makes the person receiving it a *Dwija* (a twice born)! The boy is born first into the world; now, he is born into the *Saadhaka* world. He becomes a *Brahma-chaari*—a person who walks towards *Brahman*. So, it is a very significant day in the lives of these people, a day they must long remember with joy and thankfulness. It is the day when their hearts were turned towards God; and they should try not to run away from God hereafter; that is a great responsibility.

## *Gaayathri manthra* is Universal prayer

The initiation was done by the *Upadesham* (instruction) of the *Gaayathri manthram*. The *manthram* (sacred formula) is a universal prayer that can be used by men of all climes and creeds, for, it calls upon the Glorious Power that pervades the Sun and the three worlds to arouse, awaken and strengthen the Intelligence, so that it may lead to intense *Saadhana* and *Saadhana* may lead to success.

Every little moment or incident results in sound; only, you may not be able to hear, because the range of your ear is limited. The falling of an eyelid over the eye makes a sound, the dropping of dew on a petal makes a sound. Any little agitation disturbing the calm is bound to produce sound. The sound caused by the primal movement that resulted in the enveloping of *Brahman* by self-evolved illusion is the *Pranavasabdha* or *OM*. The *Gaayathri* is the elaboration of that *Pranava* and so, it is now held so venerable that initiation into spiritual life is achieved by its contemplation.

The sound of a *Manthra* is as valuable as its meaning. Even a poisonous cobra is quietened by music; *Naadham* (sound), has that allaying property. The child in the cradle stops wailing as soon as the lullaby is sung; it may not carry any meaning; it may be a nonsensical rhyme or just a jingle, but, it quietens, soothes the nerves and induces sleep. In the case of the *Gaayathri*, the meaning too is easy and profound. It does not ask for mercy or pardon; it asks for a clear intellect, so that the Truth may be reflected therein correctly, without any disfigurement.

## Requisites of spiritual discipline

The *Brahmachaari* has vowed himself into a life of spiritual discipline. Now what are the requisites for the discipline?

First: Faith, that can stand the ridicule of the ignorant, the cavilling by the worldly, the laughter of the low-minded. When someone ridicules, you should argue like this within yourself: Is he ridiculing my body? Well, he is doing what I myself would wish to do; for, I too want to escape out of this attachment of this body. Is he ridiculing the *Aathma*? Well, he is doing the impossible, for, the *Aathma* is beyond the reach of words or thought; it is unaffected by praise or blame. Say to yourself, "My *Aathma thathwa* (Principle of the Self) is *Nischala* (immovable), it is *Nirmala* (pure)," and carry on.

Second: Do not worry about ups and downs, loss or gain, joy or grief. You are yourself the maker of the ups and downs. If you but care, it can all be one smooth level. You label something as loss and something else as gain. You crave for a thing and when you get it, you call it joy; when you don't, you call it grief. Cut the craving off, and there will be no more swinging from joy to grief.

Third: Reason out and get convinced of the truth, *Sarvam Brahmamayam* (All is *Brahman*). You know there are five elements or *bhuuthas*, which constitute, by their permutations and combinations, the world called *Prapancham*, the "Five-constituted." *Prithivi* or the Earth-element has five qualities, the maximum, and so, it is the grossest. It has its own special characteristic of *gandha* (smell), as well as the characteristic of the other four, namely, *sparsha, rasa, ruupa* and *sabdha* (touch, taste, form and sound). The next one *Jala*, the water-element has only four, its own special one---taste and touch, form So it is subtler than the Earth-element. *Agni* is subtler still, because apart from its special characteristics of form, it has only two others, sound and touch. *Vaayu*, the Air-element has touch as its special and one more quality, sound. Finally the lightest and subtlest of all the five, *Aakaasha*, the Sky-element, has only one characteristic, its own, namely, *sabdha*. Now, God is subtler than even *Aakaasha* and so He is all-pervading, even more than ether or anything more pervasive than that. His nature is beyond all human vocabulary, beyond all human mathematics. Have this conviction well stabilised in your intellect.

## Establishment of *Dharma* by Adhi Shankara

Fourth: Be steady in spiritual practice, and never hesitate once you have decided on it. When the bus is moving on, the dust will be floating behind as a cloud: it is only when it stops with a jerk that the dust will envelop the faces of the passengers. So, keep steadily engaged in the practice. Then, the cloudy dust of the objective world will not cover your face.

Shankaraacharya came to this world for the work of *Dharmasthaapana* (establishment of righteousness), but he did not wage a war against the narrow sectarians or the wild theologians who opposed him or the critics who condemned him as a pseudo-Buddhist. He won them over by argument, persuasion and preaching. He spoke softly, but, with conviction. He gave his opponents fair chances to present their cases to the best of their ability and sometimes he even helped them to clarify their own points of view. Through *Bodha* (knowledge) alone can *Dharma* be saved in the modern *Kali*-age. That is why I am engaged in *bodha* (imparting knowledge), in this task of re-constructing through *upadesha* (instruction).

When you scatter seeds on the surface of the soil, they do not germinate. You have to keep them inside the soil. So too, *bodha*, if it is scattered on the surface, it will not germinate, grow into the tree of knowledge and yield the fruit of wisdom. Plant it in the heart, water the plant with divine love, manure it with Faith and Courage, keep off pests with insecticides of *bhajana* (group singing of holy names) and *sathsangha* (company of the holy), so that you can benefit in the end. You have not yet got started in *saadhana*; still you demand *shaanthi*; you demand Grace. How is it ever possible? Start! Then, everything will be added unto you.

## Ask for the right things

God gives you whatever you pray for; so, take care. Ask for the right things. There was a man who had four wives; he happened to go to Bombay on some work connected with his business. From there, he wrote to all of them that he was prepared to bring home whatever each of them wanted. So, they all wrote to him giving a list of things they wanted. The first wife asked for some nice tonics for her health, and rugs and woollen clothing, to be of service whenever she fell ill. The second wife wanted some saris of the latest style, choli pieces, jewellery of the Bombay type and such other sundry decorative stuff. The third asked him to select for her some religious books, the *Jnaaneshwari*, *abhangs*, *Bhakthi-vijaya*, etc., available in Bombay book-shops, as well as pictures of Pandarinath, Bhavaani, Sai Baaba, etc. The fourth wife had no list at all; she simply wrote, "If you return soon and safe, that is enough for me." She got nothing but his love. The others got big packets containing whatever they had written for. So think well, discriminate clearly before you ask, before you pray.

I know how systematic you are all in eating and drinking. You take pretty good care of the body. I do not condemn it; I only want that you should take equally good care of the needs of the spirit also. Take a dose of *Dhyaanam* (meditation) and *Japam* (silent repetition of holy Names) as the morning breakfast; *Puuja* and *Archana* (ritual worship) as Lunch at noon; some *Sath-sangha* (holy company) or *Sath-chinthana* (thinking holy thoughts) or *Sath-grantha paaraayana* (reading of holy books) or *Naama likhitha* (writing of holy Names) as afternoon tea and snacks; an hour of *bhajana* (devotional singing) as Dinner; and a small ten-minute *manana* (reflection) as the cup of milk before going to bed. That dietary is enough to keep your inner being happy and healthy. That is My advice to you today.

*Prashaanthi Nilayam, 16-5-1964*

---

*There is in this world*
*no  austerity higher than fortitude,*
*no  happiness greater than contentment,*
*no  punya (good deed) holier than mercy,*
*no  weapon more  effective than patience*

**SHRI  SATHYA  SAI**

## 19. Jeeva and Dheva

**W**HEN you pour oil from one tin to another, the hand that pours must be steady and the tin from which it is poured must not shake; nor, should the tin that receives shake, for, that will also make the oil spill on the ground. You should be *nischalam* (not moving); then only can you accept the *Bodha* (imparting of knowledge) straight into your hearts.

Now, there are some who say that *Jeevi* will be *jeevi* (individual soul) and *Deva* will be *Deva* (God) and the two can never be the same or merge. If that was true, then, what is the use of *Japam, Dhyaanam, Sath-karma* (good deeds) and all the other varieties of *Saadhana* (spiritual discipline) recommended by the *Shaasthras* and the sages? There is no doubt that *Nara* (man) can become *Naaraayana* (God); *'thwam'* (thou) can become *'Thath'* (That). That is the doctrine of the *Upanishadhs* and the experience of the saints.

Once a quarrel ensued between the *Adhwaithin* (non-dualist) who said that the *jeevi* (individual soul) is really God who falsely identifies himself with the limited Name and Form which he appears to have assumed, and the *Dhwaithin* (dualist) who said that the *jeevi* is distinct from the *Dheva*. When the quarrel boiled over, the *Dhwaithin* said, "See, even this dhobi knows that *Adhwaithism* is wrong." The *Adwaithin* said that the dhobi too is subject to the *Ajnaana*, the delusion that he is the limited *Upaadhi* (adjunct) of name and form, which are but temporary adjuncts of the personality. The knowledge of the *kshethra* and the *Kshethrajna* will alone help to overcome that delusion. *Kshethra* is the field, the field of the senses, the field of the dualities, and the *Kshethrajna* is he who knows the field and is its Master.

## Human body is "God's temple"

Every word used in philosophy and even in common parlance has a deep meaning, full of significance. *Dhehi* which means, liable to be burnt, is the word for body; not merely because it is consumed by fire after the, *praana* (life) has left, but because even when alive, man is consumed by the fire of *Thaapathraya* (threefold suffering caused by oneself, nature and fate). *Sareeram*, which is another word for the body, also comes from the root, meaning that which is consumed.

The *dheha* (body) is called a *Dhevaalayam* (God's temple) for the *jeevi* (individual soul) which is the *Deva* (God). The architectural temple has three parts; the *Praakaaram* (the outer temple), the inner temple and the shrine or *Garbhagriha* (sanctum sanctorum). These three represent the *sthuula*, the *suukshma* and the *kaarana sareera* (the gross, the subtle and the causal body) of man; when you go to a temple, you should remember this symbolism. *Prakrithi* is a word that is used to indicate condition of the body, the *svabhaava* (one's nature) of the body. Well, this *Prakrithi* or Nature is also just *svabhaava* of the Lord, his *Sankalpa* (Will), a manner of His manifestation. All this is, as Kasthuri said in his speech, while quoting some experiences of *Bhakthas*, "His Hands and Feet, His manifestation." That is why it is said that *Sarvam* is *Brahmamayam*.

A *yogi* had an attack of gastritis and his comrades and co-*saadhakas* gathered round him to advise him on the treatment. One man suggested that he should always keep some salt in his mouth and swallow the saliva. He did so and was having always salt in the mouth. A few days later, he wanted to distribute some sweets to the children around his *aashram*, but, whichever item he tasted, he found it not sweet enough. At last, one sweets-vendor asked him to spit out what he had in his mouth and gargle his throat and wash his mouth and then taste the sweets. That made them taste quite nice. With all this salt taste accumulated through many births on your tongue, how can you discover the true sweetness of the Lord?

## Keep intellect free from prejudices

At one of the railway stations of North India, when a thirsty passenger asked the waterman whether the skin-bag from which he was pouring water into his cup was clean enough, the waterman replied, "The bag I have is cleaner than the bag, into which the water is being poured by you." Keep your mind clean of *Vaasanas* (tendencies caused by past deeds), your intellect free from prejudices, your character free from blemishes, your behaviour free from rudeness—then, you can attach yourself to God and God too will favour you with His affection

With just a little paint and a piece of white paper, the painter can draw a frightening picture of a demon, or a charming picture of a smiling baby or an inspiring picture of a *yogi* meditating on the Absolute. All those different reactions are the result of the combinations of colours; the basic reality is just colour. So too in the picture house, the screen is the stable substance, the shadows come and go. When the picture is being flashed on the screen, the screen is not noticed; it is the base, the foundation, the whole of it has become the picture. *Sarvam Vishnu mayam jagath* (All this Universe is pervaded by Lord Vishnu).

Every one calls himself "I," is it not? Now, who gave that possession? Was it any company? Or, did you get it as part of the dowry? Or, from the rulers? Or from some organisation? You say it is your birthright; well, let it be so. That "I" is the entity which is posited as *Brahman* in the *Mahaavaakya* (great *Vedhic* dictum), '*Aham Brahmaasmi*,' I am *Brahman*.

## See the divine in the sense-impressions

When the One became many, when the One manifests as *Prakrithi* composed of the Five Elements, do not imagine that its value is affected thereby. When a rupee is changed into ten-naya paise coins, its value is not decreased at all. So, see Nature as Supreme Soul, not as multiplicity of sense-impressions and sense-attractions. Wherever your eye turns, whatever your ears hear, your fingers touch, your tongue tastes, and your nose smells, whatever has form, sound, touch, taste and smell, take that also to be God-filled. Do not allow the mere sound, the mere taste, etc. to captivate your senses. See the divine in each, welcome and accept only that.

When Thukaaraam was asked how man can keep this monkey-mind from running after sensuous pleasures, he replied to the enquirer, "Let the monkey run; you keep quiet where you are; do not let the body go along with the monkey-mind." Tell the mind, "I shall not give you the body as your servant." Then, the mind will desist and it can be defeated. Just as there is a method to be followed even in pulling down a house, there is a method to be followed even in pulling down the complex structure of the mind.

## You can become Master of yourself

The mind can be pulled down by systematic efforts and you can become master of yourself. You might ask, can such a mighty force come down? Well. When we were nearing Rishikesh on our way back from Badhri, Governor Raamakrishna Rao also asked Me the same question. I asked every one to come beyond a certain point on the road in a matter of minutes. Everyone was surprised that I was ordering them to get down from the cars and buses and scurry forward in hot haste. I told the Governor that the projecting rock on the mountain by the side of the road will slide very soon on the road and block it. He asked Me "Is it possible?" Within a few minutes, after every one had come forward to a safe distance, the rocks fell and the road was blocked for a long time, until debris was cleared.

The ladder must be as tall as the height to which you want to climb, is it not? Your spiritual practice to curb the mind must be carried on step by step until *Saakshaathkaaram* (Realisation) is gained. The rice in the pot must be well boiled and become soft and sweet. Until that happens, the fire must burn. In the vessel of 'body,' with the water, that is to say the 'senses,' boil the mind and make it soft. The fire is the *Saadhana*. Keep it burning bright; the *jeeva* will at last become *Deva*.

*Prashaanthi Nilayam, 17-5-1964*

## 20. The Guru is the guide

THIS day is called *Vyaasa Poornima*, holy day, which must be celebrated with the prayer and contrition which alone can cleanse the heart, and not by feasting or fasting, which affect only the body. The fact that Sage Vyaasa is associated with this day or that Lord Raama or Krishna is connected with some other day is merely an opportunity to mark the day as outstandingly important, when something holy has to be done. It is full moon today, when the moon shines without any let or hindrance, when moonlight is bright and cool and full. The mind of man is compared to the moon, for it is as wayward as the moon with its swing from brightness to darkness; this day, the mind too has to be bright, effulgent and cool.

Vyaasa was born with a great urge for spiritual uplift and he entered into deep study and *saadhana*, even as a child. He acquired such divine wisdom and glory that he is identified with Naaraayana Himself. He stands out as the *Lokaguru* (World Teacher) for he codified the *Vedhic* hymns, and prepared the great *Vedhaanthic* text of *Brahmasuuthra*, besides the epic commentaries of the

*Vedha-vedhaantha* (teachings based on *Upanishadhic* philosophies) for the people whom he loved to educate, commentaries named the Mahaabhaaratha and the Shrimadh Bhaagavatha.

## You have to traverse the path

He is called *Vedha-Vyaasa* because of his service to the students of the *Vedhas*, which defied understanding, since they were countless and fathomless: *Anantho vai Vedhaah.* He composed also the eighteen *Puraanas*, on the various *Naamaruupas* (Names and Forms) of the same Godhead, *Puraanas* which are text-books and illustrative descriptions of moral codes, historical episodes, philosophical principles and social ideals. Vyaasa sought to bring home, through the *Puraanas*, the need for mastering egoistic impulses, as the *slokha* says:

*Ashtaa dasha puraaneshu*

*Vyaasaaya vachana dwayam;*

*Paropakaara punyaaya*

*Paapaaya para peedanam.*

"Two statements can summarise all the eighteen *Puraanas* composed by Vyaasa. Do good to others; avoid doing harm," says the hymn. Doing good is the drug; avoiding harm is the regimen, that must accompany the treatment. That is the cure for the disease of suffering from joy and grief, honour and dishonour, prosperity and adversity, and the dual throng, that bothers man and deprives him of equanimity.

Vyaasa is the *Lokaguru*: he is Divine Effulgence. Even Vyaasa can only show you the road. YOU have to traverse it alone. He gives you a *manthra* (a sacred word or formula), which you repeat; though you may not know its meaning, it will act as the purifier of your mind.

When a ryot has to get something done for him by the Collector, he goes to a lawyer, who knows how it has to be asked for; he writes it out in English, and gives it to him as a typed sheet, which the ryot presents to the Collector. He does not know what is written or its meaning but it does the work because it has come from the brain and the experience of a man who is his *Guru* for the purpose. The Lord is kinder than any human officer and far more eager. He takes on the roles which will save the devotee from harm, as he did to help Sakkubhai.

## Make the offerings without egoism

There was a devotee who felt that Seetha was his sister and Raama his brother-in-law; he loved Raama as Krishna loved Arjun! He came to know that Seetha had gone into the forest following Raama in exile; he imagined the distress she must be suffering, for want of sandals in the thorn-infested jungle paths and of a cot in the snake-infested depths of the forests. So, he went about in the jungle, with a pair of sandals and a cot, calling out, "Sister! Seetha!" long after his throat had turned hoarse. This happened a few decades ago. He took the Raamaayana as a contemporary event.

Raama appeared before him and consoled him. He fell before Him and prayed that He should accept the sandals and cot from him and use them, pleading that Seetha cannot walk on the hard thorny ground, or rather, that he would not be happy until she used them. "My dear brother-in-law," he addressed Raama fondly. Raama accepted them and asked him to leave happily. Offerings that are made with no defilement of egoism are gladly accepted by the Lord. If you feel proud or conceited, even the most fragrant flowers placed at the Feet of the Lord will be rejected by Him as unbearably stinking.

Man is a mixture of *dhaiva, dhaanava* and *maanava,* (god, demon and man). The wickedness of the ogre can be overcome by *dhaya* (the quality of mercy and charity), of sympathy and fellow-feeling; the pride of the god can be overcome by *dhama* (self-control), detachment, renunciation; the egoism of man can be overcome by following *dharma* prescribed by the impartial sages who have been purified by *thapas* (penance), and by canalising the instincts and impulses into fruitful fields. When these three are thus sublimated, *maanava* (man) is transformed into *Maadhava* (God). Each one must take up this process of purification, by discovering his faults and failings and realise the road to success.

## Krishna moved by devotion of Bheeshma

One morning, Dharmaraaja went to Krishna, in order to pay homage. He found Krishna seated in the *padmaasana* (lotus seat) pose, meditating deeply, with teardrops rolling over His cheeks. Dharmaraaja wondered whom He was meditating upon. At last, when Krishna opened His eyes he dared ask Him the question and Krishna replied that He was exulting over the devotion of a great soul towards Him. He said that it was no other than Bheeshma, whose mind was intently fixed on Him even while he was on the bed of arrows. It is not enough if you claim to be a *bhaktha;* the Lord must acknowledge it and exult over it, as Krishna did, when He was lost in admiration over the steadfastness of Bheeshma.

Vyaasa composed the Mahaabhaaratha, also called *jaya* (victory) with its galaxy of great persons, like Bheeshma, Bheema, Arjuna, Vidhura, Dharmaraaja, Dhroupadhi, Kunthi, all revolving around the divine

Krishna. This epic will remove the darkness of ignorance, the pettiness of selfishness, the cowardice of separation from the hearts of men. So, the title of *Lokaguru* for Vyaasa is very apt. He is extolled as Vishnu, sans *Shankha* (conch) and *Chakra* (discus); Shankara (Shiva), sans the three eyes; and *Brahma* (the Creator) sans the four heads. You must make the best use of this *Guru*, as you must, of this Puttaparthi itself. You must acquire here the skills for winning *shaanthi* and *santhosha* (peace of mind and bliss), the grace of God, the lessons of *saadhana*, the fruits of *sathsang* (company of holy men); do not fritter away your energy and time, seeking sensory satisfaction in ungodly company.

You pray, not for grace, but for petty impermanent pleasures; you do not try to know the ordinances of God and decide to follow them. Look at Dhruva. He started his penance, with the low aim of getting mastery over his step-mother's son; but as he progressed, he saw that he could get something far higher than even imperial honours, namely, the grace of God. Learn to appreciate the *Aathma* (Divine Self) and to detach your mind from that which is not *Aathma*. Become wise and discriminating.

### Leave everything to the Guru

When I was in the previous body at Shirdhi, there was a woman named Raadhabhai who yearned to get a *Manthropadhesha* (intiated into a sacred word or formula) from me. That day was also *Vyaasa Poornima*. She was so anxious to get a *Naamam* (Name) that she refused to take even food until she got it. Three days passed like this, but Baaba did not yield. At last, Syaama who was with the previous body spoke about her and pleaded for her and feared that she might even die of hunger. He said that if she died, it would be poor reflection on the broadmindedness for which Baaba was known. Raadhabhai was brought to the place in a weak condition. Baaba asked her to go to some *Guru* and get initiated into the name; she said, "I know of no other." Baaba asked her the meaning of the *slokha* "*Guru Brahma Guru Vishnu Guru Dhevo Maheshwarah, Gurusaakshath param Brahma Tasmai Shri Guruve namah.*" He asked her, "Why not take the *Guru's* name, then? Why demand another name from the *Guru*? If the *Guru* is God, obeying His orders, walking in the path He has shown, these are as effective as the *japam* (repetition) of the name."

## You are judged by your words

Once you have secured a *Guru*, leave everything to him, even the desire to achieve liberation. He knows you more than you yourself ever can. He will direct you as much as is good for you. Your duty is only to obey and to smother the tendency to drift away from Him. You may ask, how are we to earn our food, if we attach ourselves to a *Guru* like this? Be convinced that the Lord will not let you starve; He will give you not merely money but even *Amirtha*, not only food but the nectar of immortality.

Become immersed in the sweetness of the Name on your tongue. That will render your words also sweet and soft. By your words, will you be judged. A Mahaaraaja out hunting happened to ride far forward, so that his retinue could not catch up with him. He saw a blind man by the jungle road and so he accosted him, "Hallo, dear man. Did you notice any one passing along?" The blind man said "No." Then, after a few minutes, the minister came along and asked the same man, "Hey brother! Did you notice any one passing along?" and got the same answer. The commander when he saw him asked "Here, you fool! Did you notice some one passing along?" and a soldier who came last shouted, "You blind rotter, open your dirty mouth and tell me whether any one passed this way." At last when the priest of the court came along and said, "Dear brother, please tell me whether any one passed this way," he could reply that a king, a minister, a commander and a soldier had passed and had asked him the same question. For their style of speech, revealed their status and character.

If you have *dhaya, dhama* and *dharma* (sympathy, self-control and righteousness), that will take you beyond the realm of the three *gunas* (qualities of the mind); there is no need then for getting a *Naama* (Name) from the *Guru* and repeating it. The *aajna* (command) of the *Guru* or the Lord is even more important than the Name of the *Guru* or the Name of the Lord. Of what use is the repetition of the Name, without at the same time purifying the impulses by the observance of His commands.

*Prashaanthi Nilayam, 24-7-1964*

---

> Maayaa *itself has caused multifarious forms.*
>
> *This is a clever stage-play, a kind of fancy-dress.*
>
> *The objective world or Nature assumes many forms through the manipulation of* Maayaa, *the Deluding urge.*
>
> **Shri Sathya Sai**

## 21. Sravana and Smarana

THE first among the nine forms of devotion is *sravana* (hearing) and today, we have installed here at the Prashaanthi Nilayam this instrument for *sravana*, namely, the telephone. I am used to hearing not the talk that comes through this instrument, but the cries of agony, the call of pining hearts hungering for grace. Still, since it gladdens the hearts of devotees and I am never against anything that makes them glad and full-hearted, I have agreed for this installation. Just now, sitting in this hall, on this chair, you heard Me speak to Kanjilal at New Delhi and only he and I know how happy he is at the present moment, for he was able to speak to Baaba direct and to hear My voice, while in his own house.

Just see how this telephone itself came to be installed. The engineering staff were working day and night to fix it, but heavy rains interfered and even this noon, they were afraid that a connection with Delhi had become next to impossible. I had fixed the time as 5-30; but they pleaded with Me to postpone My coming into the hall for a few minutes at least, so that they could make sure that Delhi was coming through fine and clear. I said that we could speak to Delhi later, if they felt that would be better.

## *Sravana* can transform the individual

But, you saw how, as soon as I sat on this chair, Kanjilal could be heard clearly and I could inaugurate the service. It is given to these men who are here today to share in this achievement and this joy; they have the luck, the chance. Many times, people search far and wide for a groom for their daughter; but all the while, the young man might be in the neighbouring house itself. The engineers may say that they only did their duty and they might not look for any gratitude; but I am sure, you will thank them for the service they rendered, in these rains and under high pressure of work.

*Sravana*, hearing the voice of God, hearing about God, these are important events in life, events that transform the individual. Arjuan "heard" the Bhagavadh Geetha; Pareekshit "heard" the *Bhaagavatha*; both were liberated from bondage thereby. In the Mahaabhaaratha, *Karna*, meaning the Ear (!) is the most outstanding character; it is called *Karnarasaayana*, (sweet medicine to be "heard") and assimilated into daily life. The *Sabdha* (Sound), the *Pranava* (Om) are all very important keys to bliss; the *Vedhas* are to be "heard" and "recited." They are *Shruthi*, that which was heard, in moments of supraconscious ecstasy, by purified scholars doing *saadhana*. I am reminded of all this in the presence of this contrivance for *Doora-sravana*, hearing people who are far away.

*Bhaagavatha-sravana* (listening to *Bhaagavatha*) leads to *Bhaagavatha-smarana* (the constant remembrance of the Lord), and detachment from the ties of the objective world. There was famous dacoit once who advised his son while initiating him into the ancestral profession, never for a moment listen to stories of the Lord. "Do not stay to listen to any *Puraana* (mythological stories) or any reading of the *Bhaagavatha*," (tales of incarnations of Vishnu), he exhorted the young aspirant. The son scrupulously observed this injunction for years and amassed a good fortune.

## Effect of hearing the *Bhaagavatha*

One night, however, while running with his loot on his shoulder through a side lane of the city to avoid the police, a piece of glass cut into his sole; he sat for a while to pull it off and stop the flow of blood. He was then behind a house, where some one was reading and explaining the *Bhaagavatha* to a small group of listeners; he listened perforce for a short two minutes. The spark fell on the heap of cotton. During that short period, he heard the Pandith explaining the nature of God. He has no ears, no eyes, no limbs; He has a thousand forms; He is without form. "*Sarvathah paani-paadham*," (with hands and feet everywhere) as the Geetha says. That description got fixed in his heart. He could not shake it.

A few days later the police came to know of the depredations made by him as well as his associates and kinsmen. In order to know more about their activities they entered the area incognito, one constable as *Goddess Kaali* and some others as the worshippers and priests. They shouted and yelled, cursed and terrified the dacoits and called upon them to come out of their homes and fall at the feet of *Kaali*.

Many did so, but the son who heard the *Bhaagavatha* albeit for two minutes knew just enough to save his skin. He was not terrified at all. He challenged the constable who was acting the role of *Kaali* and tore off his makeup and exposed the plot and instilled courage into the hearts of the gang. Then, when the police left discomfited he argued within himself thus: "If two minutes of the forbidden fruit could help me so much, what can I not gain if I devote myself entirely to the stories of the glories of God?" He left off the evil path and became a *saadhaka* (spiritual practitioner).

## Tongue is man's biggest weapon of offence

The grace of God descends upon the eager *saadhaka*, who listens attentively to the story of that grace. The name of God, if recited with love and faith, has that power. Once the mother of Agasthya boasted that her son drank all the waters of the ocean; but the mother of Hanumaan, who was there, said: "Why go to that extent? My son leaped over it in a trice." But there was the mother of Raama with them. She said, "Your son leaped over the ocean, uttering my son's name. Without it, he was helpless." The name has that overmastering power. It can award unheard of, unimagined strength and courage. The other two women disputed the fact that it was *Raamanaama* that strengthened Hanumaan for the enterprise. So, Kaushalya asked Raama Himself. He said, "Why, it was because this body was called Raama, the name that combines the *beejaaksharas* (mystic letters) of both Shiva and Vishnu, that I Myself was able to conquer Raavana and his hordes!"

The name has much efficacy. By repeating the name, the Lord and His attributes can be easily identified. The tongue must be sanctified by the repetition of the name. It has also to use sweet expressions which will spread contentment and joy. Be very careful about your speech. Animals have horns, insects have stings, beasts have claws and fangs. But, man's biggest weapon of offence is his tongue. The wounds that his tongue inflicts can scarce be healed; they fester in the heart for long. They are capable of more damage than even an atom bomb.

When Bheema went to bring the Saugandhika flower for his beloved, he saw Hanumaan with his tail lying across the road. Bheema talked rudely to Hanumaan, ordering him to remove the tail, for he thought it mean to walk over some one else's appendage. The rudeness made Hanumaan refuse the demand and so, Bheema was humiliated for he could not lift the tail and set it aside. He learned the need for politeness in conversation.

Speak so that your language is as sweet as your feelings are. Make the words true and pleasing. (*Sathyam brooyaath; priyam brooyath*). But, for the sake of pleasing another, do not speak falsehood or exaggerate. Cynicism which leads you to speak about a thing in a carping manner and in order to bring it into disrepute is as bad as flattery which makes you exaggerate and cross the boundaries of truth.

## Bliss is man's native character

You can give *Aanandha* by your speech, only if you have attained the state of *Aanandha* yourself. A lamp burning under a pot with five holes: that is the symbol of man, who has the Flame of Wisdom shining through five senses. Cover the pot with a thick cloth and no light emerges. The cloth is the cover of *ajnaana* (ignorance), of *thamas* (inaction). Remove it; it shines feebly through the senses, that is the symbol of *rajas* (passion and activity). Remove the pot itself, that is to say, remove the identification with the body, (the *dhehaathma-buddhi*); then the *Aathmajyothi* (light of the Self) shines full and bright. The jyothi or *Aanandha* (Divine light or Divine Bliss) is ever there but, it was obstructed by the pot and the cloth. *Aanandha* is your native character, your real stamp, your very reality.

The patient must himself drink the drug. There is no vicarious cure. The balm must be applied where the pain is. The cause of the illness and of the misery is in your mental vision, for, you see many, when there is only One. You say "My God," "Their God," "Your Baaba," as if there are so many Gods existing to help you quarrel and fight among yourselves. Ask the Lord for the removal of your earthly troubles; there is no mistake in that. It is much better than asking other men, and losing self-respect and honour. For the sake of votes, people catch hold of the feet of all and sundry; if they fall at the feet of the Lord, that will bring them more votes, for the people will plead with Him to lead them as a great servant of God.

## Communicate from heart to heart

You can call Me on the phone, but I will not be available for all those who do not have the sincere and steady yearning for the Lord. For those who say "No! You are not my Lord," I say "No." For those who say, "Yes," I too echo "Yes." If I am available in your heart, I will be available over the phone. But, remember, I have My own special postal and telephone systems. They operate from the heart straight to the heart. There are rules and regulations for the operation of that system, which the *Shaasthras* (scriptures) declare. You can find them there. I am glad that devotees have today acquired this new convenience at Prashaanthi Nilayam.

*Prashaanthi Nilayam, 29-7-1964*

---

**Difficulties are created to increase the yearning and to sift the sincere devotee from the rest.**

**SHRI SATHYA SAI**

## 22. Eliminate the Ego

IT is indeed a piece of good fortune that you have been able to hear, in the midst of the many worldly worries that engross you, the valuable teachings of the ancient scriptures of this land, from these great Pandiths. This is what really confers lasting happiness. In the land which once cultivated these great ideals, weeds and thorny bushes have over-run the fields and with the decline of spiritual enthusiasm, enmity, factions, injustice and falsehood have grown wild. Indian religion and culture have treasured many folkways and customs that enshrine the lessons laid down by *yogis* and *rishis* for the good of the community. They are called *samskaaras*, (purificatory acts), acts which sublimate the baser emotions and impulses; there are 48 of these mentioned in the *Shaasthras*, but, of these, 16 are essential for the individual who strives for the higher destiny.

These have been neglected by society, since many decades, on account of a mad infatuation for the ways of the ruling race, which had come from the west. Their language slowly modified habits of living and even thinking; their dress which was adopted, changed outlooks and modes of living; their games and recreations transformed the ways in which Indians spend their leisure; their culture percolated into every field of activity and Indian culture is faced, even after the recovery of national independence, with a great danger to its continuity.

## Discard all low desires

Of course, there is no need to feel unduly depressed. One has only to recognise ignorance, in order to make it vanish. One has only to know one-self, in order to contact the springs of Bliss and Immortality and of kinship with all beings. In Sanskrit, the individual is known as *vyakthi*, because he has to make his innate divinity *vyaktha* (explicit). That is your reality; discover it, dwell in it, desire to divulge it. Discard all low desires for a few acres of land, or a fat account in the bank, or a few more bungalows or cars or radios; desire rather the joy that will never fade, that will never cloy, deep, steady and strength-giving, the joy of Divine Realisation.

Discover your holiness, your divinity, your truth. You may have doubts which is *dharma* (right conduct), which is *sathya* (truth), which is *prema* (Divine love), etc.; I admit; but, you can have no doubt about yourself, is it not? So, find out who you are and be fixed in that truth. That is enough to save you, to give you everlasting joy. That is why the *Vedhas* and the *Upanishadhs* teach, what the sages and the saints experienced, what these *Pandiths* (scholars) remind you in their discourses.

Remember the God in whom you move, the God who makes you move, the God who is all this vast universe, every atom, every huge star. Select some Name and Form for this all-pervasive immanent God and keep those on your tongue and before your mental eye. That is what is called *japasahitha dhyaanam* (meditation-cum-recitation of the Name).

## Discover the truth in silence

You are now more interested in listening to film-songs on the transistor radios which you carry round your necks. A villager came to Madras recently and his educated son-in-law went to the railway station to meet him and take him home. While they were proceeding homewards in a taxi, the father-in-law asked the son-in-law a rather strange question: "How much do the barbers here charge per shave?" The son-in-law was amazed at his curiosity; he asked why he was so eager to know this particular fact, more than anything else. The villager replied, "I saw a few barbers going along the road now; they are all wearing rich clothes, and they are carrying their equipment not in tin boxes as our village barbers do, but, in fine shiny leather boxes." The old man had seen people carrying these transistor radios. People miss a very valuable thing if they do not listen in, even while they are moving about or resting in the park or beach! They are afraid of being alone; they avoid silence as something detestable! But, you can discover your own truth only when you are alone with yourself and there is silence all around you.

Justice Sadhaashivam said now that he had seen huge gatherings of eager listeners at religious meetings like this and so, he was led to the conclusion that atheism is not gaining ground in this country. The gatherings are certainly large but they are not very encouraging if you consider what a small percentage actually pay attention and of those who attend, what a small percentage cherish the teaching in the heart and strive to regulate their lives accordingly.

As a matter of fact, there are no atheists at all but, only ignorant people. They do not know that God is their innermost core. They deny God because they do not know that their very breath is God. It is like fish denying the existence of water. You have to pity them for their colossal ignorance, not get angry with them for saying things you do not like. God dwells in you as *aanandha* (divine bliss); that is why you seek *aanandha* automatically, always, in every object around you. To become as full of *aanandha* as Raadha (the consort of Lord Krishna) or as Raamakrishna Paramahamsa or as Vivekaanandha, you have to sacrifice your ego and saturate yourself with the consciousness that the Lord is your very being.

## Krishna and Aanjaneya

You must have heard many stories of *garvabhangam*—the suppression of conceit or egoism by the Lord. One day, Aanjaneya appeared in a garden on the outskirts of *Dhwaaraka* (abode of Lord Krishna). Krishna who heard about the pranks of the strange monkey, directed Garuda to proceed and scare the animal out of the city limits. Garuda failed, even though the later took the entire army with him for the fray. His pride was humbled. Krishna sent a message through him to the monkey, who had declared himself as Aanjaneya, that he should deign to come to Krishna's court. But, Aanjaneya recognised only Raama and would obey only the orders of Raama. So, Krishna had to send another message that Raama was calling him to His audience hall! Devotion compels the Lord to yield to the whims of His servants. Aanjaneya hurried to see Raama and Krishna gave him the *darshan* of Raama Himself. Sathyabhaama had offered to change herself into Seetha and when she stood by the side of Raama, Aanjaneya could not recognise in that form his

Seetha. He was bewildered at this apparition. He asked Krishna, "O Lord Raama! Where is my Seetha? Who is this substitute?" Thus, the conceit of Sathyabhaama was broken by the Lord. He then asked Rukmini (Krishna's consort) to come forward and Aanjaneya immediately saw in her the Seetha he adored.

So long as you have a trace of ego in you, you cannot see the Lord clearly. That is the *thera* (curtain), which Saint Thyaagaraaja prayed Lord Venkateshwara to remove from his mind. Egoism will be destroyed if you constantly tell yourself, 'It is He, not I.' 'He is the force, I am but the instrument.' Keep His Name always on the tongue; contemplate His glory whenever you see or hear anything beautiful or grand; see in every one the Lord Himself moving in that form. Do not talk evil of others, see only good in them. Welcome every chance to help others, to console others, to encourage others along the spiritual path. Be humble, do not become proud of your wealth, status, authority, learning or caste. Dedicate all your physical possessions and mental skills and intellectual attainments to the service of the Lord and to the Lord's manifold manifestations.

*Prashaanthi Vidwanmahaasabha (Madras),*
*Inauguration by Shri M. Bhakthavatsalam,*
*President: Mr. Justice Sadhaashivam, 13-8-1964*

---

Mother is Love. Worship the mother as God.
Father is Truth. Worship the father as God.

SHRI SATHYA SAI

## 23. The Rain Clouds

For the last two hours, you were fully immersed in the *aanandha* of *Krishnathathwa* (Reality of Krishna) and of *Vedhasaara* (essence of *Vedha*), which are both the same. How grand it would be if all the moments of life you were imbibing this *aanandha* undisturbed! Iyengar spoke on Krishna-*thrishna*, the thirst for Krishna! What an appropriate word, that! The thirst for worldly goods can never be allayed; trying to satisfy it makes it only more acute. Thirst can never be quenched by drinking salt water, which is the objective world. Human desire is illimitable, without end. It makes you pursue the mirage in the desert; it makes you build castles in the air; it breeds discontent and despair once you succumb to it. But, develop the thirst for Krishna, you discover the cool spring of *aanandha* within you. Krishna *Naama* (name) makes you strong and steady; it is sweet and sustaining.

Gouranga, the great example of this thirst, is so called because his heart was so pure that it had no touch of blemish at all. He is called Krishna *Chaithanya*, because he lost his *chaithanya*, that is, became unconscious of the world outside him, when he heard the name Krishna and became Krishna-conscious!

## Yearning of *Gopees* for Krishna

Look at the *gopees* (milk maids of Gokulam) and their yearning for the Lord! They never swerved from the path of *bhakthi*, of continuous *smarana* (remembrance) of the Lord. When in pain you shout "*Ayyo, appa* or *amma*"; but the *gopees* always called on Krishna only, whether in joy or in grief. A *gopee* was moving along the streets of Brindhaavan selling butter and ghee and milk; but, she was not crying aloud the names of her ware; she was calling aloud the names of Krishna: "Govindha! Dhamodhara! Maadhava!" The *gopees* forgot the very purpose of their visit to Brindhaavan, their very livelihood, their task of selling and earning. They stood watching Krishna, running along with a hoop and ignoring all else, they ran behind him with a ball of butter in the hand, offering it to the Divine child who had captured their hearts, calling on Him to receive the gift; "Govindha!" Dhamodhara! Maadhava!"

When one of them was rolling on the ground in terrible anguish at the separation from Krishna, they sat around her and instead of assuaging her grief by turning her thoughts away from Krishna, they augmented it because they themselves could not think of any other subject to talk to her than Krishna's glory and Krishna's *prema*! They sat around and sang, "Govindha! Dhamodhara! Maadhava!" Whoever has the thirst, Krishna will quench it; whoever calls on Him in the agony of that thirst, Krishna, the rain-cloud, will answer that call and appear.

You can understand Raadha (Krishna's consort) only if you can fathom the depth of that thirst. Raadha believed that Krishna is the *Aadhar* (basis); she did *aaradh* (worship) to Krishna in a continuous *dhaara* (stream); in fact, she is *Dhaara* or *Prakrithi*, which is another form of the Lord or *Pursuha* Himself. How can those who are full of evil tendencies and impulses grasp that relationship?

In this *Kaliyuga*, the principle of *Prema* (Divine Love) is not in evidence. It is smothered in jealousy, conceit, hatred, fear, falsehood and greed. That is why it is best referred to as the *kalaha-yuga* (the age of faction), marked by fights between mother and daughter, father and son, teacher and pupil, *guru* and *guru*, brother and brother. The recitation of the name of Krishna is the best method for cleansing the mind of all these evil impulses.

You may ask, "If we engage ourselves in this pastime, how can we earn our livelihood?" Well, let me assure you, if you have pure and steady faith in the Lord, He will provide for you, not merely food, but the nectar of immortality. You have that mighty potentiality in you, to discover the Lord within and compel Him to grant you that nectar.

## Make the thirst for Krishna grow in you

When you say that Krishna was born in Gokula, that He grew up in Brindhaavan, that He ruled over *Mathura* and that He later reigned at Dhwaaraka, what do those statements signify? The *manas* (mind) is the *Gokula* where He was born (where He is born even now to whoever takes the spiritual path); the heart is the Brindhaavan where He grows, where *prema* (divine love) for Him develops; the *Chith* is the *Mathura* which He rules over and the *Nirvikalpa* stage is Dhwaaraka where He installs Himself, as the reigning monarch. Make the *Krishna-thrishna* (thirst for Krishna) grow through these stages and you will be saving yourself! You will be joining the ranks of Raadha, Meera and Sakkubhai (devotees of Lord Krishna).

Once upon a time, we used to hear of three famous names Lal, Bal and Pal; they were famous in the days of the national struggle. But many do not know now who they were. At least, Lal and Pal have disappeared from the memory of the people; a large percentage of even educated persons will flounder if you ask them who Lal and Pal were. Bal, meaning Bala Gangaadhara Thilak, is still known to many, because he has made a contribution to spiritual knowledge, being a *saadhaka* himself and a good student of Geetha for which he wrote a commentary. So, *saadhana* alone makes life worth while; the rest is mostly froth or fake or failure, flashes of the moment.

## Three principles to guide you

The mind must become *bhakthimaya* (saturated with devotion to God); the intelligence must be transformed into *jnaana-dheepthi* (the splendour of universal wisdom), or *jnaana* (Divine Knowledge); the body must be a willing and efficient instrument for *saddharmacharana*, (the practice of righteousness). Such a life is indeed the crown and glory of humanity. The rest are contaminated, contained, caged lives!

There is no use asking a doctor to advise you about the plans for the building you propose to raise; nor is it wise to ask the engineer for a balm to assuage pain. Go to the proper *Guru* and learn from him about at least three principles to guide your lives.

(1) **Dharma** : What is *dharma*, why should it be followed, what does it allow, what does it condemn, etc.?---these have to be clearly known. The Geetha is the best text on *Dharma*: the first word in it is *dharma* and the last word is *mama* (mine). So, it teaches each student what exactly he should consider as "the *dharma* which is mine!" Each one must evolve his own *dharma* based on *Aathmadharma*, the faith that the *Aathma* (soul) is his true reality.

(2) **Bhakthi** : *Bhakthi* (devotion) is like a king, who has two aides-de-camp called *jnaana* (divine knowledge) and *vairaagya* (non-attachment). Without these two bodyguards, *bhakthi* is never secure or safe. *Bhakthi* must be built upon the foundation of *jnaana*; it must flower as "detachment from the world." The *jnaani* is the *sthitha-prajna* (unmoved by agitating feelings and emotions), unshaken by the storms of fortune, good or bad; the *vairaagi* (the detached), is the person who has rid himself of the three *gunas* (qualities of the mind); and the *bhaktha* (devotee) is he who is all *prema* (Love). *Bhakthi, jnaana* and *vairaagya* are three peaks of the same Himaalyan range. *Prema* creates *dhaya* (compassion); *vairaagya* induces *dhama* (tolerance); and, *jnaana* leads you along the path of *dharma*.

## Put out the fire raging within you

(3) **Saadhana** : When the house catches fire, you run about in desperate haste to get succour and to put out the flames; but, you do not realise that the fire raging inside you is even more devastating and devouring. You must take up the duty of fire fighting in right earnest and never rest until the flames are put out. Start the fight right now. Start serving your parents, your teachers, the elders, the poor, the diseased, the distressed. Do not foster factions and divisions. Promote love, concord, co-operation, brotherliness. Do not look upon people as belonging to this state or that; all are in the state of bondage to the senses, to the objective world. Join the company of the good, the striving, the yearning *saadhakas* and you will soon reach the stage of peace within and harmony without.

*Madras, 14-8-1964*

## 24. The sandalwood tree

THE importance which *Sanaathana* culture (unchanging truth) gives to *dharma* was explained to you by the Pandith; he outlined some of the main principles of that subtle ideal. *Dharma* (righteousness) is the feet and *Moksha* (Realisation) the head of the human community, while the other two *purushaarthas*---*artha* (wealth)and *kaama* (desire)---form the trunk and limbs. Now, feet and head are ignored and the other two reckoned as vital. That is the tragedy of modern times. Enough warning against this tragedy has been given in the ancient texts of this country. The Kauravas are useful examples of the calamity that awaits those who pursue the ideals of *artha* and *kaama*, without the regulating influence of *dharma* and *moksha*. They were drunk with power; they were overcome by greed and pride; they had insatiable desire; they suffered untold misery and were destroyed.

Raavana fell because he strove to accumulate *artha* and was carried away by covetousness, *kaama*. His "ten heads" indicate his mastery over the four *Vedhas* and the six *Shaasthras*; but, of what avail was all that learning? Aanjaneya reported that Lanka was echoing with the recitation of the *Vedhas* and the air was thick with sacrificial smoke. But, the *raakshasas* (demons) were wicked, in spite of all that ritual exactitude. Ritual must result in righteousness; otherwise, it is only rigmarole. Raavana sought to gain *Prakrithi*, not *Purusha* (the manifestation not the manifestor); Seetha not Raama! And, so his life became futile.

*Kaama* is the three-headed demon; when you win your desire, you develop *lobha* (miserly greed), to retain the gain and see that it multiplies; when you are defeated in desire, you develop *krodha* (resentment, anger); even *thapas* (penance) might not transmute such a character, as seen in the case of Bhasmaasura, who sought to destroy the very Lord who granted him the boon he was after! *Kaama*, *lobha* and *krodha* are all forms of *rajoguna* (quality of passion and activity), the feverish activity that ignores the "means" while concentrating on the "end." *Rajoguna* pursues the goal, but is not particular about the correctness of the path.

## Qualify yourself and desire

There is a story of some monkeys who planted a mango garden. They planted the saplings, watered them a few days, and plucked them from off the ground to see how deep the roots had gone! They wanted them to grow fast and yield fruits, but they were unaware of the processs by which alone they could get the fruits they craved for! Act right; then, claim the fruit. Cultivate with care, and collect the harvest.

What is good of burdening yourself with desire when you do not have the qualification to fulfil it? Madhuranaath once asked Raamakrishna Paramahamsa for a chance to enjoy what was known as *Nirvikalpa samaadhi* (superconscious state of Bliss), about which he had heard. Though Raamakrishna demurred because he had no qualification and preparatory training for it, he insisted; so when at last, the Master acceded, and made him lose consciousness for three days, the poor man protested and appealed for an end to that experience. It was a burden too heavy for his weak shoulders.

The three *gunas* (qualities of the mind) have to be transcended one after the other; *thamas* (lethargy) being transmuted into *rajas* (passionate activity) and *rajas* into *sathwa* (serenity and poise) and *sathwa* too, at last into characteristiclessness. The *gunas* bind man and leave impressions. *Thamas* is like the worms that creep and crawl in offal; *rajas* is like the fly that sits on foul things as well as fair; *sathwa* is like the bee that visits only fragrant flowers. But, all three are drawn towards objects, whereas one should be free from all traces of attachment. When hearts are infested with flies and worms, the flit of *Naamasmarana* (constant remembrance of God's name) has to be used for disinfecting the place. You must recognise the high purpose of this human body and the unique chance man has. Then only will you strive to benefit by this hard-won piece of luck.

## The magnanimous king

A *Raaja* (king) was out hunting in the forest and while pursuing the deer, he went too far and discovered that his retinue was left behind. He lost his way and was overcome by hunger and thirst. At last, he saw a tiny hut where lived a poor wood-cutter and his wife selling fuel in the distant villages. Their larder was almost empty, but the wife managed to bring out a *roti* (bread), which the king ate with avidity. He had never known such taste, for he was never so hungry as then. and, he slept soundly that noon, for he was never so tired as then. By that time, the courtiers and soldiers came upto where he was and the astounded wood-cutter learnt that his guest was no less a person than the monarch of the realm. He apologised for the poor fare he offered, though the king never uttered a harsh word.

## Tragedy of man everywhere

Next day, a man came from the capital to take him to the court and the poor fellow was certain that he was going to be punished for insulting the ruler. His wife accompanied him, for she offered to share the misery with her lord. The Raaja gave him a seat and insisted upon his sitting, an honour which the wood-cutter knew was usually given to animals that were about to be sacrificed. He was fed nicely, along with his wife, another honour which such animals usually get.

Then the king asked him what boon he would ask from him, and the terrified man could ask for only this: "Please allow me to go home alive, with my wife! Please do not cut off my head," he cried. The Raaja said, "I am not an urgrateful wretch to treat you so cruelly. If I give you an estate you will ruin it, for you are unaware of agriculture. If I give riches, thieves will carry it away, for you live alone in the jungle. Well, I shall give you a sandalwood plantation in that forest, thirty acres in extent. Make good use of it and prosper." The wood-cutter felt relieved and he went away into the woods.

After about six months, the King went to the forest again for a hunt and remembering the bread, he went in search of the wood-cutter. He found him quite happy for he said, that he had started selling charcoal instead of fuel. The sandalwood trees were being reduced to charcoal by that man; he did not know the value of the gift he had received. Man too does not realise the value of the precious gift of "the number of days" of life he has received from the Lord. He fritters them away for temporary earnings. That is the tragedy of man everywhere.

*Sanaathana Dharma* has laid down the rules and regulations for the best possible utilisation of life, but for want of teaching, exposition and example, they have been sadly neglected. This is like inflicting injuries on oneself, this neglect of the rules, which give real happiness and peace. This is like the foolishness of living upon your neighbour's leavings, while your own home has a relishing, nourishing banquet ready!

## Regulate the way of living

Reform the body, reconstruct the mind; regulate the way of living; then, the country will become automatically strong and prosperous. Do not wail that it is a mud pot if it contains nectar; it is far better than having a gold pot with poison in it. The land may be rich, but, if life is mean, it is deplorable. It does not matter if the standard of life is poor, provided the way of life is pure, full of *prema*, humility, fear-of-sin, and reverence towards elders.

It is easy to restore this way of life, provided the *Vedhas* are once again studied and followed. The *Vedhamaatha* (mother of *Vedhas*) will foster in you love and kindness. Have faith; do not discard a diamond, dismissing it as a piece of glass. The *Dharma* laid down in the *Vedhas* is the best armour to guard you against sorrow.

Women should observe *sthree dharma* and men *purusha dharma*, the householder, *grihastha dharma*, the monk *sanyaasa dharma* (the path of righteousness presecirbed for each category of persons. The outward symbols like shave head, the ochre cloth, *kamandalu*—these are like the barbed wire erected to protect the crop from depredation. But, what we now find is, there is plenty of fence without, but no crop within!

You may have a grand feast on the plate, but, unless you have hunger, you will not be tempted to eat. There are qualifications for every task, be it eating or fasting, be it leading a householder's life or monk's life. Only a stone that was once Ahalya and was saturated by *dhyaana* (meditation) and remorse can be transmuted into human form and only the feet of a Divine incarnation can so transmute it. All stones trodden by Raama did not get transformed into women; nor did any of the feet that trod upon that stone had the power of giving life. The *Guru* must have the awakening touch and the *sishya* (disciple) must have the eagerness to awake. The relationship should not be like the snake with a frog in the mouth, the frog too weak to escape, the snake too full to swallow. The *Guru* must be able to save; the *sishya* must be ready to be saved.

## Hanumaan's dedicated service

Dedicate all tasks of offerings to the Lord. Never deviate from that attitude. Hanumaan was such a *bhaktha*; Raama was the very life-breath for him. After the coronation, one day, Seetha and the three brothers of Raama met and planned to exclude Hanumaan from the *seva* (service) of Raama and wanted that all the various services for Raama should be divided only among themselves. They felt that Hanumaan had enough chances already. So, they drew up a list, as exhaustive as they could remember, of the service from dawn till dusk, down to the smallest minutiae and assigned each item to one among themselves. They presented the list of items and assignees to the Lord, while Hanumaan was present. Raama heard about the new procedure, read the list and gave His approval, with a smile. He told Hanumaan that all the tasks had been assigned to others and that he could now take rest. Hanumaan prayed that the list might be read and when it was done, he noticed an omission---the task of 'snapping fingers when one yawns.' Of course, being an emperor, Raama should not be allowed to do it himself. It has to be done by a servant, he pleaded. Raama agreed to allot that task to Hanumaan!

It was a great epic piece of good luck for Hanumaan, for it entitled Hanumaan's constant attendance on his Master, for how could anyone predict when the yawn would come? And, he had to be looking on that heart-charming face all the time, to be ready with snap, as soon as the yawn was on! He could not be away for a minute nor could he relax for a moment. You must be happy that the seva of the Lord keeps you always in His presence and ever vigilant to carry out His behests.

## Select a Name and a Form

The Lord cares for *ekaagratha* and *chittha-suddhi* (concentration and purity of mind). You need not feel that you are physically away from Him. He has no 'near' and 'far.' Provided the address is clear and correct, your letter will be delivered, either at the next street or at Calcutta or Bombay for the same stamp. *Smarana* (remembering) is the stamp; *manana* (recapitulaiton) is the address. Have the Name for *smarana*; the Form for *manana*, that is enough.

Select one Name and one Form for *smarana* and *manana*; but, do not talk ill of other names and forms. Behave like the woman in a joint family; she respects and serves the elders of the family such as the father-in-law, and his brothers and her own brother-in-law, but her heart is dedicated to her husband, whom she loves and reveres in a special manner. If you carp at the faith of others, your devotion is fake. If you are sincere, you will appreciate the sincerity of others. You see faults in others because you yourself have those faults, not otherwise.

While in Dandakaaranya forest, Raama was once reclining with His head on the lap of Sugreeva and the *vaanara* (monkey) leaders were around Him. The moon was shining overhead in full glory, but, there was the tell-tale spot which marred the fullness of the effulgence. Raama asked each one of them what the spot indicated. Each one gave a different explanation; the reflection of the sea, one said; a deep pit, said another; a mountain range, said a third; but, Aanjaneya said, "It is your reflection I see on the moon, your colour, nothing else." That was the measure of his devotion. He saw everywhere, everytime only Raama.

Have faith in your culture, which emphasises the path of self-control and discipline. Do not be led away by the tinsel attractions of foreign cultures. Indian customs, like the wearing of the sari are now adopted by western women, while Indian women are wearing gowns! Indian women bob their hair and discard the *kumkum* (vermilion dot on the forehead), in order to look fashionable; but, every Indian custom has deep significance, ignored in this imitative rush. A vessel of sweetness can be spoiled by a drop of kerosene. Accept good things from other cultures, the things that help you to control the vagaries of the senses and the mind, to investigate and discriminate more clearly.

Of the many lakhs of people who dwell in this city, you alone had the great chance to come and hear the advice given today. So make the best use of this treasure and decide on leading more useful lives from this very moment. Listen to all who speak of the glory of the Lord, who is in you, as in everybody else. Learn from all the methods by which you can discover Him and reach Him. That is my advice to you.

*Madras, 15-8-1964*

## 25. The bubble of pride

MAN is a pilgrim towards *Dharmakshethra*, the pride of *dharma*, which is the abode also of *Shaanthi;* but, on the way, he is led into the bylanes and alleys of objective pleasure by the senses to which he has become a slave. Man is eager to know about all kinds of trivialities, like the details of other lives and other places, but, he has no keenness to know about himself or the place from where he himself has come. Man is sunk in ignorance about himself, his source and substance, his goal and fate. He reduces himself to just one individual; he, the inheritor of unlimited wealth and fortune, feels himself a pauper. Remove this ego boundary; then only can you recognise the vastness of yourself.

This microphone before Me must have been made by someone, is it not? He is not seen or known by you, but of his existence, there can be no doubt. Besides, it is certain he must be knowing all about this microphone which he has made. So too, there must be a creator for this universe and He must be knowing all about it. This universe is composed of the five elements and He is the master of all the five, their manipulator, aware of their subtle characteristics and properties. He is the *kshethrajna* (Indweller), he who knows this *kshethra* (field). When I speak into the mike, all of you can hear Me clearly; but the tape recorder here, the fan, the bulbs, the tube-lights, all operate on account of the self-same unseen electric current that animates each of them.

Diwan Bahadur Raamaswamy Shaasthry, *Yogi* Suddhanandha Bhaarathi, and others addressed you now, each one on a separate note, but, all described only the self-same *Kshethrajna*, the Universal knower, who is known by all names and who is in all forms. He is the impersonal person described in a hundred different ways in the *Vedhas*, the *Shaasthras*, the *Mahaabhaaratha*, the *Raamaayana* and the *Bhaagavatha*. Hold on to Him and live your lives; you will not slip. Build your activities on that basis; your career will not cave in. You will also develop courage, consolation and faith in yourself and in your destiny.

## Krishna's lessons to control the ego

Krishna addresses Arjuna in the Geetha sometimes as *Kaunteya*. Now, what does that appellation mean? It means, "One who assimilates quietly" as you are doing now. You are seated comfortably under this pandal, in fine weather and you can afford to listen in silence. But remember, Arjuna was between two opposing armies, eager for the fray for which they had prepared for years with unquenchable vengeance. It requires extraordinary self-control and yearning to command concentration at that time. Krishna addresses him as *Kurunandhana*, which means that he takes delight in *karma* dedicated to the high ideals he had in view. Every mode of address of Krishna has an inner meaning and appropriateness, as well as a lesson for others.

Arjuna was trained by Krishna, without break, to control his egoism. Before the *Mahaabhaaratha* war, Arjuna once happened to be at Raamasethu, near Raameshwaram. Arjuna spoke of the bridge with some scorn in the hearing of Aanjaneya who was there and said that he would have built a bridge of arrows, single-handed and not bothered about subduing the sea and getting monkeys to pile up rocks one over the other. Aanjaneya asked him to build one. When Aanjaneya walked gently over the bridge, the arrows broke under his weight!

Krishna suddenly presented Himself and suggested that it should be done in his presence, for there was no witness when the challenge was made and accepted. In order to save Arjuna from humiliation, Krishna bore the second bridge on His back, when Aanjaneya walked on it, so that Arjuna saw the tell-tale streaks of red, where the arrow points had pierced the Lord's back. Thus, Arjuna's pride was humbled. He prayed to Aanjaneya to fight on his side at Kurukshethra; but Aanjaneya said that the Kaurava army would be too infinitesimal a foe for his prowess; it would not be fair to pit him against such a weak enemy; he would only watch the fight, from the flag of Arjuna's chariot, he said; and the offer was gladly accepted.

## Egoism is a tough enemy

Arjuna's pride was humbled during the war in another interesting manner by Krishna. About the end of the war, one evening, Arjuna felt proud that Krishna was his charioteer, and his 'servant.' He felt that as master, he should get down from the chariot after Krishna and not before Him. So, that day he insisted that Krishna should get down first, that he should come down only afterward. But, Krishna was adamant; Arjuna must come down first, he said. After wasting a long time, pleading and protesting and praying, Arjuna got down, very unwillingly, swallowing his pride. Krishna then came down, and, immediately the chariot went up in flames! Krishna explained the reason. The incendiary arrows and missiles that had stuck on the chariot were powerless so long as He was on it; but, when his presence was no longer there, they set the chariot on fire. Thus, Krishna showed that every act and word of the Lord had significance and a purpose, which mortals cannot gauge. Egoism is a tough enemy and it requires constant vigilance to conquer it.

## Conquer the foes of the inner realm

Pride raises its head in every stage and state. Like grass which covers the earth with a green carpet, as soon as the rains fall even in places which appeared dry waste, pride thrives upon opportunity. Sikhadhwaja, the King, got a feeling of extreme renunciation and left for the forest for ascetic practices. His queen Choodala had the spirit of detachment in greater measure, but, she did not make a show of it as her husband did.

The queen put on a male attire, wore ochre, spelt a rosary and sought him in the jungle. Discovering him at last, she asked him who he was. The king replied that he was the ruler of the realm, that he had given up his riches, his treasure, his army, his court, etc. "For the sake of what did you give up these?" asked Choodala. "For the sake of peace," replied the king. But, he had to confess that he had not attained it. Then, Choodala taught him that the giving up of "things" will bear no fruit, that the desire for things, the pride of possessing things, of having once possessed them, has to be given up, that one must be detached from the objective world so that he might turn his eyes inward and conquer the foes of the inner realm and become a master of himself. When the king attempted to fall at the feet of the new *Guru* that had come to him, Choodala revealed her identity. She was a *sathi* (virtuous wife) who was the *Guru* of her *pathi* (husband); there were many such women in ancient times, when they were honoured and educated much better than today.

## Tremendous power of mind over body

You must develop the devotion of the *gopees*, of Raadha, of Uddhava, of Hanumaan. Raamakrishna Paramahamsa did intense *saadhana*, transmitting himself into the attitude of Hanumaan and even his physical attributes changed to suit the role. He developed a small tail during the period; such is the tremendous power of mind over body. Many husbands and mothers-in-law tried to scare away the *gopees* from Krishna by spreading scandals about Him but how can any one keep the *Jeeva* (individual soul) and the *Jagadeeshwara* (Lord of the Universe) apart? *Vyaasa*, the great saint, says that words are inadequate to describe the intensity of that devotion, the devotion of the *gopees* to the Lord. They had no egoism left in them and that is why they became the supreme devotees of the Lord.

Learn the art of overcoming the ego from the *Shaasthras*, whose repositories are here before you, in the Prashaanthi Vidwanmahaasabha. There are still many such in our land, in spite of decades of neglect and the glitter of other studies. You must have heard of Bhojaraaja, the great patron of Pandiths, such as these. He was at first not so considerate; but an incident happened which turned his attention to this essential task. The Pandiths of his realm had the grace of God in good measure, no doubt; but, they were extremely poor and had to struggle to keep their families above starvation. One Pandith was so down and out that he decided to turn thief and steal, not from any poor man's house, but from the king's palace itself, for the king cannot be made poorer by the loss. He crept into the private apartments at dusk and though he had access to a large quantity of silverware and gold cups and plates, he felt that he should carry away with him only what he needed most and so, he stole only a few seers of wheat flour. While moving about with the bag of flour in a dark corridor he heard noises and so he entered a room whose door was ajar, and hide himself under a cot. It was the bedroom of the king!

## Scholars must have faith in their learning

The Pandith spent the night under a cot, unable to move or cough or sneeze or even breathe aloud. An hour before dawn, the king rose and sat upon the bed, reciting aloud a stanza he had composed at night, while trying to sleep. There was a gap in the last line which the king could not fill; the appropriate word was evading him. The Pandith heard the stanza; he had the word on his lips and he could not but shout it out from underneath the cot. He forgot for the moment that he was a thief with the tell-tale bag in his hands. The king peeped under the cot, and welcomed the Pandith and honoured him for his scholarship and poured largesses on him in sympathy for his plight. It was thus that Bhojaraaja learnt of the misery in which the scholars of his kingdom lived.

The Pandiths also must have this faith: that their learning will never injure them, never destroy them, that it will sustain them, provided they follow them strictly, gladly, sincerely and in the fear of God. The faith in God will be instilled by *naamasmarana* (the repetition of the

Name of God)---the remembering of the glory of the Lord and of his infinite mercy and power.

When a mother is feeding her child, you can see her with the child on her hip and the plate in her hand, inducing the child to eat, by means of harsh words or a smile, a joke, a threat or a story, diverting its attention, showing the child a dog or a flower or the moon. I have also to adopt the same tactics to make you listen and assimilate the valuable food that is so necessary for your growth. That is the reason why I relate stories, sing, recite poems, etc., in My discourses!

Madras, 16-8-1964

> *Birth and death are*
> *two high cliffs between which*
> *the river of life flows.*
>
> *The force of Aathma-shakthi is the bridge*
> *that scans the chasm, and*
> *for those who have developed*
> *that force and faith,*
> *the floods are of no concern.*
>
> *With Aathma-shakthi as their safe support,*
> *they can reach the other bank,*
> *braving all dangers.*
>
> **Shri Sathya Sai**

## 26. True remorse and false

THE Pandith who spoke about the Geetha explained how it summarised the *Upanishadhs*. In fact, the people of Bhaarath can be said to be residing in Geetha Mahaal itself, whether they know it or not. The entrance to that Mahaal is through *vishaadha* (remorse), discovery of the tawdriness of sense pleasures and searching out for something more substantial and satisfying. The most satisfying prize is *Purushoththamapraapthi*—the attainment of the Lord, the Supremest *Purusha*. The *purusha* is "he who lives in the *pura*," namely, the body, the physical body. He who lives in the universe which is His body He is the Supremest, the *Purushoththama*. A tiny ant creeping over the foot is cognised by your consciousness; that is to say, the *purusha* had consciousness filling the entire body. The *Purushoththama* has consciousness filling and activating the entire universe, which is His body. The individual tree is the *purusha*, the forest is the *Purushoththama*. The *jeeva* is the *vyasthi*, the *samashti* is God. For the *purusha* to become *Purushoththama*, the path is *yoga*, or *jnaana* won by action and devotion to God.

He said that there can be no vision of unity when the *jeeva* is scattered in five directions by the five senses which drag him. Really, it does not matter if a person has five rupee coins or the same amount in small change. All the five senses subserve the same *Purusha*. It is one family, under one master. The senses need not necessarily be inimical; they can be trained to co-operate in the *saadhana*. Why? Even intellect can become an enemy, if it promotes conceit and competitive exhibitionism.

The gods once imagined that they were able to get victory over the demons because of their own prowess. When they were celebrating the victory, a deity appeared before them and cast a blade of grass on the ground. It asked *Agni* to burn it; but it could not. It challenged *Vaayu* to lift it, but he could not. It provoked *Varuna* to wet it, but, in spite of his best efforts, he could not. Then when their pride had been pricked, the deity taught them the *Brahma Vidhya* (science of *Brahman*), which reveals the inner source of all strength. This is no ordinary story; *Agni* is the presiding deity of *vaak* (speech) and so it tells us that speech has to be humble, that it derives its power only from the basic Universal Principle. *Vaayu* is *praana* (the vital air); Indhra is *buddhi* (the intellect).

## A person is judged by his conduct

After all, it is behaviour and practice that count. In the case of *dharma* and of *saadhana*, this is specially true. You judge a person by his conduct and character as revealed in his actions. No other witness or proof is needed. There were two women, living opposite each other in a bazaar; one had five cows and the other had just one. The richer woman was wasteful in habits, very extravagant and careless. So, she used to borrow milk from the woman with one cow, and the latter was helping her, in spite of the fact that she had a larger family. When she had thus borrowed about 50 seers of milk, the cow of the poorer woman died, and she went to the other woman and wanted her to return the milk loaned, at the rate of a seer per day. At this, she got wild and deposed in court that she had never borrowed any milk.

"Why should I, owning five cows, go to this woman with one cow for the loan of milk?" she asked. The magistrate was a shrewd man who sympathised with the woman whose cow had died. He knew how to get at the truth. He gave each of them five vessels full of water and asked them to wash their feet and come back to court. The five-cow woman poured all the five vessel-fuls in one stream on her feet and came in with all the dirt intact. The one-cow woman cleaned her feet by skillful use of one vessel-ful only and she left the other four vessels untouched. The act of washing the feet revealed their character and the magistrate had no hesitation in convicting the culprit. The one-cow woman must have saved and the five-cow woman must have wasted and been in perpetual want.

### The two poison fangs of man

Arjuna's *vishaadha* (dejection) is also a case of finely disguised egoism, which revealed a fault in his make-up. He was a *dheera* (hero) until he came on the battlefield and was transformed into a *bheeru* (a coward). It was all a case of I and Mine. "I will go to hell, I would rather beg. I will not fight my *Guru*, my uncle, my cousin, etc." I and Mine are two poison fangs; they have to be removed to make man harmless. Once Naaradha told Brahma of a ridiculous situation in the world; those who are dying are weeping for those who have died! That was what Arjuna too was doing, but, this foolishness is clothed in the language of renunciation and charity. The question on the battlefield was not who was the kin of whom, but who was right and who was wrong. Fight for justice, fight for truth, fight for these, as a *kshathriya* (warrior) is in duty bound, and leave the result to the Dispenser of all.

Krishna told Arjuna, "I am surprised that you should weep so, for you are *Gudakesha*, the conqueror of sleep, of ignorance. You do not kill, don't be so conceited as all that; nor do they die, 'they' have many more things to do, and the real 'they' are deathless. The sentence of death has been already pronounced on their bodies by Me and you have but to carry out My orders."

## You are only an instrument

Krishna made Arjuna aware of himself; so, the delusion that made him believe that he was a great bowman, a foe of Dhuryodhana, etc., disappeared from his consciousness; he came to know that he was but an instrument in the hands of the Lord.

You too must learn that lesson; for, otherwise there is no end to misery. *Thamaso maa jyothirgamaya*---"Lead me from darkness to light"---is the prayer. Egoism is *thamas* (darkness); *sharanaagathi* (surrender) is *jyothi* (light). There is an easy way to illumine the inner consciousness and the outer behaviour, with the light of God. Put the lamp of the name of the Lord, the illumining flame, on the tongue! That is the door-step; that light will drive out the darkness from both inside and outside. Have it ever burning, clear and bright. You will soon reach remarkable heights and enjoy happiness, the like of which you cannot get by sticking to the senses.

*Madras, 17-8-1964*

## 27. The I behind the Eye

THIS gathering is like the confluence of two rivers, the Yamuna and the Ganga, of people speaking Thamil, and Thelugu. I always speak in one language, and I am not inclined to change the language to suit the audience. I am sure even those who do not know Thelugu will understand the gist of what I say.

Whenever *ashaanthi* (absence of peace) overwhelms the world, the Lord will incarnate in human form to establish the modes of earning *prashaanthi* (tranquillity) and to reeducate the human community in the paths of peace. At the present time, strife and discord have robbed the family, the school, the community, the society, the villages, the cities and the State, of peace and amity. Anxiety and fear have contaminated the very food one eats. Therefore, the Prashaanthi Vidhwanmahaasabha has been established, and Pandiths have been entrusted with the task of revitalising the dry sources of *Shaanthi*, by the teachings contained in the *Shaasthras*.

Why is *ashaanthi* harassing the world? Because of *raaga*, *dwesha* and *moha* (attachment, hate and infatuation). These are born out of ignorance, which cause delusion.

Things seen in darkness cannot be clear; they are mistaken for something else. A rope is mistaken to be a snake; a stump is mistaken to be a thief. A piece of glass may be coveted as a diamond. So, this mistaken notion, this indistinct light, must go. It can go only if methods of discovering the truth are learnt. That is what the *Shaasthras* teach and what these Pandiths are commissioned to instruct you. They will tell you that the outward-seeking senses must be directed inwards; the inner realm of impulses, instincts, habits, prejudices, attitudes must be cleansed before God is reflected clear and bright therein. How is this to be achieved? The *Vedhas* explain how.

## Falsity of dualistic experience

The *Vedhas* tell you those things that cannot be known by anything else. The word *Vedha* means 'knowledge', knowledge that cannot be acquired by the senses or the intellect or even by unguided intuition. *Adhwaitha* is something that no one in the dual world can understand. It is *'apraapya manasa saha:'* "beyond the reach of even the mind." In fact, intellect and mind must each be transcended, before one can grasp the magnificence of that Unity. If *dhwaitha* has to be taught, why should the *Vedhas* take up that task? *Dhwaitha* (duality)—the seer and the seen, the creator and the created, the good and the bad, the right and the wrong—this is the actual daily concrete experience of every one. *Prakrithi* (Nature, Creation) is patently dualistic. The *Vedhas* endeavour to open the eyes of man to the falsity of dualistic experience, the reality of the only One, *Adhwaitha* (the non-dual One). They proclaim it, loudly and with enthusiasm.

Appanna Shaasthry said that the deer, the elephant, the moth, the fish and the bee are drawn to death by the senses of hearing, touch, sight, taste and smell respectively. If each of these falls a victim to one sense, how much is man to be pitied for he has all the five to drag him to perdition! Arjuna too had the same combination of foes. He had the urge to give up his mission and take up another's mission, namely, an urge to give up fighting, which is the mission of the *kshathriya* and a temptation to take to *sanyaasa* (asceticism), which has to be earned by further evolution. To overcome these obstacles, one must have both *saadhana* and a *sankalpa*, self-effort and grace.

## Lord's hands and feet are everywhere

Arjuna aspired to give up *karma*, momentarily fascinated by the ideal of *sanyaasa*. It is only through action that devotion can be deepened. Action cleanses the mind and makes it fit for spiritual knowledge. *Sravana* (hearing) is a *thaamasik* act, *manana* (recapitulation) is *raajasik*, while *nididhyaasana* (concentration) is *Saathwik*. When you are simply listening, quietly receiving without responding, you are just dull (*thaamasik*); when you turn it over in your mind, attempting to assimilate it, then you are active (*raajasik*); when you are sunk in the sweetness of experience in *dhyaana* you are having pure exultation (*saathwik*). That is the fruit of *bhakthi*, this *nididhyaasana*.

There is no need to fight against the fundamental delusion of *dheha bhraanthi* (attachment to body) with overwhelming force and argument! As Agnihothram Raamaanuja Thaathaachaariar said now, the delusion will disappear only if one sits quietly for a minute and analyse for himself the world and his experience of the world. *Jnaana* is not *Apraaptha-praapthi*, something new that is acquired, like gifts by some one, of money that the donor had, but which the recipient did not have. It is *praptha-prapathi*, like some one giving you a ten-rupee note which you had kept between the pages of a book you were reading. You had lent him the book; when you needed a loan, you asked him for a tenner; and he gave you back your own note. That is how *jnaana* reveals to you your own glory. The *Guru* gives you from out of your own *hridhaya-pustaka* (heart-book) the treasure which was there unrecognised by you. You are afraid because you have forgotten your own strength. Agnihothram Thaathaachaariar said that the Lord had *sarvathaah paani paadham*: "His hands and feet are everywhere." It is through Him that you are able to see; your eye required His eye in order to function. It is the reflection of the *Aathma* in the *anthahkarana* (inner conciousness) that activates it and makes it flow through the senses towards the objective world.

Liberation is attained when the *Aathma* shines in its own glory; it is not a colony or a suburb where aristocratic residents have secured good sites in paradise. It is the condition of the *jeeva* which has shed delusion.

## It is not easy to become a *bhaktha*

When delusion is shed, grief gets destroyed; joy is established: *dukha nivritthi* (removal of grief) and *aanandha praapthi* (attainment of bliss) both happen at the same time. The mind is the villain; it is another name for desire; the texture of the mind is just desire; both warp and woof are desire and nothing else. If desire goes, the mind disappears. When you pull out all the yarn from a piece of cloth, you have no more cloth. So too, pull out desires from the mind, it disappears, and you are free. Grief and joy are the obverse and reverse of the same experience. Joy is when grief ends; grief is when joy ends. When you invite a blind man for dinner, you must set on the table two plates, for he comes along with another man who will lead him in. Grief and joy are inseparable companions.

*Bhakthi* is very difficult to acquire; do not think it is easy to become a *bhaktha*. As a matter of fact, it is even more difficult than *jnaana*, for it means complete surrender, full contentment whatever may happen. The river must flow back to its source; it must turn back and up. If you flow down, you will have to go down, down, down, and water becomes undrinkable. But, do not despair; you have to win some day. The sooner, the better. A mango seller may seek to sell four for a rupee; if three of them get spoiled, he should not give up hope, for, a person may come and offer a rupee for the fourth one.

Having come here and listened, and secured *dharshan* and read about Me, put into actual practice at least one of the good counsel you got; one stick is enough to light a fire; the entire box of matches need not be used. Have faith that you will win; have steadiness in the pursuit of the goal.

## *Bhakthi* has stages in its growth

For, like the body which passes through childhood, boyhood, adolescence, middle age and old age, *bhakthi* too has stages in its growth. The tender fruit is love, the grown one is devotion and the ripe fruit is surrender. There is a type of *karma* which will melt the heart of the Lord. It is the type which does not inflict pain on any one. When Raama met the armies of Khara-Dhuushana single-handed, He did so in order to demonstrate his valour and His divinity to the demons and the sages of the forest.

My coming here and speaking daily at these meetings is the consequence of your merit and My grace. You had fine *dharshana* and *sravana* (audience and listening) in this silent gathering, silence which beats even the silence of Prashaanthi Nilayam. I am glad so many of you have been prompted by the desire to know about spiritual discipline. The committee too has the energy and enthusiasm needed to continue these *Sapthaahams;* such chances may be given to you in a larger number in the coming months. This extensive area round the Venkatagiri Raaja's bungalow is always available for your meetings; imagine what a great piece of good fortune it is for him. That so many thousands of you could gather here and hear the elevating discourses of Scholars and get started on the path of spiritual progress must indeed be very satisfying to him. The *aanandha* that you experienced here now is not something that came from outside; it was your own *aanandha* that you experienced; you are *Aanandhaswaruupa* (bliss personified); and so it welled up from inside your own heart.

*Madras, 18-8-1964*

---

*Have faith in His Grace, and lead a virtuous life, a life devoted to the service of the weak, life spent in the thought, about the might and glory of God.*

*Pray that you may carry out your duty well. God will certainly answer your prayers.*

**Shri Sathya Sai**

## 28. Be a caretaker

TODAY this *Saptaaha* (seven-day discourse) celebrates its *Samaapthi* (conclusion). That word means, according to most people, the final function; but it has a profounder meaning too. *Samaapthi* means, the attainment (*Aapthi*) of *Samam* (*Brahman*). That is the final fruit of *sravana, manana* and *nididhyaasana* (hearing, recapitulation and concentration) of spiritual lessons and discourses. In the worldly sense, it means the conclusion of a period of time; in the spiritual sense, it means transcending time!

What is the sum and substance of all these discourses? It is that man has to give up his pursuit of sensory objects if he seeks lasting peace and joy. Material wealth brings along with it, not only joy but grief as well. Accumulation of riches, multiplication of wants—these lead only to alternation between joy and grief. Attachment is the root of both joy and grief; detachment is the Saviour. *Aashakthi* (attachment) is *maaraka* (death); *anaashakthi* (non-attachment) is *thaaraka* (saviour).

A millionaire pays income-tax with tears in his eyes; a headmaster joyfully gives up the furniture and laboratory appliances of his school when he is transferred to some other place. Why? Because the headmaster knows that he is only the caretaker, not the owner. He is not attached to these articles; he knows that they belong to the government. So, too, feel that your family, your house, your fields your car, are all the Lord's property and that you are only the trustee; be ready to give them up without a murmur at a moment's notice.

The sacred literature of our country, the *Vedhas*, the *Shaasthras*, the *Ithihaasas*, the *Manusmrithi* and the *Puraanas* contain the drugs to cure attachment and endow you with the strength of detachment. Drugs available at other places though they may be more pleasant, cost time and money and do not assuage pain. *Thyaaga* (sacrifice) does not mean that you should not value things; you may, even care for them. But, remember always that they are transient, that the joy they give is trivial and temporary. That is to say, do not develop *moha* towards them. Know their real worth; do not over-estimate them.

## Subject yourself to vigilant scrutiny

A thirsty passenger asked the water-career at an up-country railway station whether his leather bag was clean. The reply he got was, "As regards cleanliness, all I can say is that the bag which pours is cleaner than the bag which takes in." You must care more for the cleanliness of your mind and intellect than for the external body. Instead of criticising others and finding faults with the actions of others, subject yourself to vigilant scrutiny, understand yourself well, and correct your own faults; do not be like the dancer who blamed the drummer for her wrong steps.

This objective world is as ageless as God. Who knows when God resolved upon the Universe? It is as *anaadhi* (beginningless) as God; we cannot determine when it came into being but we can determine when it will end, at least for each of us. When you look into the well, your reflection is always there; so far as you are concerned, your reflection can be removed from the well moment you decide you will no more seek the well, or pay attention to it.

The Shaasthri who discoursed today gave a very learned and convincing disquisition on the concepts of *Aarya* and *Anaarya* as depicted in the Raamaayana; but, you must now concentrate on the illness from which you are suffering and on its cure. Foolishness, egoism and sheer ignorance are the causes of the misery of man today. The eye, the ear and the tongue lead man to anxiety and malice, instead of making him the messenger of peace and harmony. Intellect is the root of pride and envy. Vishnu is *Jagannaatha* at Puri; at Kaashi, Shiva is *Vishweshwara* (both Lords of the Universe); where, then, is there any room for rivalry between those who worship at Puri and those who worship at Kaashi? Vishnu is *Gopaal* (protector of cows) and Shiva is *Pashupathi* (master of cows). Still, the innate urge to fight comes up in the heart of man and he uses the names of the Lord as excuses for provoking the fighting he relishes.

## Limit the desires to your capacity

It is difficult to put into practice even the truths of which you are intellectually convinced. Look at Dhrona on the battle-field. When he heard that Ashwatthama had been killed, he was so overcome with sorrow that he did not pause to consider where he was and for what end; even if the news were true he should not have laid down arms, forgetting the task upon which he had come to the field. Delusion (*moha*) induced him to do so; that was the reason for his discomfiture and death.

There are many thousands of people here today, the final day, as there were all these days and so, I would like to tell you that it is not what you hear that is beneficial, but what you put into daily practice. Develop renunciation about your own needs and wishes. Examine each on the touchstone of essentiality. When you pile up things in your apartments, you only promote darkness and dust; so also, do not collect and store too many materials in your mind. Travel light. Have just enough to sustain life and maintain health. The *pappu* (dhal) must have only enough *uppu* (salt) to make it relishing; that is to say, do not spoil the 'dhal' by adding too much salt. Life becomes too difficult to bear if you put into it too much of "desire." Limit your desires to your capacity and even among them, have only those that will grant lasting joy. Do not run after fashion and public approval and strain your resources, beyond repair. Also, keep to your own *dharma* and the code of rules that regulate life or the stage you have reached.

## Cow : symbol of selfless service

Do not place your needs first, your joy first. Consider the needs of others, the *aanandha* of others, as even more important. Respect elders and cultivate cordiality between brothers and sisters, teachers and students, employers and employees, etc.

Tend the cow, for, the cow is the symbol of selfless service of *Dharma*. That is why when a newly built house is ceremonially entered, the owner first takes into the house a cow. Once a *rishi* was taking a ritual bath at the Thriveni Sangham at the confluence of the Yamuna, Ganga and Saraswathi. While he was submerged in the holy water some fishermen threw the net and he was dragged ashore by them as a rare catch. He was claimed by the fishermen and the *rishi* told the king, who was in a fix, that they should be paid the price of the catch before he could order them to release him. Now, what was the price of the "*rishi-fish*?" A thousand *varaahas*? The *rishi* protested that he was not so cheap. Five thousand? It was too small, the *rishi* remarked. Then a *yogi* who was at the palace suggested a fair solution. He said "Give a cow, that is enough" and the cow was considered fair compensation for the *rishi*. That is the measure of the value of a cow.

Observe the rules laid down in the *Shaasthras*, respect the culture of your land and bring honour to the land of your birth. Belief in providence is native to an Indian and fear of sin is inherent in him. Nourish your aged parents; revere them. If you honour your mother, the mother of the Universe will guard you against harm. If you honour your father, the Father of all beings will guard you. This is as true as the fact that if you honour your parents, your children will honour you.

## Distinctions of different Incarnations

While speaking of God as guarding you, I am reminded of a note that some one has sent Me from this gathering. The note wants Me to explain why I have not mentioned Sai Baaba in any of my discourses so far, though I bear the name as the *avathaara* of Sai Baaba. Evidently, the writer of the note had in mind the people who engage themselves in publicity work of Raama or Krishna or Sai Baaba.

For those who know, Sai Raama, Krishna Vishnu, all are One; the distinction is only in the *Upaadhi* (the form and the name). The power, the glory, the mission, the message are all the same, though the particular achievements may be different, according to the needs and purposes of the age. That is why, though you believe that Raama and Krishna are the same, you do not approve when some one says that Raama lifted the Govardhanagiri or that Krishna broke the *Shivadhanus* (Shiva's bow). I do not appreciate in the least, the distinction between the various appearances of Godhead, Sai, Raama, Krishna, etc. I do not proclaim that this is more important or that the other is less important.

There are many attempts to construct *mandhirs* (temples) for Me, and people go about collecting donations for the same. I do not like this enthusiasm. Worship in any temple, any form, under any name. You neglect the ancient temples of your town, and start building new ones. And, very soon, the new ones too will be neglected, when you discover reasons for building newer ones. People who plan the new *mandhirs*, and form committees, and go about collecting contributions, help only to spread atheism, for they are urged by egoism, greed and malice, rather than genuine devotion and spirit of service.

## Be an example to others

*Dhana* (money) is the currency of the world; *Saadhana* is the currency of the spirit. When these self-styled *bhakthas* come to you with their lists and books, do not give even a paisa. Why do you need a hall to do *naamasmarana* or *japa* or *dhyaana*? The presence of others will more often be a hindrance rather than help; make your house itself a *mandhir*, meditate in your own shrine-room. Sing *bhajans* in your own home; above all, be an example to others by means of sweet speech, humility, reverence to elders, truthfulness, faith and steadfastness. That way you will bring more into the fold of theism than by establishing societies, collecting donations and running *mandhirs*.

The Lord looks for sincerity, simplicity and steady joy in the contemplation of His name and form. If you keep awake throughout the twelve hours on *Shivaraathri* (festival of Lord Shiva), because of illness, the vigil will not win His favour. If you quarrel with the wife and desist from food for one full day, it will not be recorded in the book of God as a fast. If you lose yourself in the depths of unconsciousness after a bout of drink, you will not be counted as a person who has achieved *Samaadhi.* No *bhuktha* (enjoyed) can be a *bhaktha* (devotee); that is to say, he who has an eye on the profit he can derive from service to God, cannot be a true devotee. They praise Raama to the skies one day and decry Him the next, if their fortune gets dry. Those who declare that Sai Baaba is great and others are small, do not know the elements of spiritual discipline. They are unfit for entering the field of spiritual service. I want to warn you against a set of people who have emerged nowadays using My name for such personal purposes. Be careful about these and treat them as they deserve.

Treasure in your hearts the *Amrithavaakyas* (death-destroying message) that you have heard during these seven days; ponder over them in the silence of your *dhyaana*; and, endeavour to realise the precious Goal of this invaluable 'Human birth.' I bless you all.

*Madras, 19-8-1964*

> *Past is past, it won't come.*
> *Future, you are not sure of.*
> *The given moment is now (Present).*
> *This Present is Omnipresent.*
>
> **Shri Sathya Sai**

## 29. Japa and bhaja

TWO Ministers, P. K. Savant and Lakshminarasiah, one from Andhra and the other from Maharaashtra, spoke informatively and enthusiastically to you, on health administration and on the part that spiritual discipline plays in the upkeep of mental and physical health.

Savant spoke about the work being done in the Maharaashtra State to eradicate disease in the villages and to persuade doctors to settle in the villages. He said that the ancient Ayurvedhic system of medicine was more suited to the food habits and the climatic peculiarities of this country and since it used the drugs available in the neighbourhood of the village, it was cheaper and more easily available. He also said that he has never been a patient so far, because he has been able to resist disease by means of strict observance of the rules regarding food, sleep and recreation. His faith in Baaba, he said, has proved a great reserve of strength to overcome illness.

Lakshminarasiah is himself a doctor; he spoke in praise of the quiet atmosphere of the hermitages of India and he wanted that the simple living of the ancient seers be revived. He said that deep down in the heart of every Indian there is a stratum of faith in *Sanaathana Dharma* which has to be tapped for all kinds of reconstruction.

Being the anniversary function of the hospital, I have to say something about physical ailments, their treatment and cure. Health is sought by man, not for its own sake; he tries to cure his illness, for illness means grief; he tries to secure health, for health means joy. He is after *Aanandha* (joy). At all times, through all acts, he seeks only *Aanandha*. A fish thrown on the bank of the lake wriggles and struggles to enter the water again. Man's struggle to get back into *Aanandha* is also of the same nature; he was in *Aanandha* and he has been thrown into misery. His native element is *Aanandha*. He was calm, and experienced concord, *Shaanthi* and *Prema*, when he was in the realm of *Aanandha*. Now, this *Aanandha* has to be won back, each for himself. No other can get it for him. The minister described how the Plan is providing food, clothing and shelter for all. But, even those who have these three in ample measure are not free from misery; they have not been restored to *Aanandha*. *Aanandha* is an inner treasure, won by detachment and discipline. We must have a Plan for *Aanandha*, a Plan for *Shaanthi* and *Santhosha* (Peace and Contentment).

## Consider first things first

A person may be sitting on a soft-cushioned sofa in an air-conditioned room, but his heart may be burning with unspeakable anxiety and fear. The body is as the cart and the mind as the horse. Now, planning places the cart before the horse. It gives first place to body and its needs. Consider first things first. Then only can the true culture of India be restored in all its ancient vitality. The sages of this land had known of the mine of *Aanandha* that lies in every human heart and they had discovered methods of developing that mine and working that gold. They said that if *Bhoomaatha* (Mother Earth), *Gomaatha* (Mother Cow). *Nijamaatha* (one's own mother) and *Vedhamaatha* (Mother Scripture) were revered and fostered, and used as best as they could be, happiness is certain and liberation is assured. It is because the people of India followed this path that India has remained India and not become either Europe or China.

## Inner harmony is what really matters

Even the scarcity of food about which the minister spoke is due to the decline in *shraddha* (faith) which was the hallmark of the ryots. When the strength that comes from the enthusiastic pursuit of one's profession wanes, when the courage of self-sacrifice is absent, all activity suffers. Have faith in the Lord or the *Aathmathathwa*; it will vitalise you. A fakir went to Akbar and he was told that Akbar was at his prayers and so could not give audience for some time. He was asked to wait in the ante-room. But, he refused to wait. He said, "What can this beggar get from that beggar?" All are beggars at the gate of God. The hero is he who does not beg or cringe or flatter or fawn. He knows that the Lord knows best. If it is His will, He will grant food and raiment; if not, well, let His will prevail. That is the path of *Sharanaagathi* or *Prapatthi* (absolute surrender).

There should be no begging or bargaining; surrender, submit to His will. Some people bargain with God and promise to give Him this or that costly article or their own hair, if a certain illness is cured or a certain calamity is averted. Lord Venkateshwara or any other form of the Lord does not need the hair of your head, but He wants you to respect the plighted word, to whomsoever given.

So in order to be true to your word and not incur the sin of falsehood and deceit, you have to offer it to Him, whatever the lapse of time. Shaving off the hair of the head is a sign that you have lost the delusion that it is physical beauty that counts; you make yourselves willfully ugly, so that you can demonstrate that it is inner harmony, inner charm, that really matters. *Sanyaasins* (ascetics) too have to shave likewise, in order to escape from a similar delusion, and equip themselves with the proper attitude.

Even the best of doctors will not be able to save a man when death calls. Men have to respond to that call, whether they are on a pilgrimage to Kedhara or Badhri or Rameshwaram, whether they are bridegrooms in the ceremonial seat before the ritual fire. Death brooks no delay; death accepts no excuse. Tears do not move His heart, nor can threats keep Him away.

## The waking and dreaming stages

Emperor Janaka was listening to the soothing strains of music in the Durbar Hall, and he fell asleep on his throne. Slowly and silently, the courtiers and musicians slid out of the hall leaving him to himself. He had a dream. His kingdom was invaded, over-run, pillaged. He was captured and imprisoned. But he escaped, he was wandering alone, in enemy territory, overcome with hunger and thirst. The jungle was dark. He groaned aloud. The queen heard the groan and woke him! He saw himself as Emperor on the throne, surrounded by servants. Then, a doubt started haunting Janaka: "Which is true, that or this?" While dreaming, the dream was as true as the experience of the palace when awake. This is true, while awake; that was true, while dreaming. Each has only relative value, while at that stage. Nothing is absolutely true, really real. The waking experience is as unreal as the dream experience. When you are in deep sleep, there is no world at all. When you attain the super-conscious fourth stage, the 'I' alone remains, the Universal 'I', which was mistaken even in the sleeping stage as limited and particular.

## Fix responsibility for your health on Him

A few minutes of quiet thought will convince you of this. But you are too busy with trivialities to pay attention to the vital needs. Plant the seed of the name of the Lord, any one of His thousand names that appeals to you, in the well-prepared soil of your heart and let it sprout in the silence there; water it with love and service to fellowmen; guard it against pests and cattle, the outward dragging emotions and passions, by putting up the fence of *japa* and *dhyaana*, then you will get the harvest of *Aanandha*.

Minister Savant said that faith in Sai Baaba is keeping him fit, the mind and body, all these years. He was the chairman of Shirdhi Samasthan for many years. His devotion and attachment to that body are known only to him and Me. So, when he says that Baaba has been keeping him healthy and strong, I know that it is true and that his faith is deep and sincere. If you have sincere devotion you will fix the responsibility for your health on Him and He will also accept that responsibility. Your mind will be so full of happiness that your body will be fit instrument for *Saadhana*.

*Shri Sathya Sai Hospital Day,*
*Prashaanthi Nilayam, 8-10-1964*

## 30. Genuine kinsmen

THESE Pandiths, scholars in Bhaagavatha lore, have spoken to you so far on many sweet and wholesome topics taken from that great and inspiring work. The teachings of the Bhaagavatha are the mainstay of all *bhakthas*, the strength with which they walk the path of God. If only the culture of India, which is based on the *Vedhas* and expounded in the Raamaayana and the Bhaagavatha, is practised with a true understanding of its value, people can ensure for themselves perpetual joy or bliss. Grief is the illness; it has to be cured. The medicine is prescribed in the *Vedhas*; it is taught in the *Shaasthras* and *Puraanas*; it has to be discovered and taken in; then the experience of *Aanandha* will certainly follow. Of this, there is no doubt.

Samskrithi, the word for culture and cultivation, is derived from the word, *samskaara*, which means the dual process of removing the dust and dirt of vice and planting the virtues of *Sathya, Dharma, Shaanthi* and *Prema. Samskaara* is also the name for certain obligatory rites of initiation and purification prescribed by the *Vedhas* for the spiritual upliftment of man. Their number is forty-eight in all; but, they could be reduced to ten and, if needed, even to one; the final and fulfilling One, of recognising one's identity with Maadhava or Shiva or *Brahman*. *Nara* (man) is but Naaraayana (God); *Jeeva* is *Brahman*, seen through the limitations of primal ignorance.

## Forms of devotion revealed by Bhaagavatha

Though the tongue of the penitent might repeat the *sloka*, "*Paapoham paapakarmaanaam*," (I am a sinner, committing sins) the inner Dweller, as the real You, will not agree to the description and that self-condemnation! Hence, you turn round in anger when you are accosted as a sinner (*paapi*). In your heart of hearts, you know that you are the Pure, the Full, the Eternal. You are the limitless, timeless, spaceless *Aathma*, the changeless, characteristicless Self. That *Aathma* persists in your dreams, in deep sleep, in the varied activities of the waking stage. It persists during childhood, youth, middle age, old age and senility. It is the entity which declares itself as I: I slept, I dreamt, I awoke, I was a child, I am too old to walk erect, etc. My eye, my word, my idea, my plan, my resolution, my experience, you say; thereby, you announce that you are not any of these. You are separate from these, but yet, you are involved with them. How to experience the *Aathma*? The *Vedhas* say, "*Sathyam vadha; Dharmam chara*." (Speak the truth; practise righteousness).

What is *Sathya* and what is *Dharma*? The Raamaayana and the Bhaagavatha reveal this knowledge, through story and example, so that any one, however poor or illiterate he may be, can understand it and practise it and benefit by it. So it is enough if these are taken to the door of every home in this land. The Bhaagavatha will reveal the fortune of Nandha and Yashodha who reared the Lord as their own child; the supramental Love that bound the simple cowherds of Brindhaavan with the Lord; the deep self-abnegating devotion of Raadha; the reverent affection that Uddhava had towards the Lord; and a variety of other forms of devoted service which brings God nearer to man. If you revolve these relationships in your mind and ruminate over the sweetness, it is freed from inferior impulses and your faith in the Supreme deepens.

## Remove the dirt of envy from the mind

You will have to re-live the Bhaagavatha in your own experience; become a Nandha or Yashodha fondling the child Krishna; become a *Gopee* yearning for the company of the Lord, as the soul craves for the Supersoul, as the river craves for the sea; become one with the cows whom He tended, or the boys with whom He played, or the *Murali* (flute) which He breathed through to give the world the music that captivates. Mere reading the Bhaagavatha is not enough; seeing the picture of grand banquet in the cinema will not appease hunger. Eat a meal and it is appeased.

*Samskaara* means first removing the dirt from the mind. Know that envy is the stickiest dirt! You must be happy when others were happy. Raama is said to have been happy when others were happy; the Raamaayana says that He was then as happy as if, the event that made the other man happy, had happened to Him. That is the true test. Krishna speaks of Arjuna as *An-asuya* (envy-less). What a great compliment! Therefore, He proposed to teach him the mysteries of spiritual discipline. Dhroupadhi is extolled as an ideal wife, for she served her five masters, who were the five vital airs or *Praanas*, without the least trace of envy or pride. Sathyabhaama has become famous for jealousy and there are many stories current about Krishna's attempts to put down this vice and teach her humility.

Have Love towards the Lord, but do not become depressed with envy when others also love him or get attached to Him. The Kuchipudi Party acted the musical dance-drama *'Bhaamakalaapam'* here very nicely and artistically. They demonstrated both the love and the jealousy of Sathyabhaama. Try to have Love without the canker of jealousy.

You come often to Puttaparthi; you hear the *pandiths* expounding the scriptures; you observe Me and My activity; what is the benefit you derive? How have you improved by all this? Have you succeeded at least in recognising your *thaamasik* and *raajasik* habits and tendencies? Recognising them as deleterious is the first step in removing them. Have you become more and more *saathwik* (serene and poised) as the years go by, or are you the same dull or perhaps, fiery individual? If you must know the Lord, you must love the Lord and live the good way. Hatred or even indifference will result only in misunderstanding. Develop close association with Him and He will reveal Himself to you.

## Grace is won by suffering only

Walk in the path laid down in the Raamaayana, and Mahaabhaaratha and the Bhaagavatha. Proceed along that path, inspite of halts and handicaps, inspite of the approval or disapproval of kith and kin, of praise or blame from society. What exactly is praise or blame? Words, sound waves coming from across the air; waves that strike your ear. Let them strike only the outer ear. Do not welcome them in.

The other speaker said that the lament of Dhroupadhi in her helplessness brought her the grace of the Lord. Yes, grace is won by suffering only. The Incarnation of the Lord comes upon the world when *Adharma* (unrighteousness) becomes rampant. Therefore, *adharma* has to be suffered so that one may have the joy of welcoming the Lord in human form. You can experience the *swabhaava* (nature) and the *swaruupa* (form) of the Lord through the experience the *avathaara* confers. That is the greatest gain. If the place you must reach is very near, you can just step across; if the distance is more, you may need a vehicle, bullock-drawn or horse-drawn; for longer distances, you may require a car or a plane. But, the Lord is nearest to you. Slide ajar the door of delusion; part the curtain of ignorance; open the closed eye; He is right there, before you! The fog of sensual pleasure is hiding Him from you. Switch on the light; the darkness disappears and He becomes visible.

## Know your genuine kith and kin

Revere Knowledge as you revere your father; adore Love as you adore your mother; move fondly with *Dharma*, as if it is your own brother; confide in *Dhaya* (compassion) as if it is your dearest friend; have *Shaantham* (calmness) as your better half; treat *Sahana* (fortitude), as if it is your own beloved son. These are your genuine kith and kin. Move with them, live with them, do not forsake or neglect them.

Arjuna asked Krishna how the ever-restless mind could be controlled. Living with these kinsmen is the best recipe. That is the best atmosphere to ensure the discipline and detachment needed for mind control. Mere prayer will not do. You will have to swallow and digest the morsel that is put into the mouth; repetition of the name of the dish is of no use. Hearing discourses and nodding approval or clapping in appreciation are not enough. The mother feeds lovingly, but the child must take it in with avidity and relish. When this earthly mother has so much love, who can estimate the love of the Mother of all beings, the *Jagathjanani*.

You heard the Bhaagavatha, portions of it, today. All the teaching you need for liberation from grief and worry, you can get in that one book. Read it every day, bit by bit, page by page and ruminate over the lessons you find there. Gradually, you will earn detachment from worldly sense objects; the book will take you in hand and lead you Godword. It is a better guide than many of the so-called *gurus* who ply their trade today. They welcome you with great gusto and proclaim the excellence of their wares, condemning those of the others and set about the profitable task of hooking you as a disciple, so that they may extract funds from you or fame through you. Like shopkeepers clamouring for customers, manufacturers of patent medicines competing for customers, they try to sell their prescriptions to you, before you discriminate and escape.

## The four-storeyed mansion

Whichever the book, whoever the *guru*, whatever the *peetam* (institution), the goal is the same. The path is the ancient one, laid down by the saintly pioneers. Or, you can picture it as a four-storeyed mansion, the ground floor being *karmayoga* (union with God through action) and the succeeding ones being *bhakthi*, *jnaana* and *vairaagya* (devotion, spiritual knowledge and non-attachment). When it is just a nascent fruit, it is *karma*. That is, the activity that all are capable of, and so it is the first step in *saadhana* as well. When it matures and is rendered free from egoism and greed, it becomes worship, and so, it leads one on to the second floor, *bhakthi*. When it is ripe and sweet, that is to say, when the *bhaktha* (devotee) achieves complete self-surrender, then, it is the acquisition of *jnaana*; when the fruit drops from the tree, it marks full detachment (*vairaagya*); the fourth floor of God's mansion is then reached.

*Prema* (divine love) is the motive power in *Karma Yoga*; it is the very breath of *Bhakthi Yoga*. It is universal and infinite, in *Jnaana*; it sees the Lord everywhere and in everything, when *vairaagya* has been achieved. The Bhaagavatha is saturated with the sweetness of *prema*.

The sweetness of Krishna is filling this Nature or objective world and Raadha is tasting it and being thrilled by it. Who is Raadha? She is Nature, the *Prakrithi*, the *Maayaa Shakthi* (power of delusion), the *Hlaadini Shakthi* (power of joy) of Krishna Himself, His *Mahaabhaava* (Great State). She has stolen and treasured in her heart the *aanandha* of Krishna which manifested as *prakrithi* and so, like the owner who roams round and round the house of the thief until he gets back his property, Krishna too is ever around Raadha's residence, seeking His *aanandha*.

## Be like the flute on Krishna's lips

If you have the capacity to draw the Lord to yourself, He will Himself come to you and be with you. Be like the flute, a hollow reed, straight, light, with no substance to hinder His breath. Then, He will come and pick you up from the ground; He will breathe divine music through you, playing upon you with a delicate touch; He will stick the flute into His sash; He will press his lips on it. In His hand, the infinitesimal will be transmuted into the Infinite, the *anu* (light atom) will be transformed into the *ghana* (heavy solid).

One day, Krishna pretended to be fast asleep, with the flute carelessly thrown aside by His side when Raadha approached the fortunate flute and asked it in plaintive terms, "O lucky Murali! Tell me how did you earn this great good fortune. What was the vow you observed, the vigil you kept, the pilgrimage you accomplished? What was the *manthra* you recited, the idol you worshipped?" The Flute got a voice through His grace and said: "I rid myself of all sensual desire, of envy, greed, of ego, that is all. I had no feeling of ego left to obstruct the flow of His *prema* through Me to all creation."

Intensify the *prema* that is within you, as a sacred gift. Expand it so that all beings can share in it. Raamakrishna Paramahamsa had that *prema*; when someone around him was sad, he felt sad; when some one was glad, he felt glad. He made himself one with all, in his great *prema bhaava* (state of Love). Have your *prema* fixed on the Lord, whether your petty wishes are fulfilled or not. Do not let slip the treasure, on some silly excuse or other. When Sai Baaba confers success after success on you, you are foremost in singing "Sai Shankara, Sai Shankara;" but let the shadow or disappointment fall on you, immediately you turn round and declare, "This Sai is not God."

## *Kali Yuga* is conducive to win liberation

Your worldly intelligence cannot fathom the ways of God. He cannot be recognised by mere cleverness, which is what your intelligence mostly is. You may benefit from God, but you cannot explain Him. You may benefit from electricity, and use it in a thousand ways, but you cannot explore and explain its mystery. How it works so and why it works so and not in any other way, is beyond your ken. Your explanations are merely guesses, attempts to clothe your ignorance in pompous expressions. The mistake is, you give the brain more value than it deserves. The *Parathathwa* (Supreme Truth) is beyond the reach of the brain; standing on the rock, you cannot lift it! Standing in *Maayaa*, you cannot discard it.

The present age is described in the *Shaasthras* as very conducive to liberation; for, while in past ages, rigorous penance was prescribed as the means, the Kali age in which you are, requires only *Naamasmarana* to win liberation! When the name of the Lord is remembered with all the glory that is associated with it, a great flood of *aanandha* wells up within the mind. Vyaasa himself knew this; for, when some sages once went to him to find out which *yuga* is most conducive to success in man's efforts for liberation, Vyaasa anticipated their question and repeated to himself aloud, "O, how fortunate are those destined to be born in the *Kali Yuga!*" It is so easy in this *Kali* age to win the grace of the Lord.

But, how do you profit by this luck that you have come across? How far have you progressed using the chance of these discourses and the *dharshan* and *sparshan* (seeing and touching)? Bring something into your daily practice, as evidence of your having known the secret of the higher life from Me. Show that you have greater brotherliness, speak less with more sweetness and self-control, that you can bear defeat as well as victory with calm resignation.

You read these great books, the Raamaayana and the Bhaagavatha many times, for they are now easily available at a cheap cost. But, what proof can you give for having profited by the hours that you have spent with them? To digest the food you have taken, you have to engage in some physical activity. To digest the lessons that you imbibe through holy company or through the study of great books, practise them in daily life. *Manana* (recapitulation) is a very important *saadhana*; dwell in silence on the implications of the lessons you have come across.

Keep up the enthusiasm that has given you the patience to sit through these discourses here for the last five hours. Develop it, and seeking the company of pious men, strengthen your *saathwik* (serene and poised) tendencies and progress in the spiritual path. You have my blessings.

*Prashaanthi Nilayam, 9-10-1964*

## 31. How old are you really?

THE wrold is full of sorrow and strife; man tries to avoid these and somehow derive a little joy and peace, in the midst of grief and disappointment. It is like digging a well in a sand heap; the deeper you dig, the faster it caves in. And, the whole process has to be repeated again. The piles of sensual desires overwhelm the aspirant and drag him down into grief. The only means of getting lasting joy is *bhakthi*; that is the best among the *yukthis* (the paths dictated by intelligence). That alone gives the *shakthi* (the strength needed for acquiring unshakable joy). *Bhakthi* can grow only on prepared ground. The method of preparation is given in the *Vedhas*, which speak also of things that have to be avoided. The *Vedhas* lay down the lines of conduct, the method of living, the ideals to be followed. You may not all be able to study the *Vedhas* and grasp the meaning. But those who have studied and who are following the teachings and who are overcome by the joy of that experience are here to tell you, in terms that you can understand.

Today, for example, we had the Shaasthri, who spoke of the four *Purushaarthas* (goals of human life), as mentioned in the Bhagavadh Geetha, which itself is the essence of the *Upanishadhs*, the latter part of the *Vedhas* called *Vedhaantha*. Of these goals, the final consummation is *moksha*; that is the very crux of the problem of life. *Moksha* means liberation from bondage to both joy and grief, which are the obverse and reverse of the same coin. *Moksha* is the recognition of the truth; but, though it is so simple, it required the cultivation of *viveka*, *vairaagya* and *vichakshana* (discrimination, detachment and ability), to know the Truth and escape from the temptation to hug falsehood. *Viveka* is necessary to decide what is *dharma*---the very first of the *Purushaarthas*. Each one must decide for himself the *dharma* he must choose for his uplift; this required *viveka*, the recognition of the permanently beneficial source of pure and lasting joy.

## Walk with the help of *Bhakthi* and *Karma*

Kurukshethra must be made a *Dharmakshethra*. Kurukshethra is the field where brothers fought over a handful of earth; but, it must be made a field for the uplift of man through the practice of *dharma*. It is for the sake of *jnaana* that *dharma* has been laid down. *Bhakthi* and *karma* are the two feet and the head is *jnaana*; walk on with the help of these two.

Now, about *vairaagya*. When you go to a temple you break a coconut before the idol. Now, if you try to break the nut as it has fallen from the tree, will it break? No; the fibrous cover has to be removed, and the shell exposed. The fibre protects the shell and prevents the blow from affecting the shell. *Moksha* (liberation) results from the breaking of the mind with all its vagaries and wishes. You have to break your mind but, how can you do it, when the fibrous armour of sensual desires encompasses it? Remove them and dedicate the mind to God and smash it in His presence. That moment, you are free.

The toughest fibre is anger, it is the stickiest dirt. When you get angry, you forget mother, father and teacher; you descend to the lowest depths. You lose all discrimination in the excitement; even Hanumantha set fire to the whole of Lanka when he was incensed by the demons who set fire to the tip of his tail; he lost sight of the fact that Seetha was in the Ashokavana. It was only when he had exulted in achievement for a little while that he remembered it and then he started condemning himself for his anger.

## Feel an inseparable unity with the Lord

Another fatal weakness is *dambha* (conceit, egoism, pride), the desire to be talked about, to be praised; people take delight in tom-tomming their achievements and capacities. This makes them ludicrous and pitiable. They want that their names and deeds should appear in the daily papers in big bold letters, as big as My head of hair! But it is not in the newspapers that you should strive to get attention. Earn status in the realm of God; earn fame in the company of the good and the godly, progress in humility, in reverence of elders and parents. If you are for ever in the primary class poring over A B C and D, how can you make out the meaning of what these Pandiths say? These are all subjects beyond the reach of the senses and you must garner them and cherish them in your minds. Practise them and live in joy.

When the discourses are on here, I find many running about with their beds and reserving space for spreading them. When you go to a temple, you see the idol within but your thoughts are with your footwear that you had to keep outside the outer gate. These are matters that reveal the concentration that you are capable of. Every little point has to be taken care of, lest the benefit of *saadhana* be lost. You cannot get liberation by merely coming here; you cannot get it even by *dharshana*, *sprashana* and *sambhashana* (seeing, touching and conversing). You will have to follow the instructions, the *Aajna* (the order) and the directions.

You will have to follow the path of Raadha, Meera, Gouranga and Thukaaraam. You must feel an inseparable affinity with the Lord, as inseparable as the wave and the sea. You are really of the same essence, the same taste, the same quality as the sea, though you have the name and form of the wave. The Lord is the *Saguna* aspect (Form with attributes) of the *Paramaathma*, that is the Universe. Butter, when in the milk, is immanent in it, has no separate name and form; but, take it out and it has a name and form which makes it distinct from milk. Ghee too when liquid has no particular form, but when it hardens, it has a form. So too *Maadhava-thathwam* (Divine state) when it assumes a form, is *Maanava* (Man).

## Virtue is the life-breath

When you are immersed in yourself, you are happiest. The child in the womb is in *Soham* (I am He); but when it is born in the world, it starts the question, *Koham* (Who am I?). For it forgot its truth; it identifies itself with the body and the senses. Until it becomes a *jnaani* (person of realisation), it will never regain in *Soham* knowledge.

*Maanava* can become *Maadhava* by engaging himself in *Maadhava karma* (action dedicated to God); he can then discover his *Naaraayana thathwam* (Divine state). What is the use of doing only *maanava karma* (human action) or even *dhaanava karma* (demonaic action) and claiming that man is divine? Virtue is the life-breath; character is the backbone. Without that, no meritorious act will fructify.

A characterless man is like a pot with many holes, useless for carrying water, or storing it. Renounce and win peace; have and win troubles.

There was a man living in a ramshackle hut when a huge big storm came along threatening to scatter it to the far corners, he sat inside and prayed to *Vaayudheva* (wind god). "O Vaayu! Abate thy fury," but the storm raged wild and furious. He prayed to Hanumaan, the son of the wind god Vaayu. "O Hanumaan, soften the fury of your father and save this poor fellow's shelter," and the storm blew with even more ferocity. Then he prayed to Raama to command His servant, Hanumaan, to persuade the wind god to reduce His overpowering sweep. He found that too had no effect. So, he came out of the hut and coolly said, "Let it be pulled asunder and lifted by the storm out of sight. I do not care." Thus, he got his peace of mind back.

The eagle is pestered by crows so long as it has a fish in its beak. They swish past that so they could steal the fish out of its mouth. They pursue the bird wherever it sits for a little rest. At last, it gives up the attachment to the fish and drops it from its beak; the crows fly behind it and leave the eagle free. So leave off sense pleasures and the crows of pride, envy, malice, and hatred will fly away, for they want only carrion.

## Practise renunciation from now on

The snake moves in curves, not in a straight line; man too when he is following the senses has to move in a crooked path. He has greater poison in him than the snake; his venom is to be found in his eyes, his tongue, his hands, his mind, his heart, his thoughts—whereas the cobra has it only in its fangs. The cobra raises its hood and sways in joy when it hears music; so too man when he realises the stage of *niruvikalpa*—steady unchanging establishment in the Ultimate Reality—dances in heavenly bliss.

Practise renunciation from now on, that you may set out on the journey when the call comes, you don't know when. Or at that moment, you will be in tears, when you think of the house you have built, the property you have accumulated, the fame you have amassed, the titles you have won. Know that all this is for the fleeting moment: develop attachment for the Lord, who will be with you wherever you go. Only the years that you have lived with the Lord have to be counted as life; the rest are all out of count. An old grandfather of seventy was asked by his seven-year old grandchild, "Grandpa! How old are you?" and the old man replied, "Two!" The child was struck with wonder and looked a picture of doubt. The old man replied, "I have spent only the last two years in the company of the Lord; until then I was plunged in the marshland of pleasure seeking."

## Realise the Indweller in the body

Bhrigu asked *Varuna* what the Lord does and *Varuna* (rain god) replied, *Thapas* (penance). For, he explained, "He is in all the five *koshas* (sheaths)—the *Annamaya*, the *Praanamaya*, the *Manomaya*, the *Vijnaanamaya* and the *Aanandhamaya koshas* (sheaths of material, vital energy, mind, knowledge and bliss). He digests the food in the body and the food in the mind. He is ever active, creating, fostering and transforming. You must realise the *dhehi* (the Indweller), in the *dheha* (body) and the *Naami* (person designated) by the *Naama* (name). There was a wife who got bangles of gold made when she became a widow; for, she argued, her husband had now become indestructible like gold, whereas he was, while alive, breakable, like the glass bangles she wore then. He had merged in the *Akshara Brahman* (Indestructible Supreme Reality).

Develop *prema* (divine love) towards the Lord, the *Parama-prema* (Supreme divine love) of which He is the embodiment. Never give room for doubts and hesitations, for questions to test the Lord's *Prema*. "My troubles have not ended; why? Why is it that He did not speak to me? How is it I did not get a room for staying here? Why did he not call me?" you whine! Do not think that I do not care for you or that I do not know you. I may not talk to you, but do not be under the impression that I have no *prema*. As a matter of fact, it is to give you the chance of *dharshan* that I move along the verandah from this room to that. Whatever I do, it is for you, not for Me. For, what is it that can be called Mine? Only you.

## Hold fast to your chosen deity

So, do not get shaken in mind; do not allow faith to decline. That will only add to the grief you already suffer from. Hold fast—that must be your vow. Whoever is your *Ishta dhevatha* (the chosen deity)—Vishnu or Raama or Shiva or Venkateshwara—hold fast to Him. Do not lose the contact and the company; for, it is only when the coal is in contact with the live embers that it can also become live ember. Cultivate nearness to Me in the heart and you will be rewarded. Then you too will acquire a fraction of the Supreme *Prema*. This is the great chance. This chance will not come your way again, beware of that. If you cannot, if you do not, cross the sea of grief now, taking hold of this chance, when again can you get such a chance? Really you are the fortunate few; out of millions and millions of people you have come, though no one specially invited you to be present here. That is what I call the mark of destiny.

Now, engage yourself in spiritual discipline, spiritual thoughts, spiritual company. Let the past go its way. At least from now on, seek to save yourself. Never yield to doubt or unsteadiness. That is a sign of ignorance. Have faith in any one Name and the Form indicated by that name. If you revere Shiva and hate Vishnu, the plus and the minus cancel out and the net result is zero. I will not tolerate the slightest hatred of any Name or Form. The wife has to revere the husband, but that does not mean that she has to hate his parents or brothers or sisters.

You can never attain the Lord through hatred of one or more of His many Forms and Names. If you throw contempt at the God that another reveres, the contempt falls on your own God. Avoid factions, quarrelling, hating, scorning, fault-finding; they recoil on you. You find fault in others because you have faults in you. Remember every one is a pilgrim towards the same goal; some travel by one road, some by another. Raavana, Sisupaala, Danthavakra---they too reached the feet of the Lord, by inviting Him to end their earthly careers.

## Seek the good in others

Learn to speak little and to speak soft. That will reduce the chances of getting angry. Seek the good in others and the evil in yourself. When I am defamed, I never get incensed, for it is only the tree full of edible fruits that is attacked with sticks and stones. Moreover, without scorn and contempt, greatness will not shine and spread. It has always been so, whenever *Avathaars* have come. When you hear the word, Rasala mango, you conceive of a sweet juicy fruit; but, when you have the fruit actually in hand, you are pestered by doubts whether it is really Rasala, whether it will taste sweet or sour. But, I never care for praise or blame; I just discard both. I am ever intent on the task for which I have come, the laying down of *Sathya maarga* (path of truth), of *Dharma* and the spread of the knowledge and practice of *Dharma*.

The Prashaanthi Vidhwanmahaasabha is just one of the instruments for this task: the task of making the *Kali yuga* (present Iron age), a *Kritha yuga* (past Golden age). Stage by stage as the task unfolds, the sound of detractors will also cease; when fully fried, the *pappad* will make no further noise. Only the frying *pappad* makes noise. You too should avoid contact with the unfried minds; do not develop either hatred or envy. Have love and charity towards all.

## Know what exactly is your duty

This aged Shaasthry is a sweet fruit, ripe with age and experience; he knows and has actual experience of the life laid down in the Geetha. When I asked him to share his wisdom with the world, he was indeed happy beyond words. He is exulting over the opportunity he has got to partake in the revival of *Vedhic* scholarship and in the re-establishment of *Dharma*. He knows and I know, and no one else knows, the intensity of his joy at the chance he now has secured. He has but one desire in him now, a very sacred desire: to see the era of *Dharma* established on earth through My *Sankalpa* (Will). What a rare relationship is this, between him and Me! It is *Sanaathana Sambandha* (eternal relationship); hence he got Me.

Some things happened today to make Me speak in this strain and I wanted all of you to know what exactly is your duty to yourself and to others. There are some men who are like moths, who must bore through whatever they come across, silk or cotton or wool; there are others who are like bees, who seek only honey. The lotus attracts bees from afar, but the frogs that skip around it on the lake know nought of its beauty or fragrance.

*Prashaanthi Nilayam, 10-10-1964*

## 32. The path to the presence

THIS day, three learned *Pandiths* (scholars) spoke on *Adhwaitha* (philosophy of Non-dualism) and *Avathaara Thathwa* (essential nature of Incarnation) and on the Lord of Mathura. They have appeased your hunger in full. When the stomach is full anything extra is bitter. But, a bit of pickle may be welcome. That I shall give you now!

Birth as a human being is a unique chance for living beings. For, man is endowed with discriminating intelligence, the power to reason out the best among alternative courses. Man is far from the *Pashu* (animal), closer to *Pashupathi* (Lord of beings). He should not relapse into *Pashuthwa* (animality). Listening to Krishnamurthy Shaasthry expounding the Bhaagavatha—the sweet story of Krishna—told in sweet Sanskrit and explained so sweetly, you should imbibe the *prema* with which the story is filled.

The Bhaagavatha has the majesty of *seelam* (virtue); it has the majesty of *kriya* (action); it has also the majesty of *bhaava* (feeling). By majesty, I mean *Udhaaththatha* (elevation). What a grandeur you witness in the Raamaayana, for example! When Raavana fell, Raama sent Lakshmana to the place with a message to see that he is treated like the Emperor of Lanka and not a despised enemy. Lakshmana when he was called in to identify the ornaments of Seetha contained in the bundle she had thrown on the ground during the flight to captivity, declared that he could identify only the toe-rings of his sister-in-law; he saw only those ornaments, for he prostrated every day at her feet, as the consort of the elder brother is, according to the *Shaasthras*, equal to one's own mother. Now, it is impossible to find such virtue holding sway over men's minds. Now it is egoism, pride and greed that sway them.

## Importance of moral standards

Man has lost the fear of a fall; he has become worse than animals. It was not like this in the past. During previous centuries, Rajput women immolated themselves rather than fall into the hands of wicked foes. When Hanumaan offered to take Seetha on his shoulder back to Raama, the virtue of Seetha would not allow her to accept the offer. She had her husband's reputation in view. She said that it would best suit her husband's fame if he himself avenges the wrong and rescues her. Hanumaan's taking her, would be a repetition of what Raavana did, for he too stole her secretly while Raama was away. She did not consider her immediate relief as more important than the implications of that step to her virtue and her husband's fair name. That is what I call *Seelodaaththatha* (virtue in exaltation).

Or, take the Mahaabhaaratha. The Yaksha who guarded the lake had killed all the four brothers and they were lying on the ground. Dharmaraaja, the eldest brother, went there to slake his thirst and the Yaksha warned him, too. He challenged him to answer his questions, just as he had asked the others; but since he replied correctly, the Yaksha was pleased to grant him a boon; he could bring back to life one among the four who lay dead! And, whom did Dharmaraaja select? Not Bheema who would be his right hand in the coming battle against the Kauravas; not Arjuna, who was indispensable as a bowman of the highest attainments; but, Nakula, the son of his stepmother, Madri. Even the Yaksha was surprised. He asked him the reason why. Dharmaraaja said that his mother had him as the one surviving son but his stepmother too should have a son alive. That was the measure of his attachment to *Dharma*, to virtue, to normal standards. Then, people lived for the sake of *Dharma*; now, the ideal is *dhana* (riches). When Duryodhana had at last to be encountered a single combat, he himself selected a foeman worthy of his reputation, Bheema, when he could as well have chosen a weaker rival. It was considered improper to fight with a weaker foe.

## Gopees' *prema* to Krishna was super-physical

It all lies in the vision that you command, that you have equipped yourselves with. One of the Shaasthrys spoke of certain doubts which he himself had felt about Me, doubts which kept him away for some years. The love of the *Gopees* towards Krishna has led many ignorant people enmeshed in worldly attachments and physical attractions, to turn their faces away from God. Before passing judgement on any subject, you must investigate closely.

The *prema* of the *gopees* towards Krishna was super-physical, the love of the soul for the Over-soul, of the river for the sea. Persons deep in this type of love see nothing else, hear nothing else; they behave like mad persons, as the world goes. Their joy when they feel his presence is as supreme as their grief when they feel they are deprived of it. That is why among the songs of the saints, you have *Nindhaasthuthi* also; that is to say, songs, which blame Him for being cruel, partial, negligent, etc.!

You may know that the Lord of the Holy Shrine Shrisailam is called Mallikaarjuna, the white jasmine; and the Goddess, the Consort, is called most appropriately, *Bhramaramba*, the Bee! For the bee is drawn inescapably to the flower and it forgets itself while tasting the Glory of the Flower. The union of *Jeeva* and *Brahman* is of the same significance as the union of Krishna and *Thrishna*--- Krishna and the Thirst, the Lord and the Love.

## Doubt leads to perdition, spiritual ruin

The children of the Sanskrit School enacted the play Maarkandeya yesterday and you saw the boys who took the role of Marudvathi and Maarkandeya completely immersed in the role and so, they were able to make you also feel every emotion they expressed. You must fill yourself with the Form and the Glory of the Lord; you must not be aware of anything else. Then, you too can become Maadhava.

There are two eight-syllabled axioms in the Geetha, which you must take to heart: *Shraddhaavan labhate Jnaanam* and *Samshayaathma vinashyathi*. The first tells you that the person who is steady in his faith gains the knowledge of the path of liberation and the second warns against the sinister consequence of "doubt"; doubt leads to perdition, spiritual ruin. Dwell on these axioms and practise the spiritual discipline of *Naamasmarana, Japam* or *Dhyaanam*. This is the pursuit that is worthy, not the pursuit of fame, nor the friendship of the famous.

You ask for grace, which is available only at a very high cost; but, you pay only trash. It is sheer avarice, like asking a gourd as extra, when what you have paid is for a bean! You may claim that you have been coming to Puttaparthi for ten or twelve or sixteen years or that you have even stayed here long; but, it is not the years that matter; it is the depth to which the roots of *karma* have grown in previous births. They decide the ears of corn that you have to live upon. It takes a long time and systematic *saadhana* to clear the field of all those growths---the *saadhana*, as the Shaasthry said, of *Karma* and *Upaasana* which leads to *Jnaana*.

## Three stages in spiritual awareness

This is the meaning of the injunction that you should dip thrice in succession, when you take a bath in any holy river. The first dip is to cleanse the *sthuula sareera* (the gross physical body); the second is to cleanse the *suukshma sareera* (the subtle body), of the *praanamaya*, the *manomaya* and the *vijnaanamaya koshas* (sheaths of vital energy, mind, knowledge) and third is to cleanse the *kaarana sareera* (the causal body) or the *vijnaanamaya kosha*, with just a tinge of *maayaa* still left. They are also meant to consecrate the *karma* and the *upaasana saadhanas* and confer *jnaana*. *Dhwaitha*, *Visishtaadhwaitha* and *Adhwaitha* are also only three stages in spiritual awareness.

Somasekhara Shaasthry spoke of the *Dhwaitha* and *Adhwaitha* (dual and non-dual) attitudes which colour people's outlook in every field. But, they are not distinct; they are stages of mental transformation. The fruit is the same; the soil and the sun make it reach the ripe stage, through the intermediate stages of tender fruit and mature fruit. When you realise that the Lord is at the address that He has given towards the end of the Geetha in the 61st *sloka* of the 18th chapter, namely, "*Ishwarassarvabhuthaanaam hriddese, Arjuna, thishtathi*," that "He is in the heart of every being," then you know the One, with no other.

To realise the Lord in every being, you must cultivate *Prema* and drive out the bats that infest the dark caverns of your heart, the bats of hate, envy and malice. Let the light of *Prema* illumine your thoughts, your words, your movements, your activities, your judgements. When you become transmuted into *Prema*, the Lord who is *Premaswaruupa*, will reveal Himself to you, and play on the Flute, awakening your higher consciousness in the flood of Universal love.

*Saadhana* is essential because the effects of *karma* have to be removed by *karma* alone, as a thorn is removable only by another thorn. You cannot remove it by a knife or a hammer, or even a sword. The knowledge that the world is unreal was itself spread by Shankaraachaarya by means of activity in the unreal world, the establishment of *mutts* the writing of books and partaking in disputations. You cannot desist from *karma*; only, you have got to take care that it is saturated with *prema* and promotes the welfare of the world.

## The grand combination

Tomorrow again, the path of the Presence of the Lord will be explained by these *Pandiths* as well as by Me. Whoever may speak, whatever the text, the substance is the same. In no other place can you have this grand combination: *Pandiths* who expound, as if to their own kith and kin, the great truths contained in the scriptures with such faith and devotion and a congregation of listeners which listens with devoted avidity, eager to learn and practise what they learn.

You must be devoted, as devoted as a boy who studied in the *Aashram* of Dhoumyarishi. When the *guru* was conducting his lesson assiduously, the rain came in torrents and the boys ran helter-skelter to roll up their beds or collect their clothes or save their *kusa* grass bundles. But, one boy reasoned out within himself: we had heavy rain last evening too; so this downpour will certainly damage the dike. So, to save the two acres of land that the *guru* owned, he went and laid himself across the breach. You must so act that the heart of the *Guru* melts at your devotion. Only that will cleanse the mind of evil and vice. If you develop devotion and steady faith you will achieve the Glory of Self-realisation.

*Prashaanthi Nilayam, 11-10-1964*

---

*After long searches, here and there,
in temples and in churches,
in earths and in heavens,
at last you come back.
Completing the circle from where you started,
to your own soul, and find that
He, for whom you have been seeking
all over the world,
for whom you have been weeping and praying,
in churches and temples,
on whom you were looking
as the mystery of all mysteries,
shrouded in the clouds,
in the nearest of the near,
is your own self, the reality of your life,
body and soul.*

**Shri Sathya Sai**

## 33. Faith is the foundation

THIS day, you heard the Pandiths tell you about the supremacy of the *Vedhas* and the need for establishing *Dharma*. No one can break the limits of *Vedhas* and *Shaasthras* and speak here; in fact, all spiritual subjects are subsumed in the scriptures. All knowledge is derived from the *Vedhas*. You cultivate your divinity in proportion to the *Saadhana* you do and the handicaps you have brought down from previous births. It is above and beyond the intellect and incapable of being reached through the senses. Divinity is its own law; it is independent of all restrictions and modes. The senses can each perform only one operation for the gathering of knowledge: the ear can inform you of sound, the eyes can speak of colour, the tongue of taste, etc. But, the Divine is beyond all sensations and systems.

*Srishti*, *Sthithi* and *Laya* (creation, sustentation and dissolution) are the three forms of the Divine will; you have to penetrate the inner meaning of *Srishti*, by means of *Karma Yoga*; you have to grasp the significance of *sthithi*, by means of *Bhakthi Yoga* and when you master the *Jnaana Yoga*, you arrive at the experience of *Laya*, of manifoldness in the One. *Bhakthi* makes you aware of the Lord who sustains and supports every being; it is *Prema*, which is *Nithya, Sathya* and *Nirmala*; that is to say, Love which is unchanging, sincere and pure. There is no one who is devoid of *bhakthi*; deep down in his core, every one has the feeling of kinship with all creatures. It is this that makes a lonely man miserable, that makes every one likeable to some one or other. If you have no love, you are like a lamp without the flame, blind and blinding. Love of the pure type is unmixed with hate, untampered with greed.

## *Karma* is necessary for liberation

Faith is the foundation for this type of devotion, faith in doing good, faith in *punya* and *paapa* (merit and sin), so that you examine each act in the light of its long-distance consequences, and lastly faith, in the series of births through which the present life is built up. Pilgrimage was, in the years gone by, a long and arduous process, and so, the pilgrim was educated by it in humility and fortitude. Those who came with Me to Badhri were free from fear for the road, and so, they had more time to dwell on Naaraayana and His glory.

Thirupathi has been made so easily accessible now that it is fast being turned into a paradise for picnickers! The sacred hills have been scarred and the full throated exclamation, "Govindha" "Govindha" as the pilgrims climb the steps have disappeared. People go in aeroplanes to Kaashi and return after a quick round of the ghats and shrine, in a few hours. The silent communion with the Divine and the slow infiltration of elation into the inner consciousness have been lost.

Only through *karma* can liberation be effected. When *karma* is prompted by *bhakthi*, it is *samasaara bhakthi* (devotion of the worldly); when *jnaana* also blossoms a little, it is *vaanaprastha bhakthi* (devotion of the recluse); when *bhakthi* fructifies into *jnaana*, then it is *Sanyaasa bhakthi* (devotion of the ascetic) or *Moksha* (liberation) itself. Without *karma*, progress is very difficult.

## Faith is essential for consummation of *saadhana*

The *jnaani* too has to do *karma*, but, like swans coming out of the water, they can swish their feathers and wings and be as dry as when they entered it: *karma* will not affect them at all. They do it with no ego, with no desire. It is their nature to wish well of the world and to engage in work that promotes the welfare of the world. When a woman who is pregnant is widowed, she does not immediately rid herself of the marks of a married woman, for she can discard the nose-screw, the ear-rings, the *mangala suuthra* (marriage string worn by married women), etc., only after the child is born! Until then, though she has the outward marks of a woman happy with her husband, she knows she is a widow.

The *jnaani* is also of the same type; he knows that he is free, but, to the world he appears bound. Frothy youth, suffering from the fever of cynicism, laugh at *jnaanis* and treat them with dishonour. There is no use blaming them, either. The elders set the example and what else can they do?

*Prema* is the seed; *thanmayathwam*, over-powering experience of merging, is the tree; inexhaustible *Aanandham* is the fruit. For this consummation, faith is essential. Look at Arjuna! When the choice was placed before him to decide which he should receive---the army of redoubtable heroes belonging to the Yadhava clan or Krishna alone, unarmed and refusing to fight---he asked only for Krishna! He knew; he believed; he was saved. The same choice India has to make even now, when the

Lord has appeared in His *swaruupa* here. What does it profit the country if it accumulates money, gold and grain? The *aanandha*, derived from the worship of the name and form which arouses spiritual joy, is far more desirable than these. Want of faith is the source of weakness in all fields.

## Establishing the reign of *Dharma*

In the days of Ashoka, there was a poor man living in Buddhagaya. His name was Sishupaala. Though very poor, he stuck to *dharma* and was never known to forsake that path, in spite of strong temptations. Ashoka slipped into his house one night and craved for food and shelter. Sishupaala was surprised that there was someone poorer than himself. He welcomed him and fed him with his own share of the meal; he asked his son to press his feet, to give relief to the tired limb. When Ashoka spoke praising him for his hospitality, he protested and said, that it was wrong to take such extra notice of what was his duty. "It is our *dharma*," he said. Ashoka asked him what he meant by *dharma* and when Sishupaala said that the land was immersed in *adharma* and that the Emperor was not fostering *dharma*, Ashoka who was incognito, challenged him. "What Ashoka could not do, can you achieve?" he asked. Sishupaala replied, "Of course I shall; I bend only to God. I am not afraid of man. I care only for *dharma*." The guest laughed and changed the topic; but Ashoka had no sleep that night. He rose in the early morning and went out of the hut, while it was still dark

Next morning, a gorgeously dressed courtier appeared before the hut and inquired whether he had, by any chance, blamed the Emperor to someone during the night. Sishupaala said that he had done so, but that what he said was correct. The courtier was entrusted with the mission of bringing him to the palace, where Ashoka appointed him as *Dharmadhevatha* (deity of Righteousness), to establish the reign of *dharma* in the land. He told him, "If the slightest deviation from *dharma* happens anywhere you will be executed, beware. I shall give you all the military help you need to transform the conduct of the people." Sishupaala agreed. He said: "I shall do so; I do not need your army. I have full trust in God." Ashoka was rather disappointed that the man placed no trust in him! But he decided to watch the progress of this new experiment in administration, which was to last for ten days.

And the unexpected happened. There was no theft, no breach of the moral code, no violation of the *Shaasthras* anywhere in the land. Young women decked with jewels could go from one end of the empire to another, even during nights, without any fear of molestation or theft.

## Emperor Ashoka submits to *Dharma*

Ashoka really got envious of the capacity of the new administrator. He went incognito one night to the house of a prostitute and banged at the outer door, demanding entry. The lady protested and refused to admit him, since *Dharmadhevatha* ruled the land. There was an altercation between Ashoka and the hefty watchman at the door, which became hot. A fight ensued, and the watchman was slain.

That was on the seventh day of the new regime. Ashoka had it announced that since a murder had been committed in the town, the man from Buddhagaya had to be executed.

The news spread like wildfire and every one wept at the plight of the good man. Sishupaala, however, had discovered that it was no less a person than the Emperor who had done the deed; he had actually visited the house where the incident happened and recorded details of the persons involved. So, when he was about to ascend the steps and place his head on the block, he shouted "Stop," and asked that Ashoka himself be brought to the place of execution, for, it was he who had killed the watchman. Ashoka too was prepared; he had made an image of himself in gold and that was beheaded in his place, as the *Shaasthras* allow. The gold was distributed as gifts, and *dharma* was observed.

## Contribute your individual effort

You must use all the talents awarded to you in a prayerful and humble mood. Until then, you have no right to seek the help of the Lord, His intervention. A devotee of Hanumaan was once driving a cartload of grain to the market. On the way, the wheel got stuck and the cart could not be drawn forward by the bullocks. The cart slanted too far to one side and the bags fell on the ground. The devotee sat on the ground and started praying to Hanumaan. He finished reciting the *Sthothras*, the 108 names, and even the 1008 names. The cart did not regain balance. He began to blame Hanumaan and started reviling Him for not coming to his rescue. Hanumaan appeared and took him to task. "Foolish fellow; instead of applying all your strength on the job, you have reviled Me, for not doing what is really your task. Come on, put your shoulder to the wheel; engage in *karma*; contribute *purusha prayatthana* (individual effort)."

*Karma* cleanses the mind, if it is done as a dedicatory act, the consequence being left to the Will of the Lord. Repentance saves even sinners from perdition. No ceremony of expiation is as effective as sincere repentance. The shop-keeper may give short measure; but, he will not accept less cash. The bill has to be paid in full. Pay it through repentance. You cannot deceive the Lord by insincerity or by ruses. Unless you correct yourself by detachment and sacrifice, you cannot reach God. Give up egoism; then only you can see Him.

Raama taught *dharma*, treading in his own life every one of its steps. Krishna paid more attention to teaching it through Arjuna. Small people who cannot overcome their egoism dare judge Krishna and point the finger at what they call his "pranks." Such men were found then, as well as now. They are ever engaged in seeking faults in the great. They dare declare that the Lord should be such and such, of this form and with such characteristics, as if they could ever glimpse the edge of His glory, as if the Lord will assume the form these men decide.

## Feel you are the instrument of God's Will

The Lord can be understood only if you approach Him, develop attachment for Him, have faith in Him, and maintain unswerving loyalty to Him. He is understood only when you feel that you are but the instrument and that He wills every little movement everywhere. Who is there so bold that he can say, "the Lord must wear only this dress, the Lord must act only in this manner?" Who can limit His glory or set its direction! He is immanent in all beings and He gets done all activities through them, just as electricity makes the bulb shine, the mike to transmit the voice, the stove to cook, the refrigerator to cool.

The river of life has four causeways, while the river Vankaperu, which flows in this taluk, has two: one on the road to Penukonda and another on the road to Dharmaavaram. The causeways are *brahmacharya, grihastha, vaanaprastha* and *sanyaasa* (celibate, house holder, recluse and monk). Of these, the *grihastha* causeway has sunk and become impassable. Repair it and become good *grihasthas*; then the path of life is smooth for the journey.

On the road to Prashaanthi Nilayam from Kothacheruvu, the Bapanapalle culvert has broken down. But the villagers cannot of their own accord reconstruct it according to their sweet will. It has to be reconstructed by the very authority that first erected it. So too, when *dharma* has gone into disrepair, He who laid down the *dharma* has to come again and get it repaired. The four bridges were laid by the Lord, and He has come to rebuild them now. The engineers and others are here, in the Prashaanthi Vidhwanmahaasabha; very soon, the rebuilding work will be completed and the inaugural ceremony celebrated.

Cultivate faith and detachment. Revere elders and take to heart the advice they give, out of their mature wisdom and experience. Cross the ocean of death and birth and be "children of immortality," (*Amrithasya Puthraah*), every moment of your lives.

*Prashaanthi Nilayam, 12-10-1964*

---

*Once you rise to the*
*higher level of consciousness*
*and live at that level,*
*all those events cease to have the same meaning,*
*and so have less and less effect on you.*
*Instead, you remain happy and calm at all times,*
*merely observing events*
*as they come and go, for that is what they do.*

Shri Sathya Sai

## 34. Neither different nor diminished

THE Pandith spoke now about the many forms of *bhakthi*: *Nishkaama bhakthi, paraa bhakthi, madhura bhakthi,* (desireless, supreme and sweet devotion), *karma bhakthi* (devotion in action), etc. When you claim to have *bhakthi*, the question naturally arises, where have you placed your attachment, your affection, your unswerving loyalty and why. If you are drawn towards pleasure-giving objects and other material gains, you are in for unending worry, fear and anxiety, *ashaanthi* (absence of peace), in fact. The happiness they contribute is as unreal as the happiness you derive from similar things in your dreams. The experience of the waking stage is as unreal and fleeting as the dream. The seen is a dream; the unseen is the real. There is a mixture of reality and unreality in the variety of the universe. That is why it deludes; that is why joy and grief are fleeting.

*Bhakthi* is really unswerving loyalty to God with form and attributes and a name. You can grasp with the reason that you are endowed with, only concrete name-attribute-full things. So, God has to appear before you with form and attributes (*sakaara, saguna, swaruupa*) so that you can love

Him and serve Him and follow Him and get liberated by Him. But when He comes with form, do not think He is either different or diminished. Ghee when it is solidified is white and granulary. When it is heated it is a colourless liquid, having no shape or form. The *niraakaara* (formless) becomes *sakaara* (with form), when it is exposed to cold. So too, in the cool recesses of the *bhaktha's* heart, the *niraakaara* is rendered *sakaara*.

When the formless transforms itself, it may appear as *Vibhavaakaara* or as *Swaakaara* (endowed with some particular glory or power or as the full manifestation of itself). That is to say, the *avathaara* might manifest only that part of the Divine glory as was essential for the task which brought the Form, or it might exceed the limited purpose for which it came and shine in full grandeur. Raama is a good example of the first and Krishna of the second. Krishna was not satisfied with the killing of Sishupaala and Dhanthavakra, the two demons who were formerly Jaya and Vijaya, or even with the overwhelming of various other evil persons who infested the world then.

## Fame and ill-fame go together

He laid down in the Geetha and in the *upadesha* He gave to Uddhava and others, the fundamentals of spiritual life and the ways of removing primal ignorance, as a step to human liberation, ways that can be followed by various sections of the human community, from illiterate cowherds and milkmaids to learned scholars, practised *saadhakas*, ritualistic experts, adepts at social service, and experienced philosophers.

Jonnalagadda Sathyanaaraayanamurthy gave you in his speech a fine description of the pangs of separation which agonised the village folk, when the Lord kept away from them, even for a short while. When they espied a dark-blue cloud in the sky, they shed tears of joy, for it reminded them of the Krishna they adored. But Krishna was scandalised in His time and people spread wicked stories about Him! It is always so; the supply of drinking water implies the laying down of pipes for both fresh water and for drainage. Ill-fame and fame go together. Revered personalities are the targets of irresponsible irreverence.

## Dedication must come naturally

The sages declare that they become sad when worldly people call them happy or find them happy. Chaithanya felt happy when people reviled him for wasting his time in *keerthan* and when they broke his *mridang* and *tal*. He said, "These people are foolish; they think a tree can be saved if the leaves are watered; the root of joy has to be watered so that joy may grow in you. The root is Krishna, the Krishna in your heart." Water the root with tears, *tears of joy* that get the chance to sing His name, to praise His glory; not *tears of sorrow*, for such tears are a sacrilege; they should not contaminate the Lotus Feet of the Lord.

It is dedication to the Lord that sanctifies all activities. He is the *raison d'etre* for activity. He is the prompter, the executer, the giver of the required strength and skill, the enjoyer of the fruit thereof. So, dedication must come naturally to you, for, all is His and nothing yours! Your duty is to believe He is the impeller of your activities, and draw strength from that belief. Until the wound heals and the new skin hardens, the bandage must protect the place. So too, until Reality is realised, the balm of faith, of holy company, and holy thoughts must be applied to the ego-affected mind.

Every one of you has in possession a ticket for liberation from the cycle of birth and death. But, most do not know the train which they have to board; many get down at intermediate stations, imagining them to be the terminus and wander helplessly in the wilderness or are carried away by sights and scenes.

Reference was made to *ajnaana*. This *ajnaana* (ignorance) is imported from outside; what is native to man is *jnaana*. His *jnaana* is fogged by the smoke of delusion, which makes things appear many or confused. Man has burdened himself with information on a multiplicity of things; he has acquired a variety of skills, but, he has no vision to see things as a whole, to see the basic unity of the objective world. Moreover, he has no equipment to live lovingly with others, to recognise the humanity of all men, to feel that the same Lord activates each of them.

## Gifts of reason must not be wasted

How far can the learning which you acquire in schools and through books take you? There was a wife who was given a cheque-book so that she might imburse herself out of the bank account. She signed every cheque, "Your loving wife" and wondered why they were dishonoured. There must be adaptability, recognition of changed circumstances, awareness of the relative value of things, discrimination between the real and relatively real. The gifts of reason and conscience must not be wasted through neglect. Your story should not be a repetition of that of the wood-cutter, who was given a huge sandalwood forest as a reward, but, who out of sheer ignorance of the value of the trees, burnt the trees and sold them as charcoal at so much per bag!

The Divinity that is man is ignored and the opportunity to unfold it (which is called "life") is wasted.

You calculate wealth in terms of land and buildings, gold and silver, and finally, feel unhappy to leave them and go. You drug yourself in the attempt to escape from the hold of disease; but you are unaware of diseases that eat into the very vitals of your happiness and make you a social danger---the diseases of envy, malice, hatred and greed. Get the best advice to cure these. Believe that the Lord is living in every heart and so, when you inflict pain, physical or mental, on anyone, you are slighting the Lord or denying Him. He is everywhere.

## Purify the heart by being good to all

Do you say that the Lord appeared from the pillar in the palace of Hiranyakashipu though He was not there? Or do you say that He appeared there, since He was there? He was there; He is everywhere. But since Hiranyakashipu said He was not there, he could not see Him; since Prahlaadha said that He was there He could be seen there. If you are blind, how can you see Him, though He may be right in front? You are blind to His Omnipresence; how then can you see Him everywhere? When the magnet does not attract the needle, the fault lies in the dirt that covers up the needle. When the Lord does not approach the devotee, the fault lies in the heart of the devotee; it is not pure enough.

Purify the heart by being good and kind to all. Do not attempt to find fault with others. Look upon all with love, with respect, with faith in their sincerity. I would ask you to treat your servants kindly. Do not entertain hatred or contempt in your heart; show your resentment if you must, through words, not action. Repent for the errors that you commit and decide never to repeat them; pray for strength to carry out your resolutions.

*Prashaanthi Nilayam, 14-10-1964*

## 35. The bond that unbinds

THE scholarship which revels in the number of texts mastered is of no use; one may know the *Shaasthras* and the *Upanishadhs* upside down; he may have all the seven hundred *slokhas* of the Geetha in his head, but, if *aachaara* and *vichaara* are non-existent, it is a burden which is best avoided. *Aachaara* means, application in practice. *Vichaara* means continuous self-examination.

The Shaasthry spoke of the incident of the golden deer, which enticed the heart of Seetha. One would naturally wonder why Seetha should fall in for that creature, or why Raama should believe in the existence of such a strange creature. He could have convinced Seetha that it was a stratagem of the *Raakshasas* to attract their attention and bring about dire mischief. But, like any ordinary husband infatuated with his wife, Raama followed the deer promising to bring it back alive, to be kept as her pet. Of course, if He was an ordinary human being, infatuation like this would be condemned. But, being the Lord Himself, He has to be judged differently. All things are according to plan, His plan.

Know that plan; it is laid down in *dharma*, depicted in the *Upanishadhs*. The Shaasthry that spoke next elaborated upon the *dharma* as laid down for *brahmachaaris* (celibates). What is *brahmacharya*? It means *charya* in *Brahman*---moving ever in *Brahman*. Cognise that your existence is in *Brahman*, through *Brahman*, for *Brahman*. It is that awareness that makes acts sacred and successful. Feel pure; that makes your act pure. The *gopees* moved about, not in Gokula but in the Lord's residence; they did not sell butter and milk; but, used the opportunity to call out the names of the Lord. Pure words, pure speech; holy listening, holy reading, seeing holy things---these make the heart pure. The confusion and travail that now afflict you, are the consequences of impure speech and impure sight.

## Everyone must fit in with the Lord's plan

When I was in the previous *sareera* (body), Das Ganu who was a police officer came to *Shirdhi* on account of his good luck. That visit transformed him. Moreover, Baaba accosted him as Das Ganu as soon as he saw him, and this stunned him. He asked Baaba that some parties that were opposed to him might be put down and that he might get promotion in his official career. Baaba invited him to remain in *Shirdhi* itself and escape all bother. He told him: "Do not wonder why I am suggesting this, when you craved for something else."

Later, when promotions came, he ignored Baaba and his promise to come away as soon as his honour was vindicated by official promotion. So, Baaba had to bring about circumstances which compelled him to come at last, as per Baaba's plan. He composed a number of songs and *sthothras* (hymns); he began performing *Harikathas* on Baaba everywhere and he was instrumental in bringing the news of the advent of Baaba to thousands in the land. His life was spent in and through the Lord.

Upaasini Baaba was also a similar personality. He was born in 1869 and known as Kaashinaath. He married thrice; practised as a doctor; earned much money and lost all; after hard penance, chanced into Shirdhi, where Baaba accosted him. "Hallo, Kaashinaath!" He directed him to *Upaasana* (contemplation) and guided his *saadhana* and so he was called *Upaasini* Baaba. He too was a part of Baaba's plan.

## The journey towards the Source

Thus, every one must fit in with the plan; strive to know its main principles and be equipped for the task He allots you. Be ever vigilant in the tasks that the role involves, that is your *swadharma* (one's own nature and duty). Give your heart fully to the task. "*Raama*" means, he who pleases, attracts, and attaches himself through pleasing attributes. Krishna means the same thing; he who attracts. "*Hari*" means he who robs you of your self, your ego and reveals Himself as you. To attain Him you have to climb, and climbing from the animal to man and from man to *Maadhava* is a hard struggle with the forces that pull you downward.

A decrepit old car whines and groans when it has to ascend an incline; for the engine is clogged and worn out. Keep the engine of the mind free from the dust and dirt of sensory yearning and you can ascend easily the heights of spiritual progress. It is like swimming against the fast current, this journey towards the source of Being. The *Sanaathana Dharma* (Eternal Religion) teaches you how to succeed in this journey; and, due to its innate integrity, it has flourished without losing its pristine glory, even after the onslaught of wave after wave of strange cultures. It can never decline, for it is Truth. It is the sum of experience of *bhakthas* like Hanumaan, Raadha and Meera. Remember this when the *yajna* (sacrifice) here is drawing to a close for that type of *bhakthi* alone ensures the *aapthi* or 'attainment' of *Sama* or '*Brahman.*' That is the genuine *samaapthi* or finale.

Many of you are inspired to start in your own places *sanghams* and *samaajams* (associations) for doing *bhajana*, but it is difficult to get *bhakthas* who are devoted to the Lord without any ulterior desire or intention. A *bhaktha* must be full of joy, whatever may happen, for he knows it is the will of the Lord that is being worked out. I do not address gatherings as "*Bhakthulaaraa*" (Dear *bhakthas*), for, complete surrender and complete purity essential for a *bhaktha* are commodities that are absent. Ask yourself the question, whether each of you deserves the name, 'Sai *Bhaktha*,' and you will know why I do not address you so.

## Keep your devotion within yourself

*Bhajana* does not become effective through drums, cymbals, violins and other accessories. They cover up the absence of the essential thing---feeling, emotions, yearning, sincerity, faith. When you gather in groups, the evil qualities of envy, competition, pride and factionalism raise their heads. So, offer *bhajana* to the Lord in your own homes, and do not invite these obstacles by organising groups and *mandalis* and *sanghams*.

Again there are some who extol others for the absurd reason that Sai Baaba speaks through them! Baaba has entered into them, they declare from the housetops. "O, Baaba has come upon this child, this person." How silly! Am I a ghost or a devil to possess someone and speak through him? It is all drama which cheats sick minds. Do not fall a prey to these.

That is why I say, keep your devotion within yourself, under control, and not be led away by crooks and self-seekers. These lead you astray by giving you a wrong idea of the Lord's manifestation. They befoul the faith that their brothers and sisters repose in God.

Institutions, societies and *sanghams* have another fault. Religious institutions must make people aware of God and of their own evanescence. But, these create a paraphernalia of officers, various grades of members, a secretary, a treasurer, a president and a batch of committee members, who strut about with their badges and revel in their own assumed greatness. A society named after God must help in the removal of jealousy, envy, vanity, egoism and greed; but, these foster them and allow them to grow wild. Real *bhakthas* will never crave for such positions; they will avoid them as traps which could lay them low.

## Your faith must be unshakable

I do not need any publicity, nor does any other manifestation of the Lord. What are you daring to publicise? Me? What do you know about Me, let Me ask. You speak one thing about Me today and another tomorrow. Your faith has not become unshakable! You praise, when things go well, and blame when things go wrong. You flit from one refuge to another.

And even before you *bhakthi* ripens, you strive to lead others, you collect donations and subscriptions and plan *mandhirs* and *sanghams*; all this is mere show, which brings spiritual loss, rather than spiritual gain. When you start publicity you descend to the level of those who compete in collecting clientele, decrying others and extolling themselves.

Where money is calculated and garnered, and exhibited to demonstrate one's achievements, I will not be present. I come only where sincerity, faith and surrender are valued. So spend the silent hours in meditation and *naamasmarana* (remembering the Lord's name) in your own homes and deepen faith. I do not need *bhajans* which, like gramophone records, reproduce songs and *naamaavalis*, without any feeling or yearning while singing. Hours of shouting do not count; a moment of concentrated prayer from the heart is enough, to melt and move God.

## Practise detachment little by little

If you deny God, it is as if you deny yourself. There is no God, you declare; but, you assert that "I exist." Well, who is that I that exists, that exists throughout the varying stages of growth, physical and mental, in joy and grief? That 'I' is God; believe It. For that 'I' sees with eyes, tastes with the tongue, walks with the feet, argues with the intelligence; but, all the while, it is conscious that it is separate from all these. When you affirm "There is no God," you first assert and then declare the absence of that entity. You assert the non-existence of something that "is." That 'I' must be conceived as a wave of the ocean of God, not as the first person singular. That "first" person leads you into the world of fear and greed. My house, my village, my community, my district, my language—it entangles itself thus more and more inextricably.

There was a man from Puttaparthi who lived in a solitary hut on the banks of the Ganga, some miles above Haridhwaar. He was engaged in severe *thapas* and was greatly admired by other monks. One day, while bathing in the river, he overheard a party of pilgrims who had alighted from their bus at that site, talking among themselves in Thelugu. His attachment to the mother-tongue dragged him thither; he asked them where they came from. They said Rayalaseema. He probed further; they were from Ananthapur District; his ears ached for further details. They were from Penukonda Thaluk, Puttaparthi itself, in fact. So, that monk was very happy; he asked them about his lands, his family, his friends and when he was told that a few of them had died, the poor fellow started weeping like a fool. All his years of *saadhana* had come to nought. They broke down before the onslaught of language-attachment. He was so bound to his mother-tongue. What a pity!

Practise detachment from now on; practise it little by little, for a day will come sooner or later when you will have to give up all that you hold dear. Do not go on adding to the things which bind you to them. Bind yourself to the great liberator, God.

*Prashaanthi Nilayam, 15-10-1964*

---

*To describe the infinite aspects
in terms of limited words and
limited experience, is not possible.
The Maharishis who were well versed
in the Vedhas and Manthras realised
that it is not possible to explain and
describe the aspects of Brahman
in terms of words, and they were
only indicating by their silence.*

**Shri Sathya Sai**

## 36. Prick the bubble of pride

THE tongue that does not utter the name of God, the hand that knows no charity, the years of life that know no calm, talents that receive no reward, a life that has not garnered wisdom, a temple where there is no atmosphere of reverence, talk that does not communicate knowledge---all these are of no worth.

Dr. Raamakrishna Rao spoke of the teachings of Raamaanujaachaarya and of the basic principles of *prapathi*, which is another word for *sharanaagathi*---surrender of the individual will to the Supreme Will. He also spoke of the need for an attitude of gratitude to the Lord for this human existence He has vouchsafed; and for the many chances given for acquiring enlightenment. Gratitude is a quality that is fast disappearing in human relations; it is a heinous sin to neglect this obligation.

The Shaasthry elaborated on the assurance given in the Geetha, *Yogakshemam Vahaamyaham*. This does not mean that the Lord will ensure for you *sukham* and *santhosha* (happiness and joy)---but, it means that the Lord will endow you with steady unshakable peace, inner equanimity.

*Yoga* means the acquisition of that which you do not have and *kshema* means the preservation of that which you have acquired. So the assurance means that the Lord will ensure that you acquire the *shaanthi* that you do not have and create conditions under which you can preserve that *shaanthi*. For the greatest happiness is *shaanthi*, inner peace. How do you get it? By knowing that you are the *Aathma*, which has no birth or death, no joy or grief, no up and no down.

Just as underground water is the sustenance of all trees, the *Aathma* is the underlying source of all the *aanandha* that the *jeevi* experiences. You bring that subterranean water up by the process of boring; steady hitting, digging, thumping through a pipe, which contains and directs the drill. The borers have to take care that they do not allow air to go into the pipe; for, then the drilling cannot succeed. So too in the *japam* that you do, the drilling the Raam, Raam, Raam, you must be very careful not to allow *vishayavaasana* (attachment to worldly objects) to enter and interfere with the smooth working of the drill. If you do, the *Aathma* cannot be experienced.

## Paths of devotion and knowledge

Underground water is perennial; it will not dry up. The pleasure one gets through physical, mental and intellectual pursuits is transitory. Good deeds may grant heaven; but, that too is a temporary habitation, from where man has to journey down to earth, to live his life again. It is like the short term an M.L.A. gets to bask in public fame, earned by the votes cast in his favour; when the term is over, he becomes a beggar once again, begging for votes, to win again the lost status. He starts shouting the same slogans for getting popular applause.

Many people say that *Bhakthi Maarga* (path of devotion) is much easier than *Jnaana Maarga* (path of spiritual knowledge); but *jnaana* is easier. For, it comes in a flash to those who can just sit quiet for a few minutes and analyse themselves. A car moves on its four wheels, but the person who drives it is inside it, not outside. So, also, drive the intellect, the mind, the senses from inside; do not try to guide them from outside. Board the train of *saalokya*; that is to say, of constant thought of Godhead; it will take you to the station, *saameepya*, that is to say, nearness to God; then the next halt is *saaruupya*, where you earn divine attributes; finally, you reach the terminus, *saayujya*, when the individual *Aathma* is experienced as but a wave of the ocean of *Paramaathma*.

## How to destroy the mind?

You must reach the terminus where ignorance dies and *jnaana* is born; then, there is no more journey. Along the route, there are many pseudo-terminii which tantalise you; but, you would not give up the journey until you reach the real one. Calumny, scandal, loss, dishonour, poverty, distress, fame, pomp, triumph---all these call on you to alight; but you should stick fast to the seat and never give up.

Do not seek more and more *sukham*; seek more and more *jnaanam*. The mind is a fertile field for ignorance. Wipe out all traces of the mind (*Mano Naasanam*)---that is the task of the *jnaani* (man of realisation). How to destroy the mind? It is easy once you know what it is. The mind is stuffed with desire. It is a ball filled with air, like a football. Puncture it and it will not move from place to place. *Nirvaana* means, without air. In a square filled with water from an irrigation canal, it appears square; if the field is circular or oblong or rectangular or triangular, the sheet of water that fills it will have same geometrical shape. The mind takes on the form of the desire that fills it. To take another example, it is like a piece of cloth, the warp and the woof being the yarn of desire. The texture, the colour, the durability, the feel, the shine of the cloth will depend upon the desire that constitutes the warp and the woof. Remove the yarn, the warp and the woof, one by one—the cloth disappears. That is the technique of *mano naasanam* (destroying the mind).

## Terrible nature of "desire"

*Korike* (wish) is the elder brother of the mirage. You pursue it and suffer. It enters the consciousness softly, silently; it holds out prospects of pleasure and joy; it draws fine pictures in attractive colours; it gains a foothold, strikes root; then, it strangles, swamps and destroys relentlessly, unintermittently. That is the terrible nature. Raamakrishna Rao gave the instance of Yamunaachaarya conquering the nefarious hold of desire. Be a hero like him. If you entertain desire, you will lose contentment and peace.

In the *Thretha Yuga* (Silver Age), there was a king called Vijaya ruling over his empire from the city of Chandhragopaalapuram. He was steadfast in the observance of truth, morality and peace. He was known far and wide for his deep sympathy with the poor and distressed. He was overcome with desire to widen his sway and conquer the border regions. His spiritual teacher, Garga, permitted him to essay this adventure, for he knew that he would not overstep the limits laid down by the scriptures. He even initiated him into a *manthra*, which would gain for him superhuman help. When the *manthra* (sacred formula) was mastered, Vijaya repeated it, and lo, Hanumaan, Jaambavaan and Sugreeva appeared before him, with all their attendants, demanding to be told what he wanted them to do! He told them that his desire was to conquer the four quarters and that he could not rest until that wish was fulfilled. Hanumaan and others told him: "That is impossible; go back home. That is possible only in *Dwaapara Yuga* (Bronze Age)!" So, he returned to his palace and died, to be born again as Arjuna.

## Arjuna's encounter with Hanumaan

When Arjuna went South on this conquering expedition, on his coming to Raamasethu, where Raama has built the bridge to go over to Lanka, he was filled with pride at his unrivalled skill with the bow; he felt that he was superior even to Raama, for Raama had piled it up laboriously, stone upon stone. Arjuna said rather aloud "If I were he, I would have twanged my bow and built an arch of arrows across the sea over which the army could have marched safely along." Hanumaan surprised him by presenting himself before him with a grin, which Arjuna felt made him even uglier. He challenged him to build one, so that at least one monkey could walk across, not to speak of the vast host. Arjuna shot arrows one after the other and they got entangled one with the other in such strong combinations that a huge structure was formed, bridging India and Lanka. Hanumaan declared that it was too fragile; Arjuna agreed to immolate himself if the bridge could not stand his weight. Then, Hanumaan walked a few paces on the bridge, it crumpled into bits!

True to his word, Arjuna lit a fire and was about to expiate for the sin of pride that made him feel superior to Raama, when Krishna appeared and asked the reason, as if He did not know! In fact, that was the very reason why He appeared! When He was told of the wager and the failure of Arjuna, He declared that any agreement can be valid only when it was made before a witness.

How could the parties be trusted, since it was in their interest to modify the conditions to their advantage?

So, He wanted the bridge to be built again and Hanumaan to break it again. It was done and Hanumaan walked on it as before; but, try as he might with all his might the bridge was absolutely intact! Hanumaan jumped on it, but not a dent was caused. The secret was, Krishna was supporting the bridge with His back wherever Hanumaan's steps were placed, the same back that held the Mandhara Mountain in position, during the epochmaking churning of the ocean of milk by the gods and the demons. This was revealed to both Arjuna and Hanumaan, by the bleeding that was evident on Krishna's back! The Lord interceded to save the honour of His *bhaktha*!

## Hanumaan's offer of help to Arjuna

Arjuna's pride was humbled; he fell at the feet of Hanumaan and prayed that he must help him win the battle. Hanumaan agreed to be present on the flag of Arjuna's chariot, shedding his halo over the warrior within. That was how the *Thretha yuga* wish was fulfilled and the *Thretha yuga manthra* proved effective.

This relationship with the past is beyond the reach of human investigation. You can feel that you are inheritors of a long past, of a long history. You may not remember the incidents of a particular day ten years ago; but that does not mean that you were not alive that day. So too you may not recall what happened in the previous life or the life previous to that; but there is no doubt that you had those lives. If you eructate now, you will get the flavour of the food that you have consumed. This life is the eructation of the last one, which you consumed. The flavour of this is an indication of that.

A mother holds a child that has soiled its shirt and puts on it a new one; death is the removal of the soiled shirt and birth, the putting on of the fresh one. Let the mother do her will; be a child in her hands. Have full faith in her love and wisdom. Be an instrument; submerge your will in the Will of the Lord. That will save you from worry and pain. Do not lose seeing people who have gone astray; it will be like judging rain water to be dirty, seeing a stagnant pool. Rain water is pure; it is the soil that soils it.

## God is in you and in all else

I have been teaching people irrespective of age and circumstance. Years ago, there were no eating houses and the hundreds who came to this place had to be fed by Karnam Subbamma, who delighted in feeding them herself. The water in the big vessel on her hearth was always boiling and she had only to pour the washed rice grains into it in order to get a meal ready at short notice. She did this tirelessly for years; many came and learnt. Those who kept themselves at a distance then, are pining now for lost chances. That will be the fate of all who fall in faith, in spite of experiences that confirm and foster it.

*Vaasudhevas sarvamidham* does not mean that all this is just Krishna, the son of Vaasudheva. It means that all this is God, by whatever name He is known. So, if you decry any one, you are decrying God, that is, His real core. If you become aware of the God in you and the God in all else, there is nothing to equal the peace and joy that you get. I bless you that you may attain that bliss.

*Prashaanthi Nilayam, 16-10-1964*

## 37. Keep the flag flying

[*In the poem that Baaba composed impromptu and sang before commencing His speech, He announced Himself as* **Shri Naatha, Loka Naatha** *and* **Anaatha Naatha** *(Lord of Lakshmi, of the world and of the helpless), the same He, who saved the Gajendhra, the boy Dhruva, the poor Kuchela and the helpless Prahlaadha!*]

THE hearts of *bhakthas* gathered here are all blossoming now like lotuses when the sun rises, for they believe this is the day when the Lord was born in human form. I may tell them that every day is *Janmotasavam*, a *Brahmothsavam*, an *Aanandhotsavam* (different kinds of festivals), at Puttaparthi; as well as wherever *bhakthas* are. The *Niraakaara* (the Formless) comes in *Naraakaara* (form of man) when the virtue of the good and the vice of the wicked reach a certain stage. Prahlaadha's devotion and his father's disregard both had to ripen before *Narasimha avathaara* could take place. To know the truth of the *avathaar*, the *saadhaka* must culture the mind, as the ryot does the field. He has to clear the field of thorny undergrowth, wild creepers and tenuous roots. He has to plough the land, water it and sow the seeds well. He has to guard the seedlings and tender plants from insect pests as well as from the depredations of goats and cattle; he has to put up a fence all round. So too, egoism, pride and greed have to be removed from the heart; *sathya, japa, dhyaana* (truth, repetition of the Lord's name and meditation), form the ploughing and the levelling; *prema* is the water that has to soak into the field and make it soft and rich; *naama* is the seed and *bhakthi* is the sprout; *kaama* and *krodha* are the cattle and the fence is discipline; *aanandha* is the harvest.

## Knowledge is the final stage of *karma*

Of course, you will get faith in God only when you have yourselves discovered that the universe must have a creator, a protector, an agency for both evolution and involution or a power that exercises all these three functions. To grasp that idea, the heart must be pure, the mind must be clear. For this, *karma* is very important. The *Karmakaanda* (section dealing with rituals) in the *Vedhas* is the major part of the *shruthi*, for *jnaana* is but the final stage of *karma*. The army will have many soldiers but only just a handful of officers; so too, *karmas* are many, and they all obey the *jnaani*. Of the hundred parts of the *Vedhas*, 80 will be *karma*, 16 *upaasana* and 4 *jnaana*. *Karma* has to be done for educating the impulses and training the feelings. Then, you develop the attitude of *upaasana*, of humility before the great unknown, and finally, you realise that the only reality is you, which is the same as He.

You hear nowadays of equality (*Samaanathwa*), of each being equal to the rest. This is wrong notion, for we find the parents and children differently equipped; when one is happy, the other is miserable; there is no equality in hunger or joy. Of course all are equally entitled to love and sympathy, and to the grace of God. All are entitled to the medicines in the hospital; but what is given to one should not be given to another. There can be no equality in the doling out of medicine! Each deserves the medicine that will cure him of his illness.

I know that this struggle in the name of equality is only one of the ways in which man is trying to get *aanandha*. In almost all parts of the world, man is today pursuing many such short-cuts and wrong paths of achieve *aanandha*. But let Me tell you, without reforming conduct, daily behaviour, the little acts of daily life, *aanandha* will be beyond reach. I consider *pravarthna* (practice), as essential.

A man or an institution is to be judged by his or its integrity, whether acts are according to the principles professed. The mind, the body, the word---all three must work in unison. By such disciplined *karma* the senses will be sublimated and *prashaanthi* won; then, out of this *prashaanthi* will arise *prakaanthi* (the great light), and from that will emerge *Param-jyothi* (the suprasplendour or illumination). That illumination will reveal *Param-aathma* (the Oversoul), the Universal.

Now, I am hoisting on this Prashaanthi Nilayam the Prashaanthi Flag, according to the convention that has grown here, like the conventions in the material plane. The flag represents the spiritual discipline I have laid down for you: conquest of *kaama* and *krodha*, achievement of *prema* and the practice of *japa yoga*, leading to the blossoming of the lotus of the heart and the emergence of the *jyothi* of *jnaana* therein. When I hoist it over the Nilayam, you should convert your hearts into Prashaanthi Nilayams and hoist the flag there too, and keep it flying.

*Prashaanthi Nilayam, 23-11-1964*

## 38. Karma and karuna

[*After the song which Baaba opened His discourse, He thrilled every one by singing the two lines from the Bhagavadh Geetha, which declare* "Yadaa yadaa hi dharmasya glaanir bhavathi, Bhaaratha, Abhyuththaanam adharmasya tadh aathmaanam srujaamyaham," *and adding* "Parithraanaaya saadhuunaam, vinaasaayacha dhushkrutaam, dharma samsthaapanaarthaaya sambhavaami yuge yuge." "*Whenever* dharma *declines, I restore it and put down the forces which cause the decline, by assuming a form*" *and* "*I am born again and again in every crisis in order to protect the good, punish the wicked and restore* dharma." *He began His discourse after this announcement of His Identity with the source of all* avathaars].

EVERYONE is now seeking comfort and pleasure; that is the be-all and end-all. If you tell a man that he can eat whatever he likes and as much as he likes, he is delighted; if you add that he might develop, as a consequence, some illness or other, he will treat you as an enemy. No regimen or control is popular. But strength is derived only from control, from restraint, from regulation. Man becomes tough and capable of endurance only if he welcomes hardships. Struggle, and you get the strength to succeed. Seek the basis for the seen, in the unseen. The tall skyscraper has a deep base reaching into the earth. This seen world has, as its base, the unseen *Paramaathma*; your body is but the vehicle through which you can search, investigate, and discover that base.

## There is no one fully good

The body is the instrument for doing *karma*; the Shaasthry said that *buddhi* (intellect) is shaped by *karma* ---"*Buddhi karmaanusaarini*"; *japa* and *dhyaana* will purify the *buddhi* and make it an instrument for self-realisation and for winning grace. The warmth of divine grace will melt all *ajnaana* away; you can win it by engaging yourself in good deeds. Do the *karma* for which you are best fitted, which is your *swadharma* (one's duties that accord with one's nature); do it without complaint, without any malingering. That is the principle of *varnaashrama dharma* (duties of social groups and stages of life).

India was the home of peace and prosperity when this was followed by rich and poor alike; but, now, the land is plunged in darkness and confusion. Therefore, another *avathaar* has come, for teaching people of *dharma* they have forgotten. Raama, Krishna and other *avathaars* had to kill one or more individuals, who could be identified as enemies of the *dharmic* way of life, and thus restore the practice of virtue. But, now, there is no one fully good, and so, who deserves the protection of God? All are tainted by wickedness, and so, who will survive, if the *avathaar* decides to uproot?

Therefore, I have to correct the *buddhi*, by various means; I have to counsel, help, command, condemn and standby as friend and well-wisher to all, so that they may give up evil propensities and recognising the straight path, tread it and reach the goal. I have to reveal to the people the worth of the *Vedhas*, the *Shaasthras* and the scriptural texts, which lay down the norms.

The easiest path to self-realisation is the surrender of the ego, *sharanaagathi*. Arjuna surrendered and so, the war in which he was engaged was transformed into a *yajna*, a spiritual exercise! Daksha performed a *yajna*; but he did not surrender; he was so full of egoism that he slighted God! So, his *yajna* was transformed into a war reeking with hate. Do not pit your tiny ego against the Almighty; leave it to His Will and you will have lasting peace.

## Grace can countermand all effects of *karma*

You might say that the *karma* of the previous birth has to be consumed in this birth and that no amount of grace can save man from that. Evidently, some one has taught you to believe so. But I assure you, you need not suffer from *karma* like that. When a severe pain torments you, the doctor gives you a morphine injection and you do not feel the pain, though it is there in the body. Grace is like the morphine; the pain is not felt, though you go through it! Grace takes away the malignity of the *karma* which you have to undergo.

You know there are dated drugs, which are declared ineffective after a certain date; well, the effect of *karma* is rendered null, though the account is there and has to be rendered! Or, the Lord can save man completely from the consequences, as was done by Me to the *bhaktha* whose paralytic stroke and heart attacks I took over some months ago, in the *Gurupoornima* week! It is wrong to say the "*Lalaatha likhitham*" (what is written on the forehead, i.e. fate) cannot be wiped out; that what one has earned in previous births must be consumed in this birth. Grace can countermand all that; nothing can stand in its way. It is the grace of the "Almighty," remember.

Of the *avathaars*, some are for a definite limited purpose like Vaamana or Narasimha. They are just manifestations, to counter some particular evils. They are not full-fledged, long-lasting, expansive, like Raama and Krishna. The Lord has no hate in His composition; He is all mercy. That is why Krishna proceeded to the Kaurava court, as a messenger of peace, with compromise proposals. He showed man how patient he should be in spite of provocations, how self-control wins in the end.

## God has no favourites or rivals

Krishna demonstrated that if you practise the *saadhana* of the constant presence of God, you are bound to achieve victory. Take Him as the charioteer; He will steer you through the heaviest odds. He has no favourites or rivals. Like fire, He spreads warmth to all who are near Him. If you do not feel the warmth, do not blame Him: blame yourself that you are far from Him. Look at Bheeshma! He prayed to the very Krishna who had vowed to kill him; he prayed that Krishna should grant him a vision of His divine splendour! That is true *bhakthi*, real *jnaana*! He had the faith, the vision, and Krishna blessed him.

Hiranyakashipu said, 'He is nowhere' and so, He was nowhere for him; Prahlaadha asserted 'He is everywhere,' and He appeared from the pillar to prove him true. God did not have to run into the pillar in order to come out of it, to reply to the challenge of the father. He was there all along, just as in everything else. He had only to make Himself visible!

I too am like that; if you accept Me and say yes, I too respond and say S S S! If you deny and say, no, I also echo, no. Come, examine, experience and have faith; that is the method of utilising Me.

## Do not demean your talents

Dakshinamurthy taught his disciples by his silence, Shaasthry said. Yes; what he did was to make the disciples rely on their own intelligence. Do not demean your talents; when you dive deep into yourselves, you can discover the source of all strength. Ants creeping over a rock, millions of them, can carve a deep groove along their path. The minute feet of the ant have that power. You might have seen on the walls around the village wells, hollows produced on granite slabs by the continuous placing of water pots! The pots are made of mud, but, they erase even the hardest granite over the years and cause the hollows where they rest! The *Aathma-swaruupam* (embodiment of Self) is not *alpa-swaruupam* (an insignificant embodiment)! The *aathma* is not anaemic. It is a powerful dynamo, capable of generating enormous power. The *guru* (spiritual teacher) shows you the *guri* (goal); but, you must generate the power yourself, by your own *saadhana* (spiritual effort).

*Prashaanthi Nilayam, 23-11-1964, 8 p.m.*
*[Speech delivered after the offering of flower-garlands by devotees continuously at one sitting, from 10-30 a.m. till 7-30 p.m.]*

## 39. Through mirth and moan

THE revered old man who spoke of the *upaasana* of Hanumaan referred to the *Ashtotthara Sathanaama* (the 108 names) of Aanjaneya. I wonder how many of you know the significance of that number 108. Why is it that the strings of the names of the gods are always 108? They could as well be 110 or 112 or 50 or 120, isn't it? All such mystic numbers have a deep meaning. Man breathes at the rate of 900 per hour, 21,600 times per day, 10,800 during daytime. With every breath, man is supposed to repeat *Soham*, "I am He," and so, the figure 216 and its half, 108 has a deep significance. It is also 9 times 12, 9 being the number indicative of *Brahman*, since it is always 9, however many times you may multiply it (9 x 12 = 108, 1 + 8 = 9, 9 x 9 = 81, 8 + 1 = 9) and 12 is the number of the Sun; also, the Sun moves through 12 *raasis* or points, each *raasi* representing one month.

Just as 9 is the symbol of *Brahman*, 8 is the number of *Maayaa*. For, multiples of 8 go on diminishing in total value, instead of remaining the same or increasing, (2 times 8 is 16 which adds up to 7; 3 times 8 is 24 and so, the total has come down to 6; 4 times 8 is 32 which adds up to 5 and 5 times 8 is 40 adding up to only 4! 6 times 8 is 48, that is, 12 adding to 3. And 7 times 8 adds up to 2. 8 times 8 is 64 and so, only 1). This decrease in value is the best symbol of *Maayaa*. Every number has many such valuable inner meanings. It is an interesting subject. You must investigate and reason out, not laugh cynically and condemn. If you stand on the seashore and hesitate to dive into the waters, you cannot secure pearls.

## The message of the *Vedhas*

One *bhaktha* sings, "O Krishna! You are dark; the 'Kalindi deeps' in the Yamuna river into which you have descended is also dark with rain clouds; my eyeball is dark; my heart too is darkened with dark thoughts. How then can I discover You? Your secret is beyond me; your majesty is ever receding before my imagination." Now, the dark colour of the Lord is the colour of the deep sea and the deep sky. It signifies the fathomless, unfathomable. What has to be changed is the heart, the intelligence. Above all, do not be traitors to yourselves. If you say one thing and do another, your conscience will itself condemn you as a cheat. You are your won witness. Not all the stones which Raama trod on were converted into humans; only one stone changed into Ahalya, for, repentance and penance had elevated it to that status.

Nothing ever is born without the will of God, nothing ever happens without His will; that is the message of the *Vedhas*; understand the *Vedhas* well and this lesson will be instilled into you. Fleas drink only the blood of the cow; but men draw from her the sweet and nourishing milk. So, learn from the *Vedhas* the potence of the Will of the Lord. Once you are fixed in that faith, you will be able to brave all dangers. You complain that

God is invisible; but the fault is yours, not to recognise God in all His various manifestations. You are yourself "manifestation of God." But you do not know it; you call yourself a sinner, worm born in sin, wallowing in sin, essentially wicked. But, let some one, who takes you to your word, call you, "Hullo sinner!" you resent it. Why? Because your real nature is purity, peace, joy. *Manas, buddhi, chiththam, ahamkaaram, indhriya* (mind, intellect, thought, egoism and senses)---these are like the bricks, iron rods, cement, wood, etc., that go to make up a house for the *Aathma* to live in. They are jewels that the *Aathma* wears. They are not you; they are only incidental. The real you is the *Aathma*. This can be learnt only by constant meditation, by moving in good company, by listening to the talks of realised men, by following some prescribed course of discipline. That is why I lay so much emphasis on discipline.

## The co-operative commonwealth

The *Varnaashrama* (social groups and stages of life) disciplines, to which the Shaasthry referred, is very useful in this field. *Varna* or what is called caste, is a convenient arrangement for the conduct of worldly affairs; the *aashramas* or the stages of life are roots of supra-worldly joy. The four *varnas* are universal; they can be found in any country. The leaders of thought are the *Brahmins*; the fighters carrying arms are the *Kshathriyas*; the entrepreneurs and the business executives are the *Vaishyas*; the busy producers and labourers are the *Suudhras*.

Whether head or heels, it is the same blood that circulates through each; it is the same body which claims them as limbs. Each limb has to perform its task, the task for which it has specialised. You cannot walk on your head or think with the feet. It is a co-operative commonwealth, the body as well as the body-politic. The eye is the master of sight; the ear cannot question the authority of the eye, nor the eye that of the ear about sound, or the ear that of the tongue so far as the taste is concerned. Each is the master in its own field. The *aashramas* are also steps towards the attainment of detachment and fulfilment. They ensure experience and the unfoldment of personality.

## God cannot be bamboozled

Each *varna* and a*ashrama* has it own rules, regulations and restrictions. A bullock cart cannot move on rails nor a locomotive on the road. Each type of vehicle has its own type of road. But, all move forward and reach the goal in their own good time. When the heart is pure, the Lord is revealed. He is the judge; He cannot be bamboozled. The doctor may assure you that you have no fever, but the thermometer cannot lie. The doctor may say so to save you from panic, but the thermometer declares the truth. God knows and God will deal with you as you deserve. Have the faith. Repent for all wrongs done and resolve not to repeat the mistake; then God will extend His grace.

You feel that there is something behind and beyond all this fleeting fantasy; something that persists through all the successes and defeats, all the tears and smiles, all this mirth and moan; but, you are unable to grasp it and realise that it is the same entity that underlies the entire universe. You are one with most distant star and the least little blade of grass. You shine as dew on the petal of the rose; you swing from star to star; you are part and parcel of all this manifestation. The *Shaasthras* teach you this truth through many a parable and story, and even directly, supported by the experience of sages and mystics. Hanumaan may have the form of an ape; but that is simply the outer casement, the *upaadhi*. The Lord is the very breath of Hanumaan: every hair-end of his was echoing with *Raamanaama*.

## All forms of divinity are equally sweet

Through *dhyaana* and *upaasana*, you can be aware of yourselves as all this. Mud existed before plates and pots; pots and plates are mud; mud there will be when plates and pots are no more. The plate and the pot must be aware of their being always mud; that, in other words, is self-realisation. When that is achieved, wherever your eyes are cast, you find yourself; wherever your attention is directed, you find your reflection. Begin to feel for it now, this very moment.

Do not hold *japam* and *dhyaanam* as the games of 'cracks'; hold fast to them, for they alone can save you from ruin. Offer the Lord, not the flowers got in exchange for a few paise from the shop, but the fragrant flowers of your own virtues. Let tears of joy be the holy water with which you seek to wash the feet of the Lord. Let your *upaasana dhevatha* (deity being worshipped) be Aanjaneya as in the case of this Shaasthry, or any other form; treat that *dhevatha* as comprising all forms of divinity; do not argue that one form is less and another is more; all are equally sweet. Seek to identify yourself with some grand and glorious Entity, for all Grandeur and all Glory is His ultimately.

*Prashaanthi Nilayam, 25-11-1964*

---

*Life is a game : Play it. Life is Love : Share it.*
*Life is a challenge : Meet it. Life is a dream: Realise it*
Shri Sathya Sai

## 40. Naama and naami

It appears as if, in this *Bhaagavatha Bhaktha Samaajam*, they impose restrictions on all, except Myself! For, they warned all speakers so far to stop early, and now they ask Me to take as much time as I please! Of course, some 60 members of the *Samaajam* have come here and each of them wishes to partake in the three-day programme, which is possible only when severe restrictions are insisted upon the length of their speeches and musical recitals. They are masters in their own fields and endowed with *bhakthi* and *shraddha;* so I feel that they must be given longer time in the coming years when they would be here.

Man suffers from two types of agony; the first, which can be allayed through the intercession of others and the second, which can be allayed only by the individual's own effort. Hunger and thirst can be overcome only when the individual eats or drinks; however much others may eat, hunger will not abate even an iota. If your wife or father or mother or son or brother offers to take an injection on your behalf, can your illness be cured thereby? The hunger of the spirit, the illness of inner man is also the same. You must help yourself. The illness has come due to some excess, some infection, some breach of rules. The infection is produced by the viruses of *kaama, krodha, lobha, moha, madha* and *maathsarya* (desire, anger, greed, delusion, pride, jealousy). They do not allow your divinity to shine forth; they cause discontent, worry, grief and pain. You can brave them only by manifesting your inner strength. Do not yield to them; fight them with faith that you are unconquerable.

## Give up the idea that you are the body

How did this fatal ignorance enter into your makeup? Well, there was once a huge mirror inside a room in a rural home. They wanted to take it out, but the door was found too narrow and too short! Some suggested that the wall be broken open while others said that the mirror itself be cut into two! How did they place it in this room, one shrewd villager asked. Yes, how did it get in? If they only knew that, they could manage to take it out too. Before the room was ready, the mirror had got in. So too, ere this body was formed, ignorance had established itself; it is a product of the sloth of previous lives. Do not worry about the house, and the mirror will cease to be a problem. Give up the idea that you are the body and ignorance will vanish. You can see yourself in the light.

The members of the *Samaajam* enabled you to listen to very valuable discourses and inspiring *Harikathas*, which made you know many facets of the Raamaayana, Bhaagavatha, the *Puraanas*, the *Vedhas* and *Shaasthras*. You heard from them that Raama was "*Vigrahavaan-dharmah*" (*Dharma* embodied), that Krishna was "*Leelaamaanusha vigraha*" (sporting in human form), but, how does that affect you? Have you felt that you too are kith and kin of Raama and Krishna, that every *maanava* (human) can be a Maadhava, that every *nara* (man) can be a Naaraayana? Unless you adhere a little to Raama *dharma*, how can you claim to be a *bhaktha* of Raama? Unless you evince a little of the *prema* that Krishna had, how can you pride yourself on being a Krishna-*bhaktha*? Do not be different from your ideal; approach it as close as you can. You must be as golden as the gold you idealise, though you may be a tiny jewel and He, a vast treasure. The Lord is *Kavi* and Vaalmeeki is also a *Kavi*; both create---one the *loka* (world) and the other, the *slokha* (verse). The *bhaktha* must form himself on the model of Bhagavaan; otherwise, he can lay no claim for *saaruupya* (sameness of the Form of the Lord).

## *Maayaa* is a false enchantress

*Krishna-avathaara* is a *Sampuurna Avathaara*, the Lord appearing with all the 16 *kalas* (distinctive marks); whereas Raama shared the *kalas* with other brothers. Raama appeared as if He was associated with *gunas* (qualities), or as having qualitative behaviour, whereas Krishna was above and beyond such. Krishna never prayed, even in the direst crisis! But, Raama does so, to *Aadhithya* (Sun God), for instance; the intent of that *Avathaara* was different. Krishna was unaffected by the *gunas*. His relationship with *gopees* was pure. A person like Dharmaraaja selected Him above all the sages and saints of the day for special worship at the *Raajasuuya* sacrifice.

The best armour against the tendency to read gross meanings into the *leelas* of Krishna is Faith---faith in Krishna as the Lord. You can also remember that Krishna was a boy of seven, when the *raasaleela* (sportive dance) happened. King Pareekshith asked Sukha, the immaculate saint who extolled Krishna as God, the same question: How could the *gopees* attain *moksha*? Sukha replied: They knew that Krishna was the Lord and they regarded Him as God and no less. He also reminded Pareekshith that he himself owed his life to the divine touch of Krishna which changed him from a still-born child into a hefty baby. The miasma that makes you miss these points and drags your imagination into the mire is called *Maayaa*. Identify it as a false enchantress---that moment she will vanish and you are free.

There was once a *brahmin* who passed through a forest on his way to a village, with a heavy load on his head. He could not carry it any further and there was no one in sight, except a *chandaala* (outcaste) youth, who offered to carry it for him only as far as the edge of the jungle, for as an outcaste, he was afraid to enter a village of the upper classes. The *brahmin* persuaded him to accompany him into the village itself; he advised him to pretend to be dumb and not answer any question put to him. At the village all went well, until the master of the house to which the *brahmin* had gone asked the outcaste to keep aside a pair of sandals. When he hesitated, the master chided the fellow, as was his wont: "Eh, you *chandaala*." As soon as he suspected that his identity was discovered, the *chandaala* fled! *Maayaa* too will do likwise.

## *Maayaa* can be driven out

*Maayaa* can be recognised and driven out only when the mind is purified by *prema* and the avoidance of envy and hatred, born of egoism. No act done without love can be commended; there are many who come here, thousands in fact, year after year, sharing in the *bhajana*, listening to discourses, lectures, and staying put exactly where they were when they first arrived. *Naama* without *bhaava* (Godward inclination of the mind) seldom reaches the mark. The name of the Lord must be recited with awe and wonder, humility and reverence. The bow has to be drawn full before the arrow is released; then it will pierce the target. Feeling is the force that draws the string taut and makes the *Naama* reach the *Naami* (the bearer of the name).

The Lord is approachable by all; do not have envy towards others or feel that they are your rivals or your inferiors or even superiors; each has a place in His mansion. Sathyabhaama suffered from envy and so she was never happy. Dhroupadhi had five husbands, but she was able to serve all impartially without envy and so Krishna was ever rushing to her rescue. Give your heart over to the Lord and move in society as a dedicated being; then, no harm can come to you. As a *jeeva*, you may be an individual; but, as *Aathma*, you are Vaasudheva, the *Samashti* (path of the Universal whole).

## The *gopees* were sages in previous births

First save yourselves and then save others, or try to. Being yourselves caught by the wily slush, how can you pull another out? Stand firm and safe on hard dry land and then lend a helping hand to the man struggling in the mire. You may wear the ochre robe but the robe may hide an ogre! You may advise others on *yoga*, but you may be full of *roga* (disease) yourself! Be sincere; talk only about your genuine experience; do not distort, exaggerate or falsify that experience.

Have the *Aathmic* experience; only then can you understand the Bhaagavatha and explain it to others. For example: the incident where Krishna carries away the clothes of the *gopees*. The *gopees* (cow-herd girls) were *rishis* (sages) in previous *Avathaar* periods; the *vaanaras* (monkeys) of Raama *avathaara* come again under special charter; so their hearts are pure and their motives holy.

When the *gopees* pleaded, "Krishna! is it *dharma* for you to treat us thus?" Krishna replied, "My act is not *adharma*; but yours is, for body-consciousness is against the highest spiritual *dharma*."

Vyaasa once asked some persons, who came to him for advice to cross the Yamuna near his *ashram*, to bring him milk and fruits and after eating his fill, he told them, "Well! If I have maintained my vow of fasting go now and the Yamuna will make way for you!" They said, "Then we are lost; for, we saw you eat your fill with the things we ourselves brought you." But, Vyaasa said, "I did not eat them. I offered all to Krishna; I have no body-delusion. I am the *Aathma* dwelling in this body." His *Aathma*-consciousness was so well grounded that he could assert that he had not broken his vow!

## World is changing but God is steady

What is realisation? The moment you see your own beauty and are so filled with it that you forget all else, you are free from all bonds. Known that you are all the beauty, all the glory, all the power, all the magnitude of the Universe. This Nature is but an infinitesimal fraction of His Glory; yet, you feel content with the pleasure it gives, the knowledge you gather about it, the wonder it reveals. The reflection of *Shivam* (auspiciousness) in the mirror of *Prakrithi* (Nature) is *jeeva* (individual being).

Look into the mirror and see your own image; you assert : "That image within is mine; but, I am different." So too, the *jeeva* is *Shiva* but *Shiva* is not *jeeva*. The image of the Sun in the water shakes, though the Sun is steady, up above; that is the nature of water, not the Sun; so too *Prakrithi* is changing, but *Shiva* is steady, unchanging, ever the same. You do not believe that dreams indicate reality, because the dream is negated on waking. When you get knowledge, the waking experiences will also be negated. Until then, you will take all this as real; after that, you will find that this has only relative value.

The drug has to be revised, when the disease takes a turn. So, I shall tell you one more point before I close. We hear of many things and see many things. Man fills these with his own illusion and garnishes or tarnishes each thing with that illusion. A baby is born and dies within two hours or two months. If it survives and dies when it is 16 or 18 years old, the pain is greater, for the sense of "mine" has deepened its roots, through association and the development of hopeful attachment. No one is worried if the neighbour's son dies. This is due to the egoism and exaggerated attachment.

Give each problem the attention it deserves; but do not allow it to overpower you. Anxiety will not solve any difficulty; coolness comes from detachment. Above all, believe in God and the efficacy of prayer; the Lord has said that he who does good, thinks good and speaks good will not come to harm. That is the way to get Equanimity, *Shaanthi*.

## You have designed the chains that bind you

Some of you may imagine that it is a source of joy for the Lord to take a human form. If you are in this state, you will not feel so. I am always aware of the future, the past as well as the present of every one of you. So, I am not moved so much by pity. Not that I am hard-hearted, or that I have no *dhaya* (pity). If you bolt the doors fast, how can the rays of My Grace be available to you? "*Swaami*," you cry, "I have no eyes; I am yearning to see you. Won't your heart melt at my plight?" Of course, this pitiable condition melts *your* hearts; will it not melt *Mine*? But, since I know the past, the background, My reaction is different. If only you knew, you too will react differently. It is the consequence of evil, deliberately done in previous births, and so, I have to allow the suffering to continue, modified, often by some little compensation. I do not cause either joy or grief; you are the designer of both the chains that bind you.

Remove the weight from your head by transferring all burdens to the Lord; leave everything to His Will, His law. Feed your mind with sweet and wholesome food---*Sathsangha, Sathpravarthana, Sarveshwara-chintha* (company of the holy, speaking of God, thinking of the Lord of the Universe); then you are full of joy. I am of the nature of Bliss (*Aanandhaswaruupa*); come and take *Aanandha* from Me and returning to your avocations, dwell on that *Aanandha* and be full of *Shaanthi*.

*Prashaanthi Nilayam, 26-11-1964*

---

*The traits of Raavana's lust,*
*of Shishupaala's pride,*
*of Kamsa's hate,*
*of Hiranyaaksha's envy*
*are tainting every human heart.*
*Only the discipline of spirit*
*through Japam and Dhyaanam*
*can quench the flames*
*and sooth the conflagration.*

**Shri Sathya Sai**

## 41. Swinging from yes to no

THE *dharma* that is the heritage of India is the staff of life for all men; it is the backbone of morality and well-being. It is the nectar which can confer immortality. Others may in their ignorance laugh at Indians for taking a stone to be God, but, what they do is to realise even the stone as God. It is transformed into God, an act which is a grand victory. The highest energies of man in this land are used for conquering death, while in other countries, they are misused in the diabolic attempt to make weapons of mass destruction. People here offer themselves to *Mrithyunjaya* (Shiva, the conquerer of death); those others fall at the feet of *mrithyu* (death)! Others are content with tinsel and trinkets; in India, people are taught to dive deep, and win the pear, and not wander on the sandy shore, collecting shells.

But, it is a pity that here, too, the infection is spreading and people are fast losing all sense of values and running after vanities and inanities. People attach more value to the many and they forget the One; they do not seek the One Persistent Truth; they follow the ever-changing falsehood and so, naturally, fall into grief and resentment. Take the simple rite of *namaskaaram*---the folded palms with which you greet reverentially elders and others. What does it signify, that gesture? The right palm is *Thath* (that entity, the unseen base, the other) and the left palm is *Thwam* (the I, the separate, the individualised, the thing that feels limited, alone, apart). When the two palms are brought together and kept in contact, the One-ness of that and this, of all that is outside you, and all that is in you, is emphasised and demonstrated: *Aham-Brahmaasmi* (I am *Brahman*), in fact. What greater and grander greeting can human aspiration discover and prescribe? You greet the other with as much joy as you would greet yourself; no man loves another more than himself; all are loved for the sake of the self.

Or, consider another interpretation of this act of folding the palms. The five fingers of the right hand are the five *karmendhriyas* (organs of action), the five of the left are the five *jnaanendhriyas* (organs of perception); they are together ten, dedicated to sage or *guru* or elder to be used for his service or at his bidding. That is the surrender which is called *Sharanaagathi*, the same that Hanumaan practised.

## Principle of idol worship

Take the case of the Bhagavadh Geetha, to which reference was made. When and where was it taught? On the battlefield, in the midst of the opposing forces, to solve a mental crisis. It is when such crises affect man that the Lord starts His mission of instruction. For those who have realised the goal, there is no need; for those who have known neither goal nor path, neither thirst nor yearning, it is of no use. It is only to those who are afflicted by doubt, swinging from yes to no, that instruction will be useful. A mental crisis is solved by the word of God.

Again, the worship of idols has to be looked upon as but the worship of the Formless. Water or milk has no form as such; they assume the form of vessel which contains it, is it not? Take milk in a cup or a flask, or a kettle or jug or mug, it assumes those forms. So also the form of Krishna is the form of a vessel in which you fill the formless entity; the form of Raama, Shiva, Linga, Chaamundeshwari, Ganesha—all are forms of vessels in which, according to your fancy, you take the Formless, Unpicturable! The *Naama* is the nectar, the *Naami* is the cup, the idol.

## Story of crow-demon and its meaning

Take the story which the Bhaagavathar related just now: the story of Kaakaasura, the crow-demon, that wounded Seetha when Raama was sleeping on her lap, when Seetha was there helpless to ward him off. What happened to him? Raama made him and all his race one-eyed; the one eye-ball rolls from the right to the left and from left to right so that he may see this side and that. The meaning is that if you crave for Seetha (*Prakrithi*, the pleasing, the objective world) you cannot get a perfect picture, a synoptic vision; you become one-eyed, warped, defective.

Again, the Bhaagavathar who gave the musical discourse on Santh Raamadaasa described how a *vimaana* (aerial chariot) came down from the skies to carry the saint to heaven, when his earthly career was over. The word *vimaana* does not mean an aerial chariot, as Bhaagavathars describe it; it has a deeper and truer meaning. It means that a person who has given up *maana* (pride or egoism), ascends to Heaven, that is all. Or else, consider this: *Vi* means a bird, *maana* means measure, dimension. So, the idea of going in a *vimaana* means that the soul moves through the infinite, like a bird through the sky, unopposed. It has gained freedom.

You heard the stories of the lives of Saints Thyaagaraaja and Naamadheva, described by members of this *Samaajam*. I hope you have learnt the lesson of *prema*, of *Vishwaprema* (Universal Love), that they conveyed. Imagine the *prema* of the *gopees*. One noon, Krishna stealthily entered the house of a cowherd and drank all the milk in the pot. The *gopee* discovered Him and when she admonished Him, Krishna took to His heels; when the *gopee* saw Him running over the hard cobble-stones of the street she shed tears of contrition. Those lotus feet must pain much, she felt, and wept. "O, what a great sinner I am!" she wailed. Krishna will make the wickedest heart melt in repentance. He is *Premaswaruupa* and *Shaanthiswaruupa* (of the embodiment of Love and Peace) and so He makes every heart sprout into *prema* and *shaanthi*.

## Withdraw into yourself like a tortoise

His prattle, His pranks, His innocent tricks were all-conquering. He gave the *gopees* a heap of bother and a heap of joy. That was the *thapas* (penance) for them; the bother was *anugraham* (favour); the joy was *prasaadham* (grace). You cannot have only one. Bhadhram was reading from some piece of paper, on one side of which he had written the poems he hastily composed on Me this afternoon. The other side of that paper contained some scribbles, but he could not avoid bringing those also here. You cannot bring just one side of the paper, the side that you want; you have to bring the other side too though you may not like it. Do not get puffed up with pride when you succeed; do not get punctured when you fail. Be like the tortoise that is able to withdraw its feet under its shell; withdraw into yourself the outgoing senses and be happy in the contemplation of your reality. The Lord took the Tortoise *Avathaara* because it represents the true *saadhaka*. Be also like the swan, which on coming up from the lake, gives a vigorous shake to its wings, a shake which scatters the waterdrops off; so too, the *saadhaka* must shake off the attachments that are likely to grow when the world impinges on him.

## Three friends you earn in this life

Mere scholarship is of no use; it results only in swelled heads. *Vedhaantha*, really practised, makes you fearless, like the lion in the forest. You roar and they flee in terror. The *Brahma thathwam* (Reality of the Supreme Being) expounded in *Vedhaantha* will make you master of the universe. So, do not attach yourself too much to this body or to the things that bring comfort to it. You earn three friends in this life.

*The first* : The riches you accumulate, which refuse to come with you when you move out of this life.

*The second* : Kith and kin who accompany your body up to the burial ground or cremation-ghat.

*The third* : The merit and demerit you have earned, which accompany you to the last.

Sleep inside the mosquito curtain; the insects can do no harm; so also, do not allow the insects of *kaama*, *krodha*, etc., to harm you. Get inside the curtain of *saadhana* while you are in the world. Be in the world, but do not let the world into you. That is the sign of *viveka* (discrimination).

*Prashaanthi Nilayam, 27-11-1964*

## 42. Life's balance sheet

THE opening of this Shrinivasa Cloth Market is just an excuse for My coming to Kurnool and meeting all of you, including the two ministers, Dr. Lakshminarasiah and Alapathy Venkataraamiah. Life itself is a market, where giving and taking, bargaining and speculating are part of the game. Life has its ups and downs, its profits and losses, its balance sheets and disappointments, its joys and sorrows. But the giving of *bhakthi* (devotion to God) in exchange for *mukthi* (liberation) is the most profitable business of all; and I am interested in telling you about that only.

*Bhakthi* is not simply the worship of the Lord; it is much more than that. Primarily it is the control of the senses; for, when life is offered as worship, the senses do not run after transient things. They can be thus controlled, for man is not a weak animal; he is endowed with mighty spiritual power and he can learn to use it; he can tap this power through prayer, which brings down Grace to fill the reservoir of his heart. Man tames the lion and the elephant to obey his call; can he not tame his emotions and passions? Make your strength evident in the face of hardships; when all goes well, you become soft, the blows of defeat toughen you into heroes. The difficulties that the organisers of this market encountered, as described to us in the report, show that they but deepened the determination of Raamalingiah and others to plod on, until they won through.

Alapathy Venkataraamiah is the Minister in charge of temples in Andhra and the words of advice which he gave now are worthy of attention. He spoke of the culture of India and its excellence. It held up to mankind for reverence of not conquerors and millionaires but hermits and saints. He has also a great love for Sanskrit, the language of our scriptures, which give this land the inspiration to advance along the spiritual path of discrimination and non-attachment. The scriptures are so framed that they serve the highest needs of all classes of people, whatever their age, avocation or attainment. Like a loving mother the *Vedhas* guide and guard all her children, wherever they may be.

## The body is worn by the *jeeva* to realise God

Venkataraamiah also said that the attitude of *bhakthi* is the important thing, not the name and form which has drawn it out. Yes; the Lord has a thousand names. In fact, all names are His; there is no name that is not His. Krishna, Shrinivasa, Sai Baaba---all are names of the same entity. The body is worn by the *jeeva* in order to realise God, the source from which the *jeeva* came. That is why it is said that it is very lucky for living beings to get equipped with the human physique. To be endowed with a desire for things of the spirit is the height of fortune.

A grandfather was fondling his grandson, a little lad of four; the boy asked him his age; the grandfather said he was seven; the lad refused to believe; how could a boy of four have a grandfather of seven? But, the old man said, "My dear boy! I do not care for all the sixty-three years I spent in the darkness; it is only seven years since I came under the influence of a *guru*, who opened my eyes and led me along the path to realisation. I have lived only seven years so far; the rest, I could as well ignore as wasted. I speak the truth always; this the truth."

That is the proper attitude. Do not admire and gape at the engineering achievements of countries that are able to shoot a rocket round the earth or over the moon or invent a bomb that can wipe out an entire city. That is the culmination of the strife for death and for mastery over other nations. That path leads only to misery, loss, hatred, and waste. The competition is about who will earn more in less time. All this comes about because man mistakes himself to be just a bundle of the senses, packed into this body. Really speaking, he is a spark of divinity waiting to illumine the intelligence.

## Man has to develop spiritual attitude

India has been announcing this Truth to the world since ages; this is the land where holy personages, divine personalities, saints and sages, *avathaars*, carrying the authentic stamp of God, have demonstrated that nothing else can give man the peace and joy that the contemplation of the Universal *Aathma* can give.

The poor ryot who throws a paisa into the river Godaavari when he passes over the bridge might appear to the half-educated boor, smoking in the corner, to have wasted a precious coin, which he could have put to better use, perhaps, buying a *bidi*! But, what he did is a spiritual act; he felt that the Godaavari was a living mother, who gave food to men and cattle, and his paisa is not just a coin, it is an attitude of mind, a token of gratefulness, a flower of worship. He has the *Aathma-bhaava* (spiritual attitude), while the critic who sneers at him is suffering from *anaathma-bhaava* (unspiritual attitude). *Hindhu dharma* teaches man to see and develop this *aathma-bhaava* not only with all mankind who are bound by the same tie of kinship, but, with all beings and all nature. Man is not isolated; he is one with all. All have to be served, all have to be known, for he is this all.

*Kurnool, 4-12-1964*

*As the carpenter shapes the wood,
the blacksmith shapes the iron,
the goldsmith shapes the gold,
so the Lord shapes in His own way,
as the fancy suits Him.
He created the Universe, the manifold,
woven of space, time and guna.*

*Know the Lord is the basis;
and lose all fear.*

**Shri Sathya Sai**

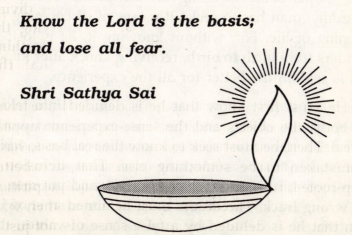

## 43. Actors and action

RARELY do I preside over a dramatic performance; I have come here tonight, because you are having a play on "Shri Sailam" and on a great devotee drawn by the deity to that temple and also because the author is a devotee for years. What exactly is a drama? It is a dream within a dream. It is a dream which unfolds before you, even while you are "awake," another dream. It tries to shed some light, some joy, some courage, some faith, some hope, some meaning on the dream called life. Naturally, man has to seek all means of discovering the meaning of life. For, without knowing it, he is lost; he wanders from birth to birth, receiving knock after knock, and is seldom the better for all the experience.

He must first know that he is deluded into taking the body, the objects and the sense-experienced world, as real. Then, he must seek to know the real basis, which is mistaken to be something else. That delusion is deep-rooted; it has warped the outlook and put man on the wrong track. The drama must be aimed at showing man that he is deluded by a false sense of values; that he is running after vanities, leaving reality behind. It should instill into man faith, strong enough to make him recoil from that pursuit, and gain the glory of discovering his great illusion.

The sorrows of life can be ended not through hatred and injustice; these only breed more of the species. They will yield only to nobler and higher thoughts and experiences, germinating from the pure heart where the Lord resides. This drama, on Hemareddy Mallamma, deals with such experiences arising from the heart of a sincere devotee and that is the reason, as I already said, why I agreed to preside over this second anniversary of the Kurnool District Kalaa Parishad and why I stayed on until the entire play was enacted.

## Service to man is service to God

Whatever talent a person has, should be dedicated to the service of the rest of humanity, indeed, of all living beings. Therein lies fulfilment. All men are kin, they are of the same likeness, the same build; moulded out of the same material, with the same divine essence in each. Service to man will help your divinity to blossom, for, it will gladden your heart and make you feel that life has been worth-while. Service to man is service to God, for He is in every man and every living being and in every stone and stump. Offer your talents at the feet of God; let every act be a flower, free from creeping worms of envy and egoism, and full of the fragrance of love and sacrifice. If you have the talent for acting dramatic roles, well, use it for the glorification of God, for the uplifting of man.

A question often raised when people talk of dramas or films is this: Are the people who flock to them bringing down the level of these items of entertainment? Or, are the artistes responsible for lowering it? I must say that your responsibility as artistes and writers is much greater; you must not stoop to methods and tricks that will bring in more money perhaps, but, which sow seeds of evil and vice in the minds of the people, who flock to the theatres. A person who comes in to see a play or a film must move out of the theatre a better man, a stronger and more courageous man, and, not a poorer and weaker man, less equipped to resist the temptations of the world. Remember this when you select a play for the stage or when you take up your pen to write one, and you will be on the right path.

To the actors, I must speak a word. You wear the dress and equipment of noble souls and saints; you impersonate even divine characters; you reel off words of high purpose and noble ideals, and exhibit deeply thrilling experiences. You do all this very realistically. It is a sign of your skill and your untiring practice. You inspire people to better their lives; from you, they learn the path of inner peace and devotion, for you re-enact before their eyes the lives of great saints.

### Develop the *saadhana* of self-effacement

All this is very good. But, is it too much to ask that you show in your own lives, outside the stage, that the godly path is the best and the safest and perhaps even the smoothest? Take this role of the actor as a good guide for your own betterment. It is a *saadhana* which will give you peace. Raamakrishna Paramahamsa actually lived the roles of *Puraanic* characters like Raadha and Hanumaan and realised Krishna and Raama through identification with the experiences of each.

Become one with the holy characters you represent; derive inspiration and joy therefrom. Your acting too will thereby improve vastly; you will earn the gratitude of thousands. Feminine characteristics appeared in Raamakrishna's physical body when he intensely believed himself to be Raadha yearning for a vision of Krishna; when he identified himself with Hanumaan and spent months on trees, uttering only *Raamanaama*, his anatomy changed; he grew an incipient tail. That was the measure of the depth of his *bhaava* (thought power), of the self-effacement. Use the dramatic art and the chances it gives you to develop the *saadhana* of self-effacement, for that is the quickest means of realisation of the real Self.

## Make the theatre holy and sanctifying

I must mention another point also. The author of this play is also here and you have this day honoured him for services to your Parishath and to the cause of "drama". Whenever you write a play, transform all that is low and worldly into the high and the other-worldly. Do not treat the low things as low; treat them as lapses, as mistakes, failures, incomplete attempts, errors to be avoided. Increase the *aloukika* (non-worldly) aspect of all relations between person and person. Human beings are not mere bodies, appetites, hungers and thirst, passions and prejudices. These are impediments, lapses.

Consider rather the aspirations, the ideals, the dreams of unity and universality, the struggle for truth, for mercy, for grace, for sympathy, for liberation, and depict these in the plays you write. That will change the atmosphere of the theatre and make it holy, sanctifying. You will then be helping men to become stronger and the nation to become more enduring. Now, people are sliding down the easy gradient of vice and vanity; arrest that process. Open their eyes to the chasm that yawns below.

I bless you that you succeed in raising the standard of conduct and behaviour, the standard of morals and manners, the standard of social and individual discipline and instill deep desire for discovering the inner Divinity.

*Kurnool, Zilla Parishad Hall, 5-12-1964*

## 44. Are words mere sound?

THOSE who listen to the teachings of these Pandiths have a great responsibility: they should not by their acts defile the lessons they learn. As you grow in years, detachment too should grow; as time passes by, the fruit must get ripe and become sweet. Life should not be frittered away in accumulating riches; it should be spent in knowing about the glory of God and in realising Him in the innermost being of oneself. No other intellectual exercise can give such joy. To discard this attempt as only seeking to discover the unknowable, as some men are prone to argue, is the height of foolishness. They are labelling the true as "trash" and cherishing the trash as "true"!

The *saadhaka* (spiritual aspirant) should be like a good farmer; he removes the thorny bushes and plants; he ploughs, waters, sows, manures, fences, destroys pests, and then reaps the harvest and fills his granary. Similarly, you have to remove wasteful and wicked thoughts from your heart, plough the heart with good deeds, water it with love, manure it with faith, plant the saplings of the Name of the Lord and fence the field with discipline, destroy pests with *shraddha* (faith) and reap the harvest of *jnaana*. Do not be content merely with being in *sathsangh* (good company) or thinking of God, or listening to such discourses; they are but preliminaries, helping to awaken interest in 'farming.' Many people spend all their time in fencing; they have little time left for attending to the crop which the fence is designed to protect!

What is the *jnaana* that you should achieve? It is the giving up of *deha* (identification), the escape from the belief that "you" are the "body." You say, "My hand," "My foot," just as you say, "My watch," "My shoe;" but, yet feel *you* are the body. Examine the reality of the body, and escape from this false identification; that is the hall-mark of *Jnaana*. The "I" that sees, experiences, feels, knows---that "I" is the *Paramaathma* (Supreme Soul).

## There are three types of men

The truth can flash only in a mind clear of all blemishes. The first blemish that I would like to warn you against is "inability to bear the success of others." Envy is the greatest of sins. Vanity, envy, and egoism---these three are kin. They cut at the root of man's real nature. To feel proud that you are a *bhaktha* is also a blot. Though you may be a mountain, you must feel you are a mound; though a mound, you should not pretend to be a mountain.

There are three types of men: Those who consider the *Aanandha* of others to be their own *Aanandha*; those who seek *Aanandha* for themselves, with no attention paid to the *Aanandha* of others; and those who try to prevent others from getting *Aanandha*, even at the cost of their own. There are no *Naasthikas* (atheists) really speaking, though some of you might aver that there are. For, when love is God and when even those, who do not assert that God exists, love some one or something, that love itself guarantees that they are capable of sacrifice, selflessness and pity. Probably, you believe that those who have no faith in *Vedhas* and *Shaasthras* and those who do not aver that there is some Omnipresent, Omniscient Being are atheists; but let me tell you, those who revere their parents and foster them, those who love and protect with care their brothers and sisters---these are *Aasthikas* (theists), believers in gratitude, love, affection, duty, *dharma*, etc., and these qualities are enough to save 'them' from perdition.

Love all; revere all; help all to the best of your ability. Endeavour to be as beneficial, as sweet, as soft as possible. Then the spot on which you stand become as sacred as Kaashi; the words that you utter will be as holy as scripture. This *saadhana* will lead you to Realisation.

## *Manthras* can reach the deities

*Aadhithya* (the Sun) must be propitiated by *manthras*, it was said, just now. *Aadhithya* is the deity presiding over time. Propitiate Him better by using time well; the *manthra* is the vehicle of prayer so that the *buddhi* which *Aadhithya* has accorded man may be put to the best use. You might ask how *manthra* can reach *Aadhithya*. I am surprised at the question, for you know already how it is possible for people in an aeroplane to communicate with the station they have left and the station to which they are proceeding. How do they do that? There are subtler waves which will carry the *manthras* too to the deities to whom they are addressed. The one is *yanthra shakthi* (power of instruments). If you trust in inert matter, life becomes inert; trust in the active principle and life is activated.

Then, there are people who dispute among themselves whether God is *Saguna* or *Nirguna*, (with or without attributes), *Saakaara* or *Niraakaara!* (with Form or formless). Now, who are you, among these? Are you *Saguna* or *Nirguna?* Are you *Saakaara* or *Niraakaara?* Of course you are *Saguna* and *Saakaara,* because you are with body. So long as you feel you are with body, you cannot transcend the *Saguna,* and realise the *Nirguna.* When you liberate yourselves from bondage to this limitation, you become *Nirguna.* That happens in a flash. When the Truth dawns, all is Light. There is no more darkness. There is no more fear or hate or even love. All are subsumed into the One without a Second.

## Words have tremendous power

You do not know the gem shining inside you, the Divinity whose effulgence is your to intellect, whose reflection is the *Prema* you evince. You know many other things other than this, but not this essential thing: you do not know where such and such a scholar lives in Venkatagiri, but know where a certain film star lives in Madras! This is something to be ashamed of---this loss of the sense of values! You must recognise the Higher, the Highest. Death stalks you at every step. Before he mauls you mortally, know the Truth and be blessed. The Name of the Lord is the rifle which guards you against beasts of prey in the jungle of life. The rifle makes a loud noise when the bullet is ejected fast. So too, along with the sound of the holy Name, eject the bullet of feeling too, so that the target is hit.

Nowadays, people laugh at the idea of *Naamasmarana* and *Naamasankeerthana* (remembering and singing God's holy Names). They ask, what is in a Name? It is just an assortment of sounds. My words too are assortments of sound, but, when they enter your hearts, you feel content, you feel encouraged, is it not? Words have tremendous power; they can arouse emotions and they can calm them. They direct, they infuriate, they reveal, they confuse; they are potent forces that bring up great reserves of strength and wisdom. Therefore have faith in the Name and repeat it whenever you get the chance.

*Venkatagiri, Prashaanthi Vidhwanmahaasabha, 12-12-1964*

---

*Reawakeing of man is at hand---*
*reawkening to the knowledge*
*that man himself is God.*
*The human body is not you,*
*it simply houses the soul, or*
*the spark of Divinity within,*
*for God dwells*
*in the heart of every man*
*and that indwelling spark*
*of the Divine is you---yourself.*
*All else is illusion.*
*Contemplate on that thought*
*and, when the truth unfolds,*
*you will find your true identity;*
*then your whole life pattern will change,*
*and you will see*
*everyone in the same light.*
**Shri Sathya Sai**

## 45. Ishwara grants Aishwaryam

I SEE that this quadrangle has become too small for this vast audience; but, if all of you exercise a little patience, you will be able to benefit by the discourses given by the Pandiths. If you allow the inconvenience to distract your attention, you will only be losing the chance of a lifetime.

What is the lifetime? Is it to struggle in the mire or march straight on to the eternal? You will get millions to tell you what is pleasing to you; but, it is difficult to get one in a million who can tell you what is good for you. What is good for you is akin to truth; truth is hard, but beneficial. It is unpleasant advice to tell a man to stick to truth at all costs; but, truth alone pays dividends that satisfy.

Sit quiet for a just a moment and inquire within yourself what is it that stays and what is it that does not. You try to know the news of the world, the changing fortunes of men and movements, in all the countries of the world; but you have no thirst to know about the conditions and conflicts of your own inner world happening against the permanent backdrop of the unchanging *Aathman*, which is your innermost core. Know that and everything becomes known; act and no other act is needed; possess that and all things are possessed by you!

That *Aathma* is the Universal *Aathma*; that "I" is the Universal "I." Consider the magnitude of the *Aanandha* that will fill you when you know that you are all this, that all this is you! The joy that you experience through the senses is a minute fraction of this *Aanandham*; you will not get it if the *Aathmic* bliss is not reflected through the senses. When a pot with nine holes is placed over a burning lamp, the light that comes through the holes is the light of the lamp, is it not? When the body is negated, that is to say, when the lamp is revealed, the *jyothi* (light) is seen fully; the *Aathma* is realised. But, when the thick cover of *ajnaana* (ignorance) is placed over the pot, you cannot even recognise that there is lamp inside, which illumines the senses.

## Get immersed in the Bliss of *Aathma*

There is a deep urge in man to visualise the One behind the many; scientists seek to find a law that will explain all sources of energy and all forms of matter. You can also know that, which, if known, all else can be known; only, you have to get immersed in the Bliss of *Aathma*. In the grindstone the base is steady, unmoving; the upper grinder moves; but both are stones. So too, the *chara* and the *achara* (the fixed and the changing), the base and the superstructure, are all *Brahman*. *Prakrithi* (objective world) moves; *Brahman* (Supreme Being) is steady; both are inextricably inter-related, the one with other in *Avinaabhaava-sambandha* (relationship of interdependent existence).

God should be the bedrock on which you resolve; then, life would be smooth. The physical, the mental, the objective world---these revolve around God, and if that close relationship with God is recognised, they lead you into Light. Like the strokes of the hammer, which lend shape and beauty to gold. *Aathma* gets Name and Form through the strokes of multifarious *karma*, from birth to birth. The *Aakaaram* makes it *Vikaaram* (Form makes it deformed). The deformity has to be set right by *Aadhyaathmic* rigour---spiritual discipline.

No effort is made now for this kind of discipline, no lessons are given in the educational institutions of the country. It is wrong to lay the blame on want of time; time can never obstruct it. Your are the obstructor, not time. The monkey that cannot pull out its clenched fist from the narrow neck of the pot lays the blame on the pot or the maker of the pot. But, if only it releases the hold on the peanuts it has grasped in that fist, it can easily take its hand out. The fault lies in itself. So too man's greed is the reason for this want of time. No one thrust the hand into the pot; no one forced the monkey to grab the nuts. It has become the victim of its own rapacity, that is all.

### Why should the Lord Himself incarnate?

Man too is suffering because he cannot rid himself of the greed for sense-objects and sense-pleasures (*vishaya vaasana*). He knows that he has to give up whatever he earns and collects, sooner or later; but, yet his attachment waxes instead of waning, as the years go by. If every man on earth could take with him on death, even a handful of mud from the Earth, there would have been nothing much left and mud would have been rationed at so many ounces per head!

When people forget the One and run after the Many, *Dharma* declines; for, there can be no love, no sacrifice, no detachment in human affairs then. So, the Lord takes human form and comes among men to restore his sense of values. You may ask, why should the Lord Himself incarnate? Why can He not set about the task of restoring *Dharma* through the many minor gods He has at His command? This question was passed before the courtiers by Akbar himself, for, he laughed at the Hindu idea of the Formless adopting Form, and descending into the world as an *Avathaar* to save *dharma*. Tansen asked for a week's time to furnish the answer and got it granted by His Imperial Majesty. A few days later, when he was in the pleasure boat of the Emperor sailing across the lake with his family, Tansen cleverly threw overboard a doll made to look like the Emperor's little son, crying at the same time, "O, the Prince has fallen into the water!" Hearing this, the Emperor jumped into the lake to rescue his son!

## The truth behind the Lord's incarnation

Tansen then disclosed that it was only a doll and that the son was safe. He allayed the anger of Akbar by explaining that he had perforce to enact this drama in order to demonstrate the truth of the Hindu belief that God takes human form Himself, to save *Dharma*, without commissioning some other entity to carry out that task. *Dharma* is as the son, God loves it so dearly. Akbar could have ordered one among the many personnel he had on board to jump in and rescue his son; but his affection was so great and the urgency so acute that the Emperor himself plunged into the lake to pull out the "son."

The decline of *Dharma* is so acute a tragedy; the intensity of affection that the Lord has for good men is so great that He Himself comes. The Lord is Love itself. He comes in human form so that you can talk to Him, move with Him, serve Him, adore Him, and achieve Him, so that you can recognise your kinship with Him.

People who discard the precious wisdom of the past are doomed to disaster. That is why, when people started decrying and disregarding the *Vedhas* and *Shaasthras*, they started to decline in morality and strength, courage and confidence. One argument used to find fault with the *Vedhas* by these conceited critics is that the *Varna* (caste) system is not found in advanced countries of the West, as if there too we have no religious leaders, social guardians, traders and workers and farmers. Inevitably, human society will get itself divided into these four sections, and they tend to harden into castes, each with its own moral code.

## God is the greatest mystery

What is the basic teaching of the *Vedhas*? It is that, to whichever economic or social or intellectual group you belong, you are child of Immortality, *Amrithasya puthraah*! It says that man is not a product of slime or mud; man is one who manages to live with *viveka*, so that he is able to attain the Divinity latent in him. *Ma* means *'Ajnaana'* (basic ignorance), *n*, *na* means 'without.' He who is without ignorance, who is wise, who knows himself, who knows that he is immortal, is Man.

God is the greatest mystery; the dark blue colour in which He is depicted is a symbol of the depth of that mystery. The sky and the sea are blue on account of their vast depth. Some one described the *Kaalingamardhana* (killing of the cobra Kaalinga) episode of Krishna as the height of mystery, for, in the dark depths of the dark Yamuna, where the dark sky was reflected, the dark Krishna was dancing on the dark hoods of the deadly dark cobra called Kaalinga! And, he blamed his eye which sought to visualise this scene as itself equipped with a dark cornea! Remove from the heart the darkness of vice and ignorance; then, in that white background, the *Meghashyaama*, (He whose colour is that of a rain-cloud) can easily be seen. Instead of this, man is further darkening his consciousness, while blaming God for evading his search. Seeking light, man's steps are moving further and further towards darkness; this is the pity. Better live a moment as *hamsa* (swan) on milk than live for a century as crow, feeding on carrion.

The tongue should be used for spelling the name of the Lord, not for hissing like a serpent, or growling or roaring with intention to strike terror. That is not the purpose for which the tongue is granted to man. Speech indicates one's character, reveals one's personality, educates others, and communicates experience and information. So, be vigilant about words. Slip while walking: the injury can be repaired! Slip while talking: the injury is irreparable!

## Meaning behind coconut breaking

The most desirable *Aishwaryam* (prosperity) is *Ishwara anugraha* (the Lord's Grace); that is to say, the most desirable form of wealth is the Grace of God. He will guard you, even as the lids guard the eye; do not doubt this. Faith in Providence is as the very breath of life. The bliss that it bestows has been experienced by many saints and sages, who have, with faith in their hearts, withstood the onslaughts of poverty, neglect and cruelty. Instead of fixing attention on this, man fritters his energy on collecting tawdry tinsel, forgetting the diamonds he could well have. Both are available on earth; but man is led by glitter and not by worth.

When you break a coconut in the temple, you should feel that your egoism is broken too. The coconut offering is not made so that God may consume the kernel! It is a symbol of the destruction of *Ahamkaara* (egoism), which has to split into two at one stroke, the stroke of wisdom. When do you get that effect? When does the coconut break at one stroke? When the fibrous cover of the shell is removed, is it not? So too, man must remove the fibrous matter that encases his heart---lust, anger, envy and the rest of the wicked brood. Man is the repository of vast power; he is no weakling. It is the *dhur-vaasanas* (vicious tendencies) that make him weak. Draw inspiration from the Divine in you and earn the glory of being good, sincere, honest, self-sacrificing, lovable. Hear good things, see good, do good, think good; then, all the evil tendencies will be uprooted.

## Training ground for spiritual life

You can be involved in *samsaara* or the qualities of life. But, remember, no harm can accrue if you consider the life of a house-holder, with wife and children, as a training ground for spiritual life. You wear glasses to correct the vision, to improve the sight. So too, enter the family, society and also politics to correct the vision and improve the sight. Use the opportunities confronting you there for developing detachment and self-sacrifice. If you don't, you are like the fool who puts on wrong glasses and spoils his vision!

This mike is in front of Me, obstructing Me from some of those before Me! But, you put up with it, because you can hear Me better on account of it. So also, you must put up with the body that you are encased in, for, it enables you to realise the Reality, the Divine that you are. It is a means to that glorious end. It is not an end in itself. It may be fed well, clothed well, kept well, housed well---but, yet, if you have not delved into the depths of Joy that lies in you, it will have no peace. That

Joy is immeasurable, indescribable. The joy derivable from material possessions is limited, in danger of diminution or destruction. Too much of material comfort is harmful to health and happiness. Too many dishes spoil the banquet, and turn the appetite askew.

There are many women present and so, I must tell them this: though they have faith and devotion, they promote *ashaanthi* (turmoil) by their attitudes and behaviour. They have a great responsibility which they have neglected; anxiety and worry are growing in the family and in society due to their neglecting the discipline that trains people to live self-controlled lives. They do not distinguish between a cinema hall, a market or an exhibition, but talk and chatter everywhere, even in a temple, or a holy gathering. Children learn from them and they too when they grow up lose all reverence for elders and holy places. They talk loud and long and very irreverently, and add to the *ashaanthi*, instead of reducing it. They were once the pillars of *dharma* but, now, do not know what it means, how it has to be practised in daily life.

## Means must be as pure as the end

Once you have tasted *Amrith* (nectar), can you relish any other food? India has once tasted the *Amrith* of *Sanaathana Dharma* (Eternal Religion); how foolish is it then to run after foulness and frivolity? There are some cynics who spurn *Sanaathana Dharma* as out of date, meaningless, foolish, etc. This is because that *Dharma* insists that the means must be as pure as the end, that every act must be done as efficiently as an act of worship, that true Love must forget all differences of status, age and wealth, that without self-control and detachment, man cannot claim humanity. A man can nowadays become a 'hero' for millions, without acquiring any virtue, being a 'zero' so far as *Dharma* or morals are concerned. That is the sad state of affairs. An image is seen as a stone; but, in the past, in every stone, they saw the Divine, lying latent. Now, intelligence is the handmaid of cleverness; then, it was the first step towards wisdom, which saw all things as permeated by the Divine Principle.

If your wish is not fulfilled, you start blaming the God to whom you prayed; the fault lies in you, in your not having the needed qualification to earn the fulfilment. Or, it may lie in the feeling at the back of the wish. You cannot discover which. My acts are the foundations on which I am building My work, the Task for which I have come. All the "miraculous acts" which you observe are to be interpreted so. The foundation for a dam requires a variety of materials; without these, it will not last and hold back the waters.

## Purpose of "miraculous acts"

When the Lord has incarnated, He has to be used in various ways by man, for his uplift. Krishna held aloft the Govardhana Giri, not to demonstrate His *siddhi* or attainment, but to protect the *gopas* and *gopees* (cowherd boys and girls) and the cattle they held dear. He had to do something which man could not accomplish. He had no intention to publicise Himself. Only inferior minds will revel in publicity and self-aggrandisement. These have no relevance in the case of *Avathaars*. They need no advertisement. Those who decry the superhuman are the ignorant or the wicked, that is, those who have no authority to judge the spiritual. The establishment of *Dharma* is My aim; the teaching of *Dharma*, the spread of *Dharma*---that is my objective. These "miracles" as you call them are just a few means towards that end.

Some people remark that Raamakrishna Paramahamsa said that *siddhis* are obstructions in the path of the *saadhaka* (spiritual aspirant). Of course they are; he may be led astray by *siddhis*; he has to keep straight on without being involved in them. His ego will increase if he yields to the temptation of demonstrating his *siddhis*. This correct advice, which every *saadhaka* should heed.

## Cynics carp without knowledge

The mistake lies in equating Me with the *saadhaka* whom Raamakrishna wanted to help, guide and warn. This is merely the nature of *Avathaara*: the creation of things, *ab initio*, with intent to protect, guard and give joy, a creation that is spontaneous and lasting. Creation, Preservation and Dissolution---these three, only the Almighty can accomplish; no one else can. Cynics carp without knowledge. If they learn the *Shaasthras*, they can understand Me, or they should cultivate direct experience.

Your innate laziness prevents you from the spiritual exercises necessary to discover the nature of Godhead. The *Guru* says, "Through *karma*, clarify your intellect." The disciple is lazy; he prefers *dhyaana*, sitting quiet in one place. After a few attempts, he asks that some other path be laid down for him. The laziness should go out of man's nature, in whatever shape it appears. That is My mission. This is the first step in converting *Maanava* into *Maadhava*---man into God.

God alone is eternal, man is a momentary flash, a tiny wavelet, that rises and falls. So, fill yourselves with vast thoughts, magnificent ideas, indefinable splendour, by reciting the Names of God, names that describe Him to your receptive consciousness. That is the main discipline for this Age.

*Venkatagiri, Prashaanthi Vidwanmahaasabha, 13-12-1964*

## 46. The human raft

MAN is the victim of many a pain; to those who identify themselves with body, life is a series of trouble and misery. But to those who know that the body is but a vehicle, these cannot cause anxiety. I must emphasise this now, when I am inaugurating this Primary Health Centre. Bodily health is important, for ill-health affects mental poise and concentration. When the body is fit, mental functions too run smooth; when the body suffers, the mind too gets unsettled. So, this raft called body which is the only means of getting across the sea of *samsaara* (worldly life), has to be kept in good trim.

Untruth, injustice, anxiety---all cause leaks and loosen the knots of the raft. With such a poor raft, it is foolish to attempt the crossing. The raft has to be cast aside when the crossing has been effected; there is no more use for it. The human raft is the most efficient, for it is built out of *viveka, vichakshana* and *vairaagya* (discrimination, ability and non-attachment), hard timber that can stand the beat of wave and the sway of current. If one does not make the best use of this chance, it may not come again for a long long time.

Devotion and morality are as important for physical health as they are for mental health. They free the mind from agitation, they feed it with joy and contentment; they quieten the nerves and help even bodily processes. The flowers of this garland were buds yesterday; they bloomed this morning; they have started to fade now and tomorrow they will rot and dry. But, the string that holds them together interpenetrating them, is not subject to such change; It was string yesterday, it is string now and it will be string tomorrow. The unchanging *Aathma* and the changing *body*---analyse them thus and be convinced of the eternal universal core of your being. As a thinking, discriminating human being, it is your responsibility to discharge this duty to yourself. And also to your country! For, India deserved the honour of the "World Teacher" because her people always insisted on this great responsibility and tried to discharge it. But, when Indians neglected this and attached value to physical comfort and social status, the land fell into the morass of competitive struggle.

## Treat your family as a sacred trust

Now, man encased in rockets takes pride in zooming round the world at terrible speeds and even racing to the moon; but he has not succeeded in penetrating even an inch into the innermost recess of his own mind and controlling the vagaries rampant there. To save yourself from being carried away by the current of change, you must swim up the river, which is a hard enterprising process, indeed.

Hold all your property and wealth in trust for the Lord who gave them to you; even your family, you must treat as a sacred trust, as persons given to you by the Lord to love, foster and guide. Thus, you must elevate your attachment into worship and make it an instrument for spiritual progress.

Minister Balaraami Reddy expressed his wish that this Health Centre, named after Velugota Venkataraaja Gopaalakrishna Yachendhra, should prosper from year to year. But a hospital's progress is to be judged, not by the number of patients coming for treatment. It must educate the people around in the principles of health and see that the area is freed from disease. And among the means to ensure health, spiritual discipline is the most important.

## Let your love flow towards all

You should not be ever entangled in the meshes of this world and its problems. Try to escape into the purer air of the spirit as often as you can, taking the name of the Lord on your tongue. Of the 24 hours of the day, have 6 hours for your individual needs, 6 hours for the service of others, 6 hours for sleep and 6 for dwelling in the Presence of the Lord. Those six hours will endow you with the strength of steel.

Gopaalakrishna Yachendhra, the Chairman, described the green fields that surround the villages and declared that there is nothing so congenial to happiness as village life. Villages are the backbone of the nation. Cities pant for the contentment and joy of villages. Cities are lost in confusion, noise and selfish fury. The ryots who till the soil and feed the people are indeed holy men, who help their brothers and sisters in their dire need. They bear hard toil, silently and gladly. But you need not feel small. Be like gods and you can partake of *Amritha* (nectar), as the gods did once. If you are like *Asuras* (demons), you can have no share in the Divine Nectar.

Let your love flow towards all; you have love but, now, it is distributed selfishly and sparingly. Or at least, do not hate other people and talk ill of them or seek to estimate their faults. Do not feel sad or hurt when others are happy; try to share their happiness and be happy yourself, when those around you are. Your speech has to be soft and sweet; do not imitate the roar of the lion or the hiss of the serpent. In a village where everybody knows everyone else and where living is so intimate and interdependent, this kind of sweet talk, motivated by love, is essential. The tongue is now the sharpest weapon in the armoury of the villager; it ruins many homes, it divides brothers and neighbours; it does more havoc than a bomb!

**Let not pests of greed spoil the harvest of plenty**

This Health Centre will become efficient if villagers appreciate its service and co-operate with these doctors and if you do not frustrate its efforts by wrangling among yourselves. Develop love and co-operation; then villages can thrive. Otherwise, even the best of intentions on the part of the Venkatagiri Royal Family or Government Agencies will be frustrated. The presence of the Minister and of the President of the Samithi here is a sign that they will do their best for you; it now lies with you whether you will make the best use of the help that they so readily grant. If you do that, I know, the Venkatagiri Royal Family will be really happy.

I have to tell you something more about this Health Centre. The Malayaala Swaami who made this place famous and popular by establishing his *Aashram* and School was desirous that a hospital should be added to the amenities of this village. Now that this Centre is inaugurated, his wish has been fulfilled. Let not the pests of anger, lust and greed spoil the harvest of plenty that you seek through your earnestness and steadiness. Do not use your hands to harm or injure another; use them rather to beat time, when you recite the Names of the Lord, Names which are redolent with His Glory. That is my advice to you today.

*Yerpedu, 14-12-1964*

## 47. You are born for your own sake

THE Prashaanthi Vidwanmahaasabha is meeting here for the second time and I am glad I am here to witness the dawn of *Aanandha* that is lighting up every face. I have also come to confer on you *Aanandham*. Really, all this misery is caused by mankind itself, not by any extraneous agency. Having all the instruments of joy and contentment in one's possession, if man is miserable, it is only due to his perverseness, his stupidity. He has been warned, over centuries, by the scriptures of all languages that he should give up greed and lust, give up the habit of catering to the senses, give the belief that he is just this body and nothing more. But, yet, he does not know the illness that is torturing him.

The disease is due to 'vitamin deficiency,' as they say; the vitamins are *sathya, dharma, shaanthi* and *prema* (truth, righteousness, peace and divine love). Take them and you recover; assimilate them into your character and conduct and you shine with fine mental and physical health. The more material wealth you collect, the greater the bother and the greater the sorrow when death calls. You have no peace if you struggle to win it through the accumulation of wealth. You have come from your villages, so many thousands of you, to this place to see Sai Baaba and to hear Him, is it not? Well, over and above those two aims, you must have a third one too. You must also see yourself, and hear your inner voice, urging you to discover your own truth. I am prompting you to discover your Reality. That is My Mission.

## Save yourself by yourself

You should not be swayed by the demon of doubt. Doubt comes only from ignorance; it disappears when knowledge dawns. When a man was riding on horseback with another carrying a bed behind him, passersby concluded that the rider was the master and the man behind was his servant. When both reached a caravanserai and when the rider was feeding the horse and the man with the bed was sleeping on it in the verandah, men thought the former was the servant and the latter, the master! Conclusions drawn on flimsy grounds are always subject to revision. You are born for your own sake, not for the sake of any one else. You have to cure yourself of the disease of ignorance, just as you have to cure yourself of the disease of hunger. No one else can save you from both. "*Uddhareth aathma-na athmaanam*": "Save yourself by yourself."

God is in you, but like the woman, who fears that her necklace has been stolen or lost, recognises that she has it round her neck when she passes a mirror, man too will recognise that God is in him, when some *Guru* reminds him of it. The joy that you then get is incomparable. Every Indian must realise that the science of self-discovery is self-heritage. He must value it and earn it. Now, there are many scholars, able to expound that heritage, but few who practise it and earn the reward. That science was explored by sages and laid down in clear and simple terms. Not to know it and not to practise it is the greatest loss that this country suffers from. Fancy for *naveenam* (the modern) in preference to the *sanaathanam* (the classical and the eternal), is the cause of this misery. Sugarcane should not be equated with any cane! Only those who do not know the taste of sugar will do so.

Seek *jnaanam* (spiritual knowledge), which is the seat of sweetness. Get rid of the desire for sense-enjoyment, which like the pleasure you get while scratching itching eczema, only makes the complaint worse. You cannot cure it by yielding to the temptation to scratch. The more you scratch, the more you are tempted to continue, until bleeding intervenes. So, desist from that vain pursuit and concentrate on spiritual matters, or at least, move in the world with the everpresent consciousness that it is a morass, a net, a trap, into which attachment and desire will precipitate you. Be a true *bhaktha* and become so small that you wriggle out of the shackles of the senses or be a true *jnaani* and become so huge, that you escape by breaking the shackles.

*Naayudupet, 16-12-1964*

---

*Every being needs Prema, inhales and exales Prema, for Prema is the basic breath;*

*everyone is the embodiment of Prema.*

*Love knows no fear, so love needs no falsehood to support it.*

*Love seeks no reward; love is its own reward.*

**Shri Sathya Sai**

## 48. Diagnose your own disease

ON My way to this place, thousands of eager men and women stood across and insisted that I should meet them at the Sai Mandhiram. Some delay was caused thereby. I could not come here in time. I have therefore to shorten My discourse to you. *Bhakthas* bind Me; I have no chance to have My way when people plead so. My *Aanandham* as well as their *Aanandham* were both indescribable. On account of this delay, I know, some people left and went home. Well; yours is the luck; you stayed on. The chakora bird gulps the first rain-drops as they fall; it waits long and with profound yearning. It is content if four drops wet its parched throat.

Life is many-directional; it has many faces. But, there are some directions which are auspicious, some which are ruinous. Most of it is spent in pursuit of mirages, in building castles in the air. Keenness to slake the thirst in the mirage-lake is never satisfied. Desire multiplies itself; the fulfilment of one leads to proliferation into many. You can never say, "That ends all my desires; I have no more wants." The love that is concentrated on oneself is as a bulb that illuminates the room only, without shedding light outside the four walls. It is confined to the senses and never opens out to others, who are your kith and kin in God.

There is another type of love, larger and deeper, which expands into the members of one's family. It is as moonlight, not strong enough to make things clear, but, enough to move about in. It also undergoes rise and fall, increase and decrease. But the most desirable type of love is as sunlight, ever engaged in purifying, activating, illumining, knowing no distinction. This love will make man act ever in the spirit of dedication to the Lord. And, so, the acts too would be elevating and holy.

## Liberation gives the highest Bliss

Dedication is different from service; in service, there is the element of ego. "I serve, He is the master, He requires my service, I am necessary for Him." But, in dedication, the I is wiped out. There is no desire for the fruit; the joy consists in the act being done. To cultivate that attitude of dedication, every one must think of God, remember the Name of God and deepen faith in God. University degrees will not give, riches cannot buy, kinsmen cannot hand over and teachers cannot confer the pre-requisites for *Shaanthi*---Faith and Devotion.

The most chronic disease of man is *Ajnaana*---ignorance of the undying *Aathma* within him. One must know the reason why he caught this aphasia and try to get cured. The general cause of this illness is infatuation for the objective world and subservience to senses. There is even a deeper cause : the undue prominence given to the body, imagining it to be the touchstone of value. The body is like a temporary shelter where you reside for a short while, on your journey. The *gamyam* is *kaivalyam*---the goal is liberation. Liberation gives the highest Bliss.

Have faith in the Ocean, not the wave; believe in the Lord, not in little things. But, the tragedy is, you put your trust in little men, in wicked men, in men who you know are vicious and greedy; but you hesitate when asked to put faith in the Lord, who is more merciful than any father, more loving than any mother, more powerful than any earthly authority, more considerate than any kinsman. You do not doubt each other; but, you develop doubt regarding God. Even laymen talk long and loud when the topic for discussion is 'God!' No one asks them their credentials.

## God asks for the heart, the full heart

'Doubt' is easy and faith difficult. Dwell on the *Naama* and its sweetness will saturate your tongue and improve your taste. Do not count the number of times you have repeated it. For, whom are you going to impress with the number? The Lord will respond even if you call Him just once from the depths of feeling; He will be deaf, even if you call Him a million times, automatically, artificially, with the tongue not with the heart. It is easy to amass figures.

When Akbar challenged his courtiers to give him the exact number of birds in Delhi, one illiterate servant offered to do it. After a few days, he came to the court and said that there were 99 lakhs 99 thousands of them! "Suppose, I have the figure verified and it is found that there are more, what punishment shall I inflict on you for your wrong calculation?" asked the Emperor. The servant said, "Some might have flown in from the surrounding areas." "What if the total number is found to be less?" asked the Emperor. "Some birds must have flown out of the City," he replied coolly. Numbers are easy to manipulate, but Grace does not depend upon them at all. He asks for the heart, the full heart and nothing but the heart.

If the heart has many leaks, the sweetness will be drained away and you cannot offer Him the full heart. Egoism, pride, thirst for fame---all these are leaks; if you donate something to a good cause, hoping that your name will appear in the *Andhra Patrika*, exulting when it is seen there, dejected when it is not found, then that charity springs a leak. Such sacrifice is superficial and selfish. The seeds will sprout only when they are well within the soil, not when they are on the surface. Karna lost his life when he recalled in despair the sacrifices he had made; they should not be counted in the memory.

## "The fever of arrogant youth"

Bargaining and calculating are useless in the spiritual field. You cannot higgle with the Lord and ask for proportionate rewards. Ask for proportionate reward and you lose all. He has his own arithmetic. Food, Head, God---that is the series; eat food for developing the intelligence, the head; then, with that intelligence, realise God. The senses can inform you only of the obvious, what comes within their ken. But, the intuition of the sages as recorded in the *Vedhas* speaks of that which cannot be reached by the senses or intellect or imagination. To treat the *Vedhas* lightly is the height of foolishness.

"The fever of arrogant youth," which I call *Youvana sannipaatham*, fogs the intellect and makes youth ungrateful and callous. Parents are neglected; elders are dishonoured; teachers are ridiculed; scriptures are scoffed at by them. They boast that they will not bow their heads to any one; but, they have to bow their heads at least to the barber! They cause grief to the very persons to whom they owe their very life. Do not be led away by the belief that this is respectable. Have as your ideal Lakshmana or Dharmaraaja or Seetha or Meera. Strive to see good things, hear good things, speak soft and sweet, instal the Lord in the altar of your heart. Believe in the consequences of *karma*, done now and in the past. No one can avoid the reactions of his actions; the effects have to be consumed by the 'actor' himself.

## Serve to share and spread *Aanandha*

You are undergoing training to become better *Graamasevakas* (village social workers); this is a great chance that has come in your way to render *seva* (service) and to share and spread *Aanandha*. The *seva* that you do will become useful and lasting, provided you invite great *Pandiths* to the village and through them instruct the villagers to cultivate contact with the Lord: devotion to God, love towards men. I wish that you strive to provide *bhajans, keerthanas* and *Harikathas* in order to inspire them towards the higher life of the spirit.

It is now rather late; the night is already far advanced. I am going to Madras right from here, but, it does not matter to Me; I do not care about the exhaustion; but, you have to reach home and many of you have gathered from the villages around. So, I shall stop now. I feel the exhaustion only when you do not practise what I tell you. If you are determined to act according to My advice, I shall be with you all the 24 hours. Now, I ask you only to ruminate, like the cow, on the precious words you have heard and assimilate them into your life.

*Village Level Workers' Training Centre,*
*Kaalahasthi, 17-12-1964*

## 49. No srama in aashrama

I HAVE been moving about in this region for fifteen years but, this is the first occasion on which I have appeared in this charming *Aashram*. I need not say that this is a great chance for you, a *Sumuhuurtham,* as they say, an event of auspiciousness. A State will have a Constitution and a set of great laws; *Sanaathana Dharma* is the law and the *Vedhas* are the Constitution of the State of Man. These were laid down by sages who "saw" them in their moments of ecstatic intuition; that is why they are called *Seers.* Hence the *Vedhas* are called *A-pourusheya* (not ascribable to any particular author). They are named *Shruthi,* that which is heard, remembered, and held as a treasure in the memories of men. The *Vedhas* are their own authority; just as the eye is the judge of what the eye reveals. You cannot smell a thing and judge its colour. So the *Vedhas* have to be judged by the *Vedhas* only; the experience of the sages has to be tested by sages who seek that experience through the processes laid down in the *Vedhas*; and, in every case the process is followed, the experience is won, correctly and clearly as described.

The *Vedhas* have to be practised; that is the purpose of these revelations. Merely learning them by rote is of no use. The *Uththarameemaamsa* section provides the knowledge necessary to liberate oneself from bondage and blindness. That is called *Brahmajnaana*, for, when one reaches a certain stage in *saadhana*, he realises that all this is identical with *Brahman*, which is cause and effect, being and becoming, both.

The *Bhaarathabhuumi* (land of Bhaarath) which is inherently *Yogabhuumi* and *Thyaagabhuumi* (land of godliness and sacrifice) is being dragged along the tracks of other *Bhogabhuumis* (lands of enjoyment), and putting on the paraphernalia of worldly happiness. This is the path of ignorance, of hatred, of greed, of wickedness, and competition. What the *Rishis* laid down is the best, for, they trained themselves to be impartial and detached. The teachings of the *Vedhas* were explained and elaborated in the Raamaayana, Mahaabhaaratha and Bhaagavatha, and in the commentaries by Shankara, Raamaanuja and Madhvachaarya. Even those who were the custodians of *Vedhic* learning have now neglected it and taken to lesser studies.

## Dedicate your work as offering to the Lord

Vimalaanandha, the Head of this *Aashram*, was in the previous status of life, at Prashaanthi Nilayam for about a year. He had asked for My Blessings when he took up this responsibility and this *Sanyaasi's* status, on the passing away of his *Guru*, the Malayaala Swaami. Like the ocean calling to the river, the role of a monk was calling him; the *jeeva* and the *Aathma* are so inextricably associated. It is the devotion and *saadhana* of aspirants that has taken such grand shape here. Do not ascribe it to one person; he inspired, but hundreds caught the inspiration, and dedicated themselves to the task. Raama did not live in the forest, away from the cities, for the sake of its charm; he took it as an opportunity to be of service to the *Maharishis* doing penance there, eager to come face to face with God. He moved about so that He could give *Aanandha* to them. Malayaala Swaami came here to help the *saadhakas* and the efforts of devotees are clear in the development of this *Aashram*.

## Have a pure sense of vision and hearing

People have read much; but, how much of their reading have they applied in life? They repeat that the senses are enemies of the higher life; but they continue to be their slaves. Have a pure vision; then, you will not find faults in others. Have a pure sense of hearing; then, you will not relish the scandals regarding others scattered by foolish men, who do not know that they are but scandalising themselves. Care more for *Sarveshwara Chintha*—thought of the Lord of All; not *Sareera Chintha*—thought of the care and upkeep of the perishable body.

Every farmer knows that good seeds must be sown for getting a rich harvest. If the seeds are bad, his efforts are fruitless. Sow the seeds called Name of God in the well-prepared field of the heart; feed it with the manure of Faith; have Discipline as the fence to keep out stray cattle. Without a fence guarding the crop, farming will be like shooting without a bullet: all sound and no game!

Prayer must come from the depths of feeling; the Lord looks for *bhaava* (sincerity of feeling), not *baahya* (outward pomp). With feeling, you can make the Divine Heart bloom in joy. The *Karma kaanda* and the *Upaasana kaanda* (sections of the *Vedhas* dealing with rituals and worship) insist on the worship of God and devotion to Him. They sing His Glory and instruct man how to meditate on His splendour. They say that He is known by many Names and appears under many Forms. *Ekam sath*, they say: only One exists; but, *Vipraah bahudhaa vadhanthi*---but, the same One is known and described in many different ways by the wise. To know that you are that One, and therefore Immortal, is your right, your heritage. That is why the *Vedhas* acclaim man as *Amrithasya Puthraah*: Children of Immortality.

## The *Guru* dispels darkness like the Sun

Act in conformity with that ancestry, that status. The generality of people are unaware of the Glory and Grace of God; the Malayaala Swaami made every one who came to him understand the Real behind the Unreal. He had known it by study and *saadhana*. The *Guru* is the teacher of *Aathma-vidhya* (science of the Self); he dispels darkness, like the Sun. His *sankalpa* (resolve) is that this *Aashram* must progress in the task of spiritual enlightenment. Vimalaanandha wrote to Me, when he was selected to succeed him as head of this *Aashram* asking for My blessings. I wrote back "Since he has selected you, his blessings will guard and guide you and you will surely achieve *Digvijaya* (conquest in all directions)." He was a little nervous, not because he had no faith in the efficacy of the *Guru's* blessings, but because he had little experience in bearing such burdens. I am glad all those attached to the Malayaala Swaami and this *Aashram* have strung together their loyalties and prepared a garland for honouring Vimalaanandha.

You have a committee of elders, who will also look after the affairs and come to his help. Every one should be prompted by reverence to the *Guru* which means not worshipping his photograph, but acting according to his orders, his commands, his *Aajna*. If you are right on the path laid down by him, then you can march boldly on, regardless of praise or blame. Do not doubt this.

Here I must tell you something about Myself, like leaving a Visiting Card, here. My task is not merely to cure and console, remove individual misery. It is something far more important. The important task of the mango tree is to produce mango fruits. The leaves, the branches, and the trunk of the tree are useful, in their own way, no doubt; but the main aim is the fruit. So also from the plantain tree, the fruit is the main gain. The leaves, the edible core of the stem, these are all incidental. So too the removal of misery and distress is incidental to My Mission.

### Lord's resolve cannot be hindered

My main task is the re-establishment of *Vedhas* and *Shaasthras* in the heart of *Bhaarathavarsha* and the revival of knowledge about them in the people. This task will succeed; it will not be impeded by any obstacle. It will not be limited or slowed. When the Lord decides and wills, His *Sankalpa* (Resolve) cannot be hindered; it will not be hindered. You must have heard people say that Mine is all magic, black or white. Well, these people may also say that Krishna lifted Govardhanagiri by means of black magic, or that Raama built a bridge over the sea, by black magic!

Of course, there is magic in the world both white and black; but, the manifestation of Divine Power must not be interpreted as magic. Can the crow's egg and the cuckoo's egg be identified as belonging to one class? Magicians play their tricks for earning a livelihood. They use it for worldly fame and wealth. They are based on falsehood and they thrive on deceit and ignorance. This Body can never stoop to that level. No; never. This Body has come through Divine *Sankalpa* (the Lord's Resolve), to come. That resolve is intended to uphold *Sathya*. *Bhagavath-sankalpa* (God's resolve) is always *Sathya-sankalpa* (resolve that comes true). Everyone knows the strict discipline of Prashaanthi Nilayam; the order is "Not even a flower is to be brought!" Due to ignorance and vicious motives they do not grasp correctly the nature of *Sai Shakthi*. They interpret it as something else. That *shakthi* (power) is unlimited; the fault lies in their vision, if they cannot see it as it is. There is nothing that Divine Power cannot accomplish.

It can transmute earth into sky and sky into earth. To doubt this is to prove that you are too weak to grasp the grandeur of the Universal.

## Honour the *Dharma* of your profession

I have come to instruct all in the essence of the *Vedhas*, to shower on all this precious gift, to protect and preserve *Sanaathana Dharma*. Each profession has a *Dharma*, a set of moral restrictions and regulations guiding its exercise; if these are honoured, then the joy of the participant will go on adding itself, plus, plus, plus. There are differences of innate characteristics, impulses, attitudes, prejudices, excellences and character tendencies which mark out man from man. You do not treat all mangoes alike and buy them in a lot; some may be sour, some small, some big, some tastier, some tasteless, some juicy, some fibrous, etc. You appreciate them by their taste, is it not? You select them according to the species, the *jaathi*.

Of course, all are equal before the Lord; no one has any special claim for preference, except probably the miserable and the distraught. But, in human societies, there must be distinction based on qualification and merit, whether it be intellectual, moral or spiritual. If all felt that the goal is the same, there will not be faction and fights on the way. The work that each does is important for the whole community; there is no high or low. It is not for this, that one has to compete with others; these earthly statuses and superiorities and inferiorities are tawdry tinsel, temporary pinpricks. Compete with others in the quickness with which you march on to God. Years ago, this place was deserted waste; today, it has become so full of promise, so rich in spiritual potentiality. How did this happen? How did the plan of Malayaala Swaami bear fruit? Because he stuck to his ideal; his spiritual authority was respected.

## Insist on discipline during student-life

You must observe strictly the *karmas* (duties) laid down in the *Vedha*, for you are teaching the *Vedhas* here. Men must observe the *Dharma* laid down for them and must be allotted the status they have to be given; women must be allotted the status allowed for them. Both are the children of God, no doubt; but, discipline demands that men and women must be allotted the spheres that are conducive to *Dharmic* life. Insist on discipline during student-life; only good can come out of this strictness. Let boys and girls grow as disciplined, self-restrained citizens; that is a greater contribution to the country than a number of well-read but ill-disciplined persons, who will plunge society into confusion. Those who are engaged in the game will be so immersed in its hurly-burly that they may not see it whole. The spectator will be able to give better directions for playing the game. So, respect the advice of those who come and see.

The *Samaadhi* (memorial structure) that you have built for your *Guru*, Malayaala Swaami, is proclaiming the devotion you have towards Him. That devotion must be evident in every act and thought of yours; see that you follow his teachings and demonstrate that you deserve to be known as his disciples, by even the smallest act of yours being filled with the Love that a true

*Adhwaithin* will have. The Malayaala Swaami had saturated his mind in the Geetha. He had dedicated himself to the Geetha ideal.

He placed this *Aashram* on the shoulders of Vimalaanandha and passed away. Now, all those who revere him must give full support to Vimalaanandha Swaami and see that the *Guru's* command is fulfilled. The *Aajna* (command) should not be neglected or ignored. I have much to speak to Vimalaanandha Swaami taking him apart. So, I shall stop now. I am happy that I came to this place and shared My *Aanandha* with you all. I changed the programme for today and came here in order to meet you and Vimalaanandha Swaami.

*Vyaasaashram, Yerpedu, 17-12-1964*

---

*Good Conduct has to be
the main key to life of men.
It is the way of living the path of virtue,
that keeps one in the memory of people
long after death.
If it is not the virtuous way,
the person is as good as dead.
It is often declared that
knowledge is power.
No, No. Character is power.
Nothing can be more powerful
on earth than character.*

**Shri Sathya Sai**

## 50. Beacon in the dark

THE reason why this land is today plunged in various types of distress is to be sought in our own deeds, behaviour and relations with others, which deny the faith in the innate divinity within us! Of what benefit is it to lament when stricken by disease? One ought to lament and be warned when the first false step was taken towards damaging the health. Ignorance of the rules of health, gleaned by the experience of generations, is the root cause of the illness which had laid India low. The ancients had discovered a cure for death itself and for birth which is the concomitant of death. They were votaries of *Mrithyunjaya* (the victor over death), not of Death which many nations worship today out of their greed for glory.

We praise our ancient seers but discard their heritage; we revere the texts they collected, but disregard their teachings. We expound their doctrines and discoveries, but decline to practise them! We are beggars living in a house of gold. The fact that it is precious metal that surrounds us is unknown. Discover it and you are saved!

This is called *Praaptha-praapthi* (attaining the already existing). This mike was purchased from a shop; it was not in the possession of the man who wanted it. But, peace and joy are not like this mike. They are not available in shops; they are in the possession of the very men who are in need of these. A friend comes into your room when you are desperately in need of money and you ask him for a loan; but, just then, quite by accident, he finds inside the pages of a book from your book-shelf that he starts reading, a tenner that you had kept there and forgotten. It is your money, but you had ignored it; it was out of sight; he drew your attention to its existence and saved you from the shame of a loan. That is an example of *Praaptha-praapthi*. The Guru reveals the treasure within.

## Spread the rules of religion

More than the *Guru*, the *Guri* (Goal) is essential for attaining the Divine. The very pursuit of the goal will evoke the *Sathwa guna* (quality of serenity) and weaken the hold of the inferior *Rajas* and *Thamas* (qualities of passion and inertia) in your composition. *Dhaanavathwam* (fiendishness) is caused by *Thamas* and *Maanavathwam* (human nature), is stabilised by *Rajas*; but, *Sathwa* alone can guarantee the elevation into Divinity. *Sathwa guna* fertilises the upward tendencies of man; it cleanses the mind, removing the weeds of evil. *Sathya* is the very basis of *Sathwa guna*. *Sathya* and *Sathkarma* (Truth in word, deed and thought) are acts, which are beneficial to others.

*Matham* (religion), wherever it is practised, by whomsoever established, lays down the rules and regulations by which the *Sathwa guna* can be fostered and the impact of the two other *gunas* (human qualities) lessened. Therefore, it is very necessary that the adherents of religion spread the knowledge of these rules, both by precept and example. Christians and

Muslims carry on this work with great enthusiasm; but the followers of *Sanaathana Dharma* have not got the faith in its excellence which alone can induce them to talk about it to others, and to make others listen to their talk. I find many are ashamed to accept the principles of *Sanaathana Dharma* (Eternal Religion), like *Varnaashrama, Vigraha aaradhana* (division of castes, idol worship), etc.

While western aspirants find the ancient texts of *Sanaathana Dharma* valuable sources of inspiration and they adore Bhaarath as a beacon in the darkness, the children of Bhaarath admire the tawdry victories in the field of material research which other countries have won. The *Vedhas* and the *Shaasthras* are the two eyes of *Bhaarathamaatha*; by neglecting both, her vision is dimmed and damaged. Her vision can regain its clarity and sharpness, only when the *Vedhas* and *Shaasthras* enter into the daily life of her children. Then, the children will have faith in the Supreme, and in their destiny of ultimate merger with it. This will make them true devotees, for they will then be devoted to their true Goal.

## *Bhaktha* is the supremest creation

When Naaradha once told the Lord that the earth was the grandest in creation, doubt was raised, because the ocean occupies more than two-thirds of it. But, the ocean was drunk dry by the sage Agasthya, who is but one single star in the vast firmament. Can we then count the sky as the grandest in creation? No, for the Lords Thrivikrama strode the sky with His one Foot! However, even the Lord, who encompasses the three regions, is imprisoned by the *bhaktha* in his heart. Therefore, it was decided that the *bhaktha* is the supremest in creation. Such is the glory of the *bhaktha*, a glory that is conferred by his close study and practise of the *Shaasthras*.

The *Shaasthras* are now kept at a distance, because people are unaware of the sweetness and light that they can acquire through them. They are condemned as outdated, as kill joys, as unduly restrictive and reactionary. But, all this is simply the patient's condemnation of the doctor and the drug that can cure him. The patient is suffering from anxiety, fear, despair, cowardice, greed, envy and the consequent weakness of mind and body. The *Shaasthras* can confer on him peace, courage, confidence, contentment and friendliness, if only he would take the first step of obeying their dictates. For, the very first lesson they teach is the Immanence of God. God is in the heart of every being, and so, one has to love another, as one loves God. God is residing in one's own heart and so there is no need to fear or despair. How can you hate another, when the God you adore is in him too? How can you covet his wealth? Or compete with him? Or be deaf to his entreaty?

## Scholars should not feel scholarship as burden

The body is the tabernacle of God, the chariot in which He is seated in all majesty. Do not identify yourself with it and its modifications and transformations. You are the *Aathma* and so, you are above these affections of the body. Cleanse your mind of the temptations and tenets of ignorance; make it free from dust, so that God may be reflected therein. God cares more for the motive behind the deed, the ideal that prompts the effort—the *bhaava* (depth of feeling), not the *baahya* (outer pomp). The goldsmith who is purchasing the golden idol offers equal sums for every gram of gold, whether the gold is the crown, the foot or the head of the idol. God too says, "I care for the depth of your thirst for Me. I do not care what Form you select for your adoration."

This Prashaanthi Vidwanmahaasabha has been formed to teach men this path and this endeavour, revive this pilgrimage which is fast being overwhelmed by the pressure of paltry journeys into the waste-land. The *Vidwaans* (scholars) are fast declining in numbers and influence. They must be revered and fostered. Do not say that this is a difficult assignment. I am not asking you to improve their material standard of living more and more; what I want you to do is to remove their fear that their scholarship is a burden. Use them, to learn the essentials of *Sanaathana Dharma* and they will feel happy and contented. Their estimate of themselves will then be proved true. They will live in peace, if not in plenty.

Any good deed done with sincerity will be rewarded. Do not have an eye on the reward when you do it, that is enough. It is natural that you are agitated by the gathering of clouds over the Indian sky; but, prayer to God and the constant remembrance of His Grace will remove all anxiety. There is no other support in times of dire need than God. To know Him, to cling to Him, to merge in His immeasurable splendour---that is the highest goal of man. The Governor, the Chief Minister and other officers who are here plan and execute schemes to keep bodies free from disease, brains sharp and skilled; but the mind has to be tended by ourselves.

*Prashaathi Vidwanmahaasabha: 1st Day*
*Hyderabad : 7-12-1964*

---

*It is easy to conquer anger through love, attachment through reasoning, falsehood through truth, bad thoughts through good and greed through charity.*
**Shri Sathya Sai**

## 51. Travel Light

THE number of those who talk pleasantly is legion; because, they need only cater to the desire of man for pleasure. But the number of those who talk usefully, profitably, beneficially is small for, few know what is really useful, profitable and beneficial for man. Most people are concerned only with the short run. The doctor who prescribes dietary and other restrictions and regimen is generally disliked by the patients. They gnash their teeth at such orders. But a doctor should ignore such responses and do his duty. He should insist on the prohibitions and preferences, even risking the consequent unpopularity.

At the present time, the learned and the scholarly in every field suffer from a dire disease, namely, "under-development of the moral tissue." No emphasis is laid on the growth of virtue in the plans for national development; the virtuous man is laughed at as an "ignoramus" who does not know the art of getting on in the world. But, as the *Karma kaanda* in the *Vedhas* proclaims, all acts must contribute to the elevation of character, the purification of the emotions, passions and impulses that infest the mind, the broadening of the vision and the strengthening of man's bonds with the Universal, of which he is a part. Arjun is addressed in the Bhagavadh Geetha by Shri Krishna as "Kurunandhana"; *kuru* means *karma*; the expression means that one is the product of one's *karma* or activities. One is shaped inevitably by the words and deeds and thoughts which one indulges in. So long as one has a trace of *Ajnaana* (spiritual ignorance) one is *kurunandhana*; so, Krishna addresses Arjuna thus in order to entice him into the realm of *bhakthi* and *jnaana*, from the region of *karma*.

## The immortal spark in Man can be discovered

Man can be certified as healthy, only when he is fully conscious of his reality and is gladly striving to reach it. Now, he is the child of Immortality (*Amrithaputhra*), swirling along helplessly towards Death! What a pitiable fate is this? The little ego in him is fed into a huge conflagration by the mind and the senses and he is caught in the fire of distress. Egoism makes him see glory in petty achievements, happiness in trivial acquisitions, joy in temporary authority over others. But, the Immortal in him is awaiting discovery to confer bliss and liberation from birth and death.

There is a definite technique by which that Immortal spark can be discovered. Though it may appear difficult, each step forward makes the next one easier and a mind made ready by discipline is able to discover the Divine basis of man and of Creation in a flash. There is no short-cut to this consummation. One has to give up all the impediments which one has accumulated so far and become light for the journey. Lust, greed, anger, malice, conceit, envy, hate, all these pet tendencies have to be shed. It is not enough if you hear the discourses of Sai Baaba and count the number that you have listened to. Thousands are here before Me now; but, that figure has no significance. Only those who practise at least one of the things I emphasise, count.

The Lord appeared before Bheeshma after the Mahaabhaaratha war, for, Bheeshma was praying to have Him before his eye when he left this world. The *bhaktha* yearns for Bhagavaan, but, believe Me, Bhagavaan also yearns for the *bhaktha*. That is why He assumes human form and moves among them. He derives as much *Aanandha* as the *bhaktha* derives when He moves with him. In fact, when the *bhaktha* takes one step towards Him, He takes ten towards him. That is the measure of His Grace and His *Aanandha*. The Lord is everywhere, in the house, outside it, before, behind, beside the *bhaktha*; but, men do not recognise Him or realise the value of so recognising Him.

## God is the mainspring of your life

The Lord is the unseen foundation on which your life is built. He is the source, sustenance and strength. Without His Will, no leaf can turn, no blade of grass can quiver. What firmer foundation can you desire than this? Once you know that the Lord, the Omnipotent Power, is the mainspring of your life, there will be no fear any more. When you suspect the strength of the foundation of a house, you are afraid to enter it; when you suspect the skill of the manufacturer, you are nervous to ride in the car. Bheeshma and other *bhakthas* as well as Shankara and other *Jnaanis* knew that the Lord is the *Aadhaara* (basis), and so they had no fear at all. But, that faith has not taken root in men today and so, this has become an Age of Fear and Anxiety, of *Ashaanthi* (absence of peace).

Gandhi relied on the Lord's Grace and the Lord's Might and he won. The atom bomb will only recoil with all its deadly potentialities on the very nations that trust in it. You know the story of Bhasmaasura, how he won from the gods the deadly boon by which he could turn to ashes all the things and beings upon which he placed his hand! In an unguarded moment, he placed his hand on his own head and the boon proved to be a bomb that finished him.

## How to purify the mind?

Know the *Aathma* which is your Reality; know that it is the same Inner Force of this Universe. Let your intelligence penetrate into the truth. Analyse yourself and discover the several layers of Consciousness—the physical, the sensory, the nervous, the mental, the intellectual—and arrive at the very core of even the last layer, the layer of joy. The five sheaths have to be transcended, so that you may attain your truth, which is *Aathma*.

The *Aathma* can be grasped only by a sharpened intellect and a pure mind. How to purify the mind? By starving it of the bad food it runs after, namely, objective pleasures, and feeding it on the wholesome food, namely, thought of God. The intellect too will be sharp if it is devoted to discrimination between the transient and the eternal. Let your thoughts be concentrated on God, His Name and His Form; you will then find that you are always with the Pure and the Permanent; you will then derive pure and permanent joy. That is the reason why I attach so much importance to *Naamasmarana* as a *Saadhana*.

*Prashaanthi Vidwanmahaasabha: 2nd Day*
*Hyderabad : 8-12-1964*

## 52. Anna and amritha

YOU must all be getting very tired by this long sitting though I know you are benefitting by these discourses since three days. To reach the goal, one must know where it is, how glorious it is, and what the obstacles are, and what the preparatory discipline is. A little tiresomeness is inevitable, in the attempt to know these. These Pandiths explained the statements of the *Vedhas* and the *Shaasthras*, which reveal these points and you must be grateful to them for the care they have taken to preserve such valuable wisdom.

The first requisite for the seeker is the quality of detachment, of *Vairaagya*, a quality that is the product of deep discrimination on the nature and characteristics of the senses, the mind and the intellect, besides the nature of the objects around us. Think deeply of the relative validity of experiences during the waking, the dream and the deep sleep stages and of the 'I' or Self that is the witness of these experiences.

That witness is you, the real you, a spark of the Eternal Universal Witness. How then can you, with such a grand heritage and such a grand destiny, run after mean ends and short-lived successes? It is by such discrimination that you get established in detachment. When you know that the 'diamond' which you treasured so carefully is just a piece of glass, you need no persuasion to cast it out. Employ yourself usefully; earn, but do not clasp the riches with fanatic zeal. Be like a trustee, holding things on trust, on behalf of God, for purposes which He likes and approves.

A headmaster when transferred from one school to another, goes to the new place, unconcerned and carefree, leaving behind him the laboratory, library, the furniture, the desks and boards which he cherished and loved; he knew even when he cherished them and loved them for their usefulness, that they were only in his custody for some time, that he held them on trust, and that a day may come sooner or later when he will have to leave them and go. Develop the same attitude towards the riches you accumulate and adore. Then, you can die in peace and live in contentment.

## Today Man is sliding into paltry pomp

One great temptation for weak minds nowadays is the opportunity for publicity. Even a gift of five rupees to some charitable organisation is announced in thick banner headlines! Conceit is thus encouraged and man slides into paltry pomp. Kindness has to be fostered in the silence of the mind. The seed should not be scattered on the rocky surface, it has to be embedded in the depths, so that it can germinate.

Life nowadays lays before man many a handicap, in his march towards God. All around, the forces of evil lie in wait to drag him down in the quest. Faith in God and in His Omnipresence has to be unshakable so that man can win. Cynicism is such a force, cynicism in conversation, in judging works of art, the achievements of science, the attainments of adventure, the heights of *saadhana*, the pronouncements of the wise. "If you sit in one place, reciting God's Name---Raama, Krishna, Govindha, etc." they ask "can they get food and clothing?" They do not know that God can give such men not merely *Anna* (food) but *Amritha* (Divine Nectar). The Name is enough; it has all the potentiality needed. A single gasp, a tiny gesture, an anguished cry, an agonised shriek, is enough to win the answer of God.

Surrender the ego, dedicate every moment and every movement to Him; He has assured mankind that He will ensure liberation from pain and evil. When asked where God is, people point towards the sky or some far distant region; that is why He is not manifesting Himself. Realise that He is in you, with you, behind you, before you and all around you; and He can be seen and felt everywhere. Realise also that He is all mercy, eager and anxious to fulfil your prayers, if they arise from a pure heart.

## Pray to God to illuminate your mind

He who tells you of this all-pervasive God is the real *Guru*; not he who promises you salvation if you place a purse at his feet. Do not be misled by such worldly men full of greed and egoism. Pray to God to illumine your mind, awaken your intelligence and be your *Guru*. He will surely guide you allright, from the altar of your own heart. For many a *Guru* today, the fence is more essential than the crop; so he emphasises the restrictions and rules, to the detriment of the *saadhana*, which they were designed to protect. So they insist fanatically on the observance of out-dated regulations and checks, while the very purpose of the regulations is allowed to decay. They magnify the role of Fate, and of the consequence of *karma*, without at the same time, consoling man by describing the overpowering might of God's grace.

If there is an iron law of *Karma* which binds man hand and foot, why do the *Shruthi* and the *Smrithi* extol the earnest efforts and penance of aspirants? Those efforts and that penance can surely transmute the evil consequence of *karma*, and save man from the fate that he has woven for himself. The story of Maarkandeya, whose date with Death was cancelled, is an instance in point. His *thapas* achieved that victory, by drawing down the Grace of God. There are countless instances in the earthly careers of all *Avathaars* to show that Grace is greater than garnered *karma*.

### God has no likes and dislikes

Whatever God grants is for your good, for your liberation, not for your fall or bondage. A God who does evil is no God at all. God had no likes and dislikes; he is above and beyond all traits and characteristics. He is *Gunaatheetha* (beyond all *gunas*). So, how can He be hating or revengeful? He is Love. He is Mercy. He is Goodness, He is Wisdom, He is Power. He gives you what you ask; (so be careful what you ask). Learn to ask the really beneficial boons. Do not go to the Wish-fulfilling tree and come back in glee, with a towel that you asked and got!

I do not prescribe elaborate *Japam* and *Dhyaanam* for you to win Grace. Control your tongue, make it sweet and soft, do not yield to the whims of the senses, dwell always in the thought of God, remind yourself always of the glory and majesty of God—that is enough religious discipline for you. Spend all the time that you can command in the recitation of His name—that is sufficient *Saadhana* for you.

*Prashaanthi Vidwanmahaasabha: 3rd Day*
*Hyderabad : 8-12-1964*

# Glossary

Meanings of Sanskrit words used in discussing religious and philosophical topics, more particularly used in the discourses by Shri Sathya Sai Baaba, reproduced in this volume, are given in this glossary. While the English equivalents for the Sanskrit words have been given in the text with reference to the context, this glossary attempts to provide comprehensive meanings and detailed explanations of the more important Sanskrit words, for the benefit of lay readers who are interested in Hindhu religion and philosophy.

*Aakaasa* - Space; ether; the subtlest form of matter.

*Aanandha* - Divine bliss. The Self is unalloyed, eternal bliss. Pleasures are but its faint and impermament shadows.

*Aaraadhana* - Divine service; propitiation.

*Aashrama Dharma* - The life of a Hindhu cosists of four stages as *aashramas*. *Aashrama Dharma* is the code of disciplines laid down for the blossoming of spiritual consciousness during the four stages—*Brahmachaari* (the student celibrate), *Grihastha* (householder), *Vaana-Prastha* (the recluse in the forest), and the *sanyaasin* (the ascetic or the monk).

*Aasthika* - One who believes in God, scriptures and the *Guru*.

*Aathma* - Self; Soul. Self, with limitations, is *jeeva* (the individual soul). Self, with no limitations, is *Brahman* (the Supreme Reality).

*Aathma jnaana* - Knowledge of the Self which is held out as the Supreme goal of human endeavour.

*Aathmaswaruupam* - Self embodied; of the nature of Self. The real man in us is the Self which is pure consciousness!

*Aathma thathwa* - Principle of the Self; the truth or the essential nature of the Self.

*Abhayaswaruupam* - Fearlessness embodied; of the nature of fearlessness. *Brahman* is fearless.

*Adhwaitha* - Non-dualism. The philosophy of absolute oneness of God, soul and Universe.

*Aham Brahmaasmi* - "I am *Brahman*". This is one of the great *Vedhic* dicta (*Mahaa Vaakyas*).

*Ahamkaara* - Egotism resulting from the identification of one's self with the body. It causes the sense of "I do" and "I experience".

*Ajnaana* - Ignorance (which prevents perception of the Reality).

*Annamaya kosha* - Material or gross sheath of the soul; the physical body.

*Antharyaamin* - Inner Motivator or Controller. (God is described thus because He resides in all beings and controls them from within).

*Archana* - Ritual worship of a deity, making offerings with recitation of *manthras* and holy names.

*Avathaar* - Incarnation of God. Whenever there is a decline of *Dharma*, God comes down to the world assuming bodily form to protect the good, punish the wicked and re-establish *Dharma*. An *Avathaar* is born and lives free and is ever conscious of His mission. By His precept and example, He opens up new paths in spirituality, shedding His grace on all.

*Bhaagavatham* - A sacred book composed by Sage Vyaasa dealing with Vishnu and His incarnations, especially Shri Krishna.

*Bhaagavath-thathwam* - The truth or essential nature of the Lord.

*Bhajana* - Congregational chant group worship by devotees with devotional music in which repetition of holy names predominates.

*Bhaktha* - Principle of God head. A devotee who has intense selfless love for God.

*Bhakthi* - Devotion to God; intense selfless love for God.

*Bhavasaagaram* - Ocean of worldly life. The worldly life of a being is considered to be the ocean which he has to cross and reach the other side for liberation from the cycle of birth and death.

*Bhoga* - Enjoyment; experience; the antithesis of *yoga*.

*Bodha* - Perception; knowledge; consciousness.

*Buddhi* - Intellect; intelligence; faculty of discrimination.

*Brahma* - The Creator; the First of the Hindhu Trinity.

*Brahmaandam* - The Cosmic egg, the Universe.

*Brahmachaari* - A celibate student who lives with and learns from his spiritual guide.

*Brahman* - The Supreme Being; the Absolute Reality; Impersonal God with no form or attributes. The uncaused cause of the Universe; Existence - Consciousness-Bliss Absolute (*Sathchith-aanandha*); The Eternal Changeless Reality, not conditioned by time, space and causation.

*Dhama* - Self-control; restraining the sense organs which run after sense objects seeking pleasure. This is an important discipline for an aspirant practising *yoga*.

*Dharma* - Righteousness; religion; code of duties; duty; essential nature of a being or thing. It holds together the entire Universe. Man is exhorted to practise *Dharma* to achieve material and spiritual welfare. The *Vedhas* contain the roots of *Dharma*. God is naturally interested in the reign of *Dharma*.

*Dhyaana* - Meditation; an unbroken flow of thought towards the object of concentration. It steadies and stills the mind and makes it fit for realisation in course of time.

*Dhwaitha* - Dualism; the doctrine that the individual and the Supreme Soul are two distinct principles.

*Gaayathri manthra* - The very sacred *Vedhic* prayer for self-enlightenment repeated piously at dawn, noon and twilight devotions.

*Guna* - Quality, property, trait; one of the three constituents of Nature (*Saathwa, Rajas and Thamas*). They bind the soul to the body. Man's supreme goal in life is to transcend the *gunas* and attain liberation from the cycle of birth and death.

*Guru* - Spiritual guide; a knower of *Brahman*, who is calm, desireless, merciful and ever ready to help and guide the spiritual aspirants who approach him.

*Hridhayaakasha* - Space in the (spiritual) heart in which the Self is imagined in meditation and prayer.

*Ishta Devatha* - The chosen deity through which a devotee contemplates on God.

*Ishwara* - The Supreme Ruler; the Personal God; He is *Brahman* associated with *Maayaa* but has it under His control unlike the *jeeva* who is *Maayaa's* slave. He has a lovely form, auspicious attributes and infinite power to create, sustain and destroy. He dwells in the heart of every being, controlling it from within. He responds positively to true devotion and sincere prayer.

*Japam* - Pious repetition of holy name or sacred manthra, practised as a spiritual discipline.

*Jeeva/Jeevaathma* - The individual soul in a state of non-realisation of its identity with *Brahman*. It is the self-deluded, bound spirit unaware of its own true nature. It is subjected to sensations of pain and pleasure, birth and death, etc.

*Jnaana* - Sacred knowledge; knowledge of the spirit, pursued as a means to Self-realisation. It is direct experience of God, as the Soul of the souls. *Jnaanam* makes a man omniscient, free, fearless and immortal.

*Jnaani* - A sage possessing *Jnaanam* (unitive spiritual knowledge and experience).

*Kaarana sareeram* - Causal body which carries the impressions and tendencies in seed state. It is the sheath of bliss; the innermost of the five sheaths of the soul.

*Karma* - Action; deed; work; religious rite; the totality of innate tendencies formed as a consequence of acts done in previous lives. Every *karma* produces a lasting impression on the mind of the doer, apart from affecting others. Repetition of a particular *karma* produces a tendency (*vaasana*) in the mind. *Karma* is of three kinds: (i) *Praarabdha* : which is being exhausted in the present life: (ii) *Aagami* : which is being accumulated in the present life, and *(iii) Samchitha*, which is stored to be experienced in future lives. *Akarma* is action that is done without any intention to gain the consequences; *Vikarma* is action that is intentionally done.

*Koshas* - The five sheaths enclosing the soul---sheaths of bliss, intelligence, mind, vital energy and physical matter.

*Kshathriya* - A member of the warrior caste, one of the four social groups (*varnas*) of the Hindu community.

*Kshethra* - Field; the body in which the *jeeva* reaps the harvest of his *karma*.

*Kshethragna* - The Knower of the field; the Spirit; the individual knowing Self.

*Leela* - Sport; play; the Universe is viewed as Divine sport or play.

*Lingam* - Sign; symbol.

*Linga sareeram* - The subtle body with its vital principles, subtle organs, mind, intellect and ego. When the gross body dies, the self departs, clothed in the subtle body.

*Loka* - Any of the 14 worlds (visible and invisible) inhabited by living beings.

*Maayaa* - The mysterious, creative and delusive power of *Brahman* through which God projects the appearance of the Universe.

*Maayaa* is the material cause and *Brahman* is the efficient cause of the Universe. *Brahman* and *Maayaa* are inextricably associated with each other like fire and its power to heat. *Maayaa* deludes the *Jeevas* in egoism, making them forget their true spiritual nature.

*Mahaabhaaratha* - The Hindhu epic composed by Sage Vyaasa which deals with the deeds and fortunes of the cousins (the Kauravas and Paandavaas) of the Lunar race, with Lord Krishna playing a significant and decisive role in shaping the events. The Bhagavadhgeetha and Vishnu Sahasranaama occur in this great epic. It is considered to be the Fifth *Vedha* by the devout Hindhus. Of this great epic, it is claimed that "what is not in it is nowhere".

*Manas* - Mind, the inner organ which has four aspects: (i) *Manas* (Mind) which deliberates, desires and feels; (ii) *Buddhi*, (intellect) that understands, reasons and decides; (iii) *Ahamkaara*, ('I' sense) and (iv) *Chitha* - (memory). The Mind with all its desires and their broods, conceals the divinity within man. Purification of the mind is essential for realisation of the Self.

*Maanava* - Man, descendent of *Manu*, the law-giver.

*Manomaya-kosha* - Mental sheath. One of the five sheaths enclosing the soul. It consists of the mind and the five subtle sensory organs. It is endowed with the power of will.

*Manthra* - A sacred formula, mystic syllable or word symbol uttered during the performance of the rituals or meditation. They represent the spiritual truths directly revealed to the *Rishis* (seers). The section of the *Vedha* which contains these hymns (*manthras*) is called the *Samhitha*.

*Moksha/Mukthi* - Liberation from all kinds of bondage, especially the one to the cycle of birth and death. It is a state of absolute freedom, peace and bliss, attained through Self-realisation. This is the supreme goal of human endeavour, the other three being, *dharma* (righteousness), *artha* (wealth and power) and *kaama* (sense-pleasure).

*Naamasmarana* - Remembering God through His Name; one of the important steps of spiritual discipline (*saadhana*) to obtain God's grace and to make progress in the spiritual journey.

*Nididhyaasana* - Concentration on the truth about the Self after hearing it (*sravana*) from the *guru* and reflecting on it (*manana*). It is thus the third step on the Path of Knowledge (*Jnaana-Yoga*).

*Nivrithi Maarga* - The path of renunciation that demands giving up desires and concentrating on God. The *Upanishadhs* which form the *Jnaana-kaanda* (the section dealing with unitive spiritual knowledge) of the *Vedhas*, deal with this path. This path is opposed to the *pravrithi maarga* (the path of desire) which worldly men pursue, seeking the good things here and hereafter.

*Praanamaya kosha* - Sheath of vital energy. It consists of five vital principles and five subtle organs of action. It is endowed with the power of action.

*Prakrithi* - Nature; the Divine Power of Becoming; also known as *Maayaa, Avidhya* and *Shakthi;* the world of matter and mind as opposed to the Spirit. *Prakrithi* has three dispositions or *gunas* (*sathwa, rajas,* and *thamas*) that go into the make-up of all living and non-living beings in the Universe, in varying proportions leading to the appearance of infinite multiplicity in form, nature and behaviour.

*Pranava* - *Om*; the sacred seed-sound and symbol of *Brahman*; "the most exalted syllable in *Vedhas*". It is used in meditation on God. It is uttered first before a *Vedhic manthra* is chanted.

*Prema* - Ecstatic love of God; (divine love of the most intense kind).

*Puuja* - Ritual worship in which a deity is invoked in an idol or picture and propitiated as a Royal Guest with offerings of flowers, fruits and other eatables along with recitation of appropriate *manthras* and show of relevant signs.

*Puraanas* - The Hindhu *Shaasthras* (scriptures) in which *Vedhic* truths are illustrated through tales of divine incarnations and heroes. Sage Vyaasa is believed to have written them. Of the 18 *Puraanas,* Srimad *Bhaagavatha* is the best known.

*Raamaayana* - This sacred Hindhu epic composed by Sage Valmeeki deals with the incarnation of Vishnu as Shri Raama who strove all his life to reestablish the reign of *Dharma* in the world. The *Raamaayana* has played a very important role in influencing and shaping the Hindu ethos over the centuries.

*Rajas/Rajo Guna* - One of the three *gunas* (qualities or dis-positions) of *Maayaa* or *Prakrithi. Rajas* is the quality of passion, energy, restlessness, attachment and extroversion. It results in pain.

*Thaapam* - Pain, misery; distress caused by the three types of agencies *(thaapathrayam)* . The agencies are *aadhyaadmika* (diseases and disturbances of body and mind); *aadhi bhowthika* (other beings); and *aadhi deivikam* (supernatural agencies like storm, floods, earthquakes, planets, etc.).

*Thamas* - One of the *gunas* (qualities and dispositions) of *Maayaa* or *Prakrithi.* It is the quality of dullness, inertia, darkness and tendency to evil. It results in ignorance.

*Saadhana* - Spiritual discipline or effort aimed at God realisation. The *saadhaka* (aspirant) uses the spiritual discipline to attain the goal of realisation.

*Samaadhi* - It is the super-conscious state transcending the body, mind and intellect, attained through rigorous and protracted *Saadhana.* In that state of consciousness, the objective world and the ego vanish and the Reality is perceived or communed with, in utter peace and bliss. When in this state, the aspirant realises his oneness with God, it is called *Nirvikalpa Samaadhi.*

*Samsaara* - Wordly life; life of the *jeeva* through repeated births and deaths. Liberation means getting freed from this cycle.

*Sanaathana Dharma* - Eternal religion. A descriptive term for what has come to be called Hindhuism. It has no single founder or text of its own. It is more a commonwealth of religious faiths and a way of life.

*Saamanya Dharma* - Code of conduct common to all persons in any one social group.

*Shaasthras* - The Hindhu scriptures containing the teachings of the *rishis*. The *Vedhas*, the *Upanishadhs*, the *Ithihasas* (epics), the *Puraanas* and the *Smrithis* (codes of conduct), etc., form the *Shaasthras* of the Hindhus. They teach us how to live wisely and well with all the tenderness and concern of the Mother.

*Sathwa* - One of the three *gunas* (qualities and dispositions) of *Maayaa* or *Prakrithi*. It is the quality of purity, brightness, peace and harmony. It leads to knowledge. Man is exhorted to overcome *thamas* by *rajas*, and *rajas* by *sathwa* and finally to go beyond *sathwa* itself to attain liberation.

*Sthitha prajna* - A man of realisation with a steady, tranquil and cheerful mind ever dwelling on God. He is a man of self-control, even-minded in all circumstances and totally free from all selfish desires. After death he attains freedom from *Samsaara*.

*Swadharma* - One's *dharma* or duty that accords with one's nature. This is an important concept in the Geetha.

*Upaasana* - Worship or contemplation of God.

*Upanishadh* - The very sacred portions of the *Vedhas* that deal with God, man and universe, their nature and interrelationships. Spiritual knowledge (*jnaana*) is their content. So they form the *Jnaana Kaanda* of the *Vedhas*.

*Vairaagya* - Detachment; desire and ability to give up all transitory enjoyments.

*Varna dharma* - The Hindhu community is divided into four *varnas* (social groups), based on *gunas* and vocations. *Braahmana* (the Custodian of spiritual and moral role), *Kshathriya* (the warrior gray which rules and defends the land), *Vaishya* (the group dealing with commerce, business and trade) *Shuudhra* (the group devoted to labour and service to the community). Each *varna* has its own *dharma* (*varna dharma*) restrictions and regulations that strive to canalise his impulses and instinct into fields that are special to his place in society, controls pertaining to the duties cast upon

*Vedhas* - The oldest and the holiest of the Hindhu scriptures, the primary source of authority in Hindhu religion and philosophy. They are four in number --- the Rig Vedha, Saama Vedha, Yajur Vedha and Atharva Vedha.

*Vedhaantha* - Means "the end of the *Vedhas*". It is the essence of the *Vedhas* enshrined in the *Upanishadhs*. The philosophy of non-dualism, or qualified non-dualism, or dualism based on the *Upanishadhic* teachings, is denoted by this term.

*Vishesha Dharma* - Code of conduct to be observed in special situations; obligations to be discharged on special occasions, or when faced with special situations.

*Vijnaanamaya kosha* - One of the five *koshas* (sheaths) of the soul. It consists of intellect and the five subtle sense organs. It is endowed with the power to know. The "I" or subject of experience or action is seated here.

*Viveka* - Discrimination; the reasoning by which one realises what is real and permanent and what is non-real and impermanent.

*Vriththi Dharma* - The moral code that regulates and enriches a person's profession.

*Yagna* - A *Vedhic* rite or sacrifice. Any self-denying act of service in the name of God.

*Yoga* - Means union with God, as also the path by which this union of the soul with God is achieved. The four important paths of *Yoga* are those of knowledge, action, meditation and devotion.

# SRI SATHYA SAI BOOKS AND PUBLICATIONS TRUST
## PRASHAANTHI NILAYAM
### PIN 515134, ANANTAPUR DISTRICT, ANDHRA PRADESH, INDIA
### IMPORTER/EXPORTER CODE NO. 0990001032
### RESERVE BANK OF INDIA EXPORTER'S CODE NO. HS-2001198

## OUR CLASSICS IN ENGLISH

********************************************************************

**THE VAHINIS SERIES:** (Books written by Bhagavan Sri Sathya Sai Baba. This collection of volumes contains the wisdom prevailed through out the ages)

| | |
|---|---:|
| Bhagavatha Vahini  (The story of the Glory of the Lord Krishna) | 24.00 |
| Dharma Vahini (The Path of Virtue and Morality) | 10.00 |
| Dhyana Vahini (The Practice of Meditation) | 12.00 |
| Geetha Vahini (The Divine Gospel) | 21.00 |
| Jnana Vahini (The Stream of Eternal Wisdom) | 11.00 |
| Leela Kaivalya Vahini (The cosmic Play of God) | 5.50 |
| Prasaanthi Vahini (The Supreme Bliss of Divine peace) | 12.00 |
| Prasnothara Vahini (Answers to Spiritual Questions) | 8.50 |
| Prema Vahini (The Stream of Divine Love) | 9.50 |
| Ramakatha Rasa Vahini part-I  (The sweet Story of Rama's Glory) | 32.50 |
| Ramakatha Rasa Vahini Part-II  (The Sweet Story of Rama's Glory) | 23.50 |
| Sandeha Nivarini (Clearance of Spiritual Doubts) | 13.50 |
| Sathya Sai Vahini (Basic Spiritual Message on Values) | 19.00 |
| Sutra Vahini (Analytical Aphorism on Supreme Reality) | 8.00 |
| Upanishad Vahini (Essence of Vedic Knowledge) | 9.50 |
| Vidya Vahini  (Flow of Spiritual Knowledge which illuminates) | 11.00 |

## SATHYA SAI SPEAKS SERIES (Four decades of Discourses by Bhagavan Sri Sathya Sai Baba) Revised & Enlarged Editions

| | | |
|---|---|---|
| Sathya Sai Speaks Vol I | Years 1953 to 1960 | 28.50 |
| Sathya Sai Speaks Vol II | Years 1961 to 1962 | 29.50 |
| Sathya Sai Speaks Vol III | Year 1963 | 32.50 |
| Sathya Sai Speaks Vol IV | Year 1964 | 34.50 |
| Sathya Sai Speaks Vol V | Year 1965 | 27.50 |
| Sathya Sai Speaks Vol VI | Year 1966 | 26.00 |
| Sathya Sai Speaks Vol VII | Year 1967 | 26.50 |
| Sathya Sai Speaks Vol VIII | Year 1968 | 34.00 |
| Sathya Sai Speaks Vol IX | Year 1969 | 28.50 |
| Sathya Sai Speaks Vol X | Year 1970 | 36.50 |
| Sathya Sai Speaks Vol XI | Years 1971 to 1972 | 32.50 |
| Sathya Sai Speaks Vol XII | Years 1973 to 1974 | 36.00 |
| Sathya Sai Speaks Vol XIII | Years 1975 to 1977 | 34.00 |
| Sathya Sai Speaks Vol XIV | Years 1978 to 1980 | 42.00 |
| Sathya Sai Speaks Vol XV | Years 1981 - 1982 | 39.00 |
| Sathya Sai Speaks Vol XVI | Years 1983* | 34.00 |
| Sathya Sai Speaks Vol XVII | Years 1984* | 35.00 |

(Newly Released for first time*)

## SATHYAM SIVAM SUNDARAM SERIES
(Life Story of Bhagavan Sri Sathya Sai Baba)

| | | |
|---|---|---|
| Sathyam Sivam Sundaram Part I | (Birth to 1962) | 20.50 |
| Sathyam Sivam Sundaram Part II | (Years 1962 to 1968) | 24.00 |
| Sathyam Sivam Sundaram Part III | (Years 1969 to 1972) | 24.00 |
| Sathyam Sivam Sundram Part IV | (Years 1973 to 1979) | 20.00 |

## SUMMER SHOWER SERIES :
(Discourses on Indian Culture and Spirituality by Bhagavan Sri Sathya Sai Baba)

| | | |
|---|---|---|
| Summer Showers in Brindavan | 1972 | 15.50 |
| Summer Showers in Brindavan | 1973 | 15.50 |
| Summer Showers in Brindavan | 1974 | 16.00 |

| | |
|---|---:|
| Summer Showers on the Blue Mountains (Ooty) 1976 | 27.00 |
| Summer Showers in Brindavan 1977 | 17.50 |
| Summer Showers in Brindavan 1978 | 13.50 |
| Summer Showers in Brindavan 1979 | 14.50 |
| Summer Showers in Brindavan 1990 | 22.00 |
| Summer Showers in Brindavan 1993 | 19.00 |

## CHILDREN'S BOOKS:

| | |
|---|---:|
| Chinna Katha - Part I | 21.00 |
| Chinna Katha - Part II | 31.50 |
| Stories for Children: part I | 12.00 |
| Stories for Children: part II | 17.00 |
| My Life is my message | 18.00 |

## OUR OTHER PUBLICATIONS:

| | |
|---|---:|
| Prashaanthi Nilayam-A dream come true-window Folder | 1.00 |
| Avtar of Love | 50.00 |
| Prashaanthi Nilayam-A dream come true | 16.00 |
| Lotus Design Book-let | |
| Baba The Breath of Sai-by Grace J.McMartin | 49.00 |
| Finding God-by Charles Penn | 62.00 |
| Seva: A flower At His Lotus Feet-by Grace J.McMartin | 33.50 |
| Spirituality and Health-by Dr. (Mrs) Charanjit Ghooi | 68.00 |
| Recapitulation of Baba's Divine Teachings | 52.00 |
| -by Grace J.McMartin | |
| Sanathana Sarathi-Commemoration | |
| Volume (70th birthday) | 25.00 |
| Benedictory Addresses-(15 convocation Discourses by | 29.00 |
| Bhagavan as Chancellor from beginning to up-to-date '95) | |
| Conversation with Bhagavan Sri Sathya Sai Baba | |
| - by Dr. John S. Hislop | 41.00 |
| Africa for Sai Baba-Volume I-by Dare Ogunkolati | 2.50 |
| Transformation of Heart - by Judy Warner | 25.00 |
| Divine Memories - by Diana Baskin | 37.00 |
| Prashaanthi Pathways | 12.00 |

| Title | Price |
|---|---|
| Bhaktodharaka Sathya Sai - by N. Lakshmi Devamma | 28.00 |
| Bhajanmala | 50.00 |
| Sathya Sai Baba God Incarnate - by Victor kanu | 30.00 |
| Easwaramma - The chosen Mother of Bhagavan Sri Sathya Sai Baba | 18.00 |
| Garland of 108 Precious Gems - (108 Holy Names of Bhagavan) | 11.00 |
| Journey to God - part I -- by J. Jagadeesan | 52.00 |
| Journey to God - part II - by J. Jagadeesan | 80.00 |
| Loving God - by N. Kasturi | 40.00 |
| Life is a game Play it - by Joy Thomas | 39.00 |
| Life is a Challenge Meet It - by Joy Thomas | 35.00 |
| Love is Love Enjoy It - by Joy Thomas | 35.00 |
| Love is a Dream Realize It - by Joy Thomas | 29.00 |
| My Baba and I - by Dr. John S. Hislop | 38.00 |
| My Beloved - by Charles Penn | 35.00 |
| Sathya Sai Education in Human Values | 22.50 |
| Sathya Sai book of Thoughts For the Day | 30.00 |
| Sathya Sai - The Eternal Charioteer | 46.00 |
| Sai Baba's Mahavakya on Leadership -by Lt. Gen. (Retd.) Dr. M.L. Chibber | 38.00 |
| Shirdi to Puttaparthi - by Dr. R.T. Kakade | 40.00 |
| Sai Messages for You and Me - volume I by Lucas Ralli | 26.00 |
| Sai Messages for You and Me - volume II by Lucas Ralli | 25.00 |
| Sai Baba and You - Practical Spirituality -by Mark and Barbara Gardner | 21.00 |
| The Greatest Adventure -by Dr. K.V. Murthy | 41.00 |
| One Single Stream of Love | 40.00 |
| To my father - by Justice Padma Kasthagir | 25.00 |
| Uniqueness of Swami and His Divine Teachings -by Dr. A. Adivi Reddy | 52.00 |
| Quiz on Bhagavatham | 10.00 |
| Quiz on Mahabaratha | 10.00 |
| Quiz on Ramayana | 10.00 |
| Quiz on Bhagavat Geeta | 8.00 |
| Quiz on Divine Life of Bhagavan Sri Sathya Sai Baba | 12.00 |

## MISCELLANEOUS

| | |
|---|---|
| Bal Vikas Observer - part I | 1.00 |
| Bal Vikas Observer - part II | 2.00 |
| Is Sai Baba God (Revised and Enlarged Edition) -M.R. Kundra | 50.00 |
| Sai Baba Manager Divine - by Ajith Haksar | 50.00 |
| Bhakti and Health - by Dr.(Mrs) Charanjit Ghooi | 51.00 |
| Bhajanmala (Australia) | 50.00 |
| Vision of Sai I - by Rita Bruce | 40.00 |
| Vision of Sai II - by Rita Bruce | 44.00 |
| Words of Jesus and Sai Baba - by Kishin Khubchandani | 60.00 |
| Sai Messages for you and Me - volume III by Lucas Ralli | 40.00 |
| Sai Messages for you and Me - volume IV by Lucas Ralli | 40.00 |
| Africa for Sai Baba-part II - by Dare Ogunkolati | 40.00 |
| The teachings of Bhagavan Sri Sathya Sai Baba -Question Answers on Prema Vahini | 30.00 |
| Love and Light of the World | 2.50 |
| Omnipresence of God | 2.00 |
| Prashaanthi Pearls - by Rosi Wickremasinghe | 10.00 |
| Beloved friend - by Little Heart | 35.00 |
| Nine Gems of Love | 30.00 |
| Sai Blossoms 1965 | 10.00 |
| Sai Blossoms 1969 | 5.00 |
| The Unique Graciousness | 40.00 |
| Why I Incarnate | 2.00 |

## OTHER BOOKS

| | |
|---|---|
| Sai Avtar Volume I | 5.25 |
| Sai Avtar Volume II | 9.25 |
| Daily Prayers to Bhagavan | 6.00 |
| Ananya-one alone - by Raj Kumari | 75.00 |
| Guide to Indian Culture and Spirituality | 8.00 |
| Sai Nandana | 35.00 |
| Trayee Saptamayee | 35.00 |
| Lokanatha Sai - by M.L. Leela | 45.00 |

| | |
|---|---|
| Compassionate Bhagavan - by Jogeshwar Gogoi | 60.00 |
| Sathya Sai Baba - Incarnation Philosophy & Teachings<br>-by Mrs. Vanathi Ravindran | 25.00 |

## FOR SALE ONLY IN INDIA

| | |
|---|---|
| A CAtholic Priest Meets Sai Baba<br>- by Don Mario Mazzoleni | 52.00 |
| Pathways to God - by Jonathan Roof | 43.00 |
| Sai Baba The Holy Man and Psychiatrist<br>- by Dr. Samuel H. Sandweiss | 58.00 |
| Spirit and the mind - by Dr. Samuel H. Sandweiss | 41.00 |
| Sai Baba Invitation to Glory - by Howard Murphet | 40.00 |
| Sai Baba Avatar - by Howard Murphet | 48.00 |
| Sai Baba Man of Miracles - by Howard Murphet | 55.00 |
| Where the road ends - by Howard Murphet | 71.00 |

## INLAND/OVERSEAS BOOK ORDERS & SUBSCRIPTION FOR MONTHLY MAGAZINE SANATHANA SARATHI

Books are despatched by Regd. Post Parcel only subject to availability. Indents and remittances within India should be received by Money Order/Indian Postal Order/Account Payee Cheques/Bank Drafts.

## REMITTANCES

Remittances from Overseas Countries towards Book Orders/ Sanathana Sarathi subscriptions (English & Telugu) can be sent by A/C payee cheque/Demand Draft/International Money Order in FOREIGN CURRENCY ONLY AND NOT IN INDIAN RUPEES.

All remittances should be in favour of THE CONVENOR, SRI SATHYA SAI BOOKS & PUBLICATIONS TRUST, PRASHAANTHI NILAYAM, ANANTHAPUR DISTRICT, ANDHRA PRADESH, INDIA, PIN CODE - 515 134, payable at State Bank of India, Prashanti Nilayam (Branch Code No. 2786) mentioning full address in capitals with Area Pin Code, Zip Code No., where the books are to be despatched.

## DELIVERY

Ordinarily time taken by Postal Services for delivery is as below:

|  | For Books Sent by Regd.post | For Monthly Magazine sent by post |
|---|---|---|
| Within India | 3 to 5 weeks | 1 to 2 weeks |
| Overseas by Sea | 8 to 12 weeks | 6 to 8 weeks |
| Overseas by Air | 3 to 6 weeks | 2 to 3 weeks |

The Monthly Magazine Sanathana Sarathi is despatched on 30th of every month by post.

## POSTAGE (INLAND)

At the rate of 50 paise per 100 grams plus Registration charges Rs.6/-. For an order of 1kg parcel (containing approximately 3 to 5 books), postage Rs.5 (+) Regn. charges Rs.6/-; total 11/-. For 2 kgs parcel (containing approximately 4 to 8 books) Rs. 16; For 3 kgs parcels (containing approximately 7 to 10 books) Rs.21/-; For 4 kgs parcels (containing approximately 9 to 15 books) Rs. 26/- and for 5 kgs parcel (containing approx. 14 to 20 books) Rs. 31/-. PACKING AND FORWARDING FREE.

While remitting, please calculate the cost of the books indented (+) postage (+) Registration charges.

## POSTAGE (OVERSEAS)

|  | By Sea Rs | By Air Rs | By Jumbo Cargo courier door delivery DHL Services up to 10kgs |
|---|---|---|---|
| 1 kg parcel (3 to 5 books) | 59.00 | 209.00 | for Middle East Rs.2000.00 |

| | | | |
|---|---|---|---|
| 2 kgs parcel (4 to 8 books) | 78.00 | 378.00 | for Asia pacific Rs.2500.00 |
| 3 kgs parcel (7 to 10 bools) | 110.00 | 560.00 | for Europe & USA Rs.3500.00 |
| 4 kgs parcel (9 to 15 books) | 140.00 | 740.00 | for any other place (overseas) |
| 5 kgs parcel (14 to 20 books) | 172.00 | 922.00 | Rs.4500.00 |

APPROXIMATE CURRENT EXCHANGE RATE:

US $ = Rs. 34.00
CAN $ = Rs. 25.00
UK pound = Rs. 52.00

# NOTES